D1535110

Presented to:

Beloved Richard

From:

Papa Tom

Date:

12-25-2016

Shalom & Blessings!

TRUSTING *in* God

I am like an olive tree flourishing in the house of God;
I trust in God's unfailing love for ever and ever.

Psalm
52:8

CHRISTIAN ART
PUBLISHERS

Published by Christian Art Publishers
PO Box 1599, Vereeniging, 1930, RSA

© 2013

First edition 2013
First LuxLeather edition 2014
Second LuxLeather edition 2016

Cover designed by Christian Art Publishers

Images used under license from Shutterstock.com

Set in 12 on 15 pt Palatino LT Std
by Christian Art Publishers

Printed in China

ISBN 978-1-4321-1779-5

16 17 18 19 20 21 22 23 24 25 – 10 9 8 7 6 5 4 3 2 1

Simply trusting every day,
trusting through a stormy way,
even when my faith is small,
trusting Jesus, that is all.
~ Edgar P. Stites

Trust in the LORD with all your heart
and lean not on your own understanding;
in all your ways acknowledge Him, and
He will make your paths straight.

~ Proverbs 3:5-6

Contents

January

Following Jesus

So, you see, it is impossible to please God without faith.
Anyone who wants to come to Him must believe that there is
a God and that He rewards those who sincerely seek Him.
~ Hebrews 11:6

Faith is not the holding of correct doctrines,
but personal fellowship with the living God.
~ WILLIAM TEMPLE

*Heavenly Leader, in Your love lead me
to unconditional certainty of faith.
I am so often like Thomas who first wants to see
and feel before I believe. I don't want to experience
my faith with my senses only, but by
first-hand experience of Your presence.
I so badly want to believe the Unseen and quietly
confess with all my heart, "My Lord and my God!"
Lead me through the words of Jesus Christ to an honest and
practical faith that binds me inseparably to my Savior.
I want to keep hope unblemished in my heart:
The expectancy that all the ideals in my life will be realized;
that my spiritual life will grow in love, knowledge and truth
so that I will always make the right choices.
Holy Lord, keep optimism burning in
my heart through Your Spirit.
I honestly want to believe that I can love like You,
Lord Jesus. I really want to say with deathbed-honesty,
"Lord, You know everything; You know that I love You."
I want to love also my fellow humans
with sincere, unselfish love that breaks down all dividing walls
and makes reconciliation a reality.
Lead me through Your Spirit to a new understanding
of faith, of what You expect from me.
In the glorious name of my Savior and Redeemer, Jesus Christ.*

Amen.

Jesus Is Baptized

Then Jesus went from Galilee to the Jordan River to be baptized by John. But John tried to talk Him out of it. "I am the one who needs to be baptized by You," he said, "so why are You coming to me?" But Jesus said, "It should be done, for we must carry out all that God requires." So John agreed to baptize Him (Matt. 3:13-15).

When Jesus came to John to be baptized, John was hesitant to do it. He felt it was not right for him to baptize Jesus. On the contrary; John was in need of what Jesus could give him. Jesus' baptism is difficult to understand and it has led to much speculation through the ages. John's baptism of people was a call to confession of guilt and the offer of forgiveness of sin. So, if Jesus is who we think He is, He didn't need to repent and He didn't need God's forgiveness.

There are a few good reasons why Jesus did need to go to John to be baptized: (a) Jesus waited in Nazareth for thirty years while the world was waiting for Him. The success of any undertaking is determined by the wisdom of choosing the right moment to start. When John appeared on the scene, Jesus knew the time had come. (b) No Jew had ever been baptized because it was meant for new converts to Judaism, especially gentiles. They were regarded as "dirty" in comparison to God's chosen people. Now, for the first time in the history of Israel, the Jews became aware of their sin and their urgent need of God. With His baptism, Jesus identified with the people He had come to save in the hour of the awareness of their sin, and their search for God.

> True believers when troubled by sin can always remember their baptism, and so be assured of eternal washing in the blood of Christ.
>
> JOHN CALVIN

I praise and thank You, Savior and Lord, that You became human for my sake.

My Dearly Beloved

After His baptism, as Jesus came up out of the water, the heavens were opened and He saw the Spirit of God descending like a dove and settling on Him. And a voice from heaven said, "This is My dearly beloved Son, who brings Me great joy" (Matt. 3:16-17).

The voice that Jesus heard at His baptism is of the utmost importance: "This is My dearly beloved Son, who brings Me great joy." This sentence is a combination of two Bible verses: Firstly, "You are My Son" (Ps. 2:7). Every Hebrew accepted this text as a description of the Messiah, the mighty King who would come. And then in Isaiah 42:1: "Look at My servant, whom I strengthen. He is My Chosen One, who pleases Me." The latter refers to the suffering of the Servant, which reaches its conclusion in Isaiah 53. Jesus' baptism confirmed two facts: First, He was truly the Son of God; and second, His road on earth would lead Him to the cross. Jesus' task was put to Him at that moment, and the manner in which it was to be brought to fulfillment.

> The death of Christ was the most dreadful blow ever given to the empire of darkness.
> WILLIAM S. PLUMER

When something comes to a person in a moment of clarity, the immediate problem is how to transform that vision in a practical way. A method then needs to be found to make the dream a reality. This is precisely the problem that Jesus was faced with. He had come to lead the people back to God. How would He do it? Which methods should He use? Should He be the mighty conqueror, or would it be better to be patient, and act in sacrificial love? Jesus was assigned the task and He had to choose the method He would use to carry out the task God had given Him.

Thank You, Lord Jesus, that You chose the path of the cross, so that my sins could also be nailed to it.

Tried and Tested

Then Jesus was led by the Spirit into the wilderness to be tempted there by the devil (Matt. 4:1).

There is one thing we should take note of before we speak of Jesus being tested. The meaning of the word "tested" is completely different to that of the word "tempted." The Greek word for temptation is *peirazein*, which has a negative meaning. It means to entice someone into doing the wrong thing; to lure them into choosing the wrong path. Being tried or tested means to test someone; not to tempt them.

A great and encouraging truth lies in this: When we are tried, the purpose is not to lure us into sinning, but to help us conquer sin; not to make us bad people, but to make us better people. It is a test from God, because He wants to use us. We should therefore see this episode in Christ's life as a time when He was not tempted, but tested.

> Those who draw water from the wellspring of meditation know that God dwells close to their hearts.
> TOYOHIKO KAGAWA

Furthermore, we must take note of where this took place. It happened in the wilderness, or desert. There is a strip of wilderness that lies between Jerusalem and the Dead Sea. It extends over an area of thirty by fifteen miles. In that wilderness Jesus could be more alone than in any other place in Palestine. He went into the wilderness because He wanted to be alone. The time had come to carry out the task God had assigned Him. God had spoken to Him and now He needed to think about how He would carry out that task. It is possible that we keep doing the wrong things because we are not alone often enough. We make many mistakes because we do not set aside enough time to be alone with God.

I kneel before You in thankfulness, Father God, for those holy and uplifting moments alone with You.

Stones into Bread

The devil came and said to Him, "If You are the Son of God, tell these stones to become loaves of bread." But Jesus told him, "No! The Scriptures say, 'People do not live by bread alone, but by every word that comes from the mouth of God'" (Matt. 4:3-4).

The devil launched his onslaught from three sides, and in each of these there was something unavoidable.

First there was the temptation to change stones into bread. The desert was literally strewn with small round lime stones that looked exactly like bread rolls. It was to tempt Jesus to use His omnipotence for selfish reasons. The temptation always exists that we will abuse the power God gives us. God gave each person at least one talent. Each of us must ask ourselves one of two questions: "What can I get out of this?" or "What can I do for others with this gift God gave me?"

> Despite the flesh, for it passes away, see to the welfare of your soul, for it never dies.
>
> St. Basil

There was also another side to this temptation. Jesus was God's Messiah. He had to decide in the wilderness how He would win people for God. How would He make His dream a reality? He could give the people bread, or other material things. But this would be bribing people to follow Him for what they could get out of it. So the reward Jesus offered them was the cross. He called on people to give and not receive. Jesus answered Satan in the same words that God taught His people in the desert: "He humbled you by letting you go hungry and then feeding you with manna. People do not live by bread alone; rather, we live by every word that comes from the mouth of the LORD" (Deut. 8:3). The only way to perfect peace is total dependence on God.

Lord Jesus, I praise Your name for Your victory over Satan.

Do Not Test the Lord

Then the devil took Jesus to the holy city, Jerusalem, to the highest point of the Temple ... Jesus responded, "The Scriptures also say, 'Do not test the LORD your God'" (Matt. 4:5, 7).

Then the devil launched an attack from a different angle: In a vision he takes Jesus to the highest point of the Temple in Jerusalem on Mount Zion. From this point there was a 450 foot drop down to the Kidron Valley. Why would Jesus want to jump from the Temple and land safely in the valley? So that people would admire Him and follow Him. A gospel that is based on sensation is doomed to fail. And, on top of that, it was a way of abusing God's omnipotence: "You must not test the LORD your God as you did when you complained at Massah" (Deut. 6:16).

What Jesus meant by what He said is that it serves no purpose to see how far you can go with God. It is not smart to endanger yourself on purpose, in a reckless and irresponsible manner, and then expect God to save you. God expects you to take risks to prove your faithfulness to Him, but not to take chances for the sake of your own prestige.

> Trust Jesus, and you are saved. Trust self, and you are lost.
> CHARLES H. SPURGEON

The kind of faith that depends on wonders and signs is not true faith. If faith cannot believe without sensationalism, it is not really faith; it is doubt in search of evidence in the wrong place. God's saving omnipotence is not something to be trifled with or to experiment with. It is something to be quietly trusted in everyday life.

Holy Father God, I rejoice in the fact that my faith is based on You and not on sensationalism.

Jesus Triumphs

Next the devil took Him to the peak of a very high mountain and showed Him all the kingdoms of the world and their glory. "Get out of here, Satan," Jesus told him. "For the Scriptures say, 'You must worship the LORD your God and serve only Him'" (Matt. 4:8, 10).

A nd so the devil launches his third attack on Jesus. Jesus came to save the world, and here He is given an image of the world. Satan says to Him, "I will give it all to You, if You will kneel down and worship me" (Matt. 4:9). Didn't God Himself say to His Chosen One, "Only ask, and I will give You the nations as Your inheritance, the whole earth as Your possession"? (Ps. 2:8).

What the devil suggests here is a compromise: "Let's come to an agreement! Don't make such high demands. Just look the other way for a moment when evil is around, and people will follow you in hordes." This was the temptation to make a compromise with the world instead of meeting God's unconditional demands. It would be an attempt to change the world by becoming like the world.

> Compromise is always wrong when it means sacrificing principle.
> DRAKE RAFT

Then Jesus answered the devil, as we read in Deuteronomy 6:13: "You must fear the LORD your God and serve Him." The Lord Jesus was absolutely convinced that no one would ever conquer evil by making a compromise. With this, He declared and proved that the Christian faith is uncompromising. Christianity cannot sink to the level of the evil world: It must raise the world to its own level. Nothing less would be good enough. For Jesus, this choice meant the cross – but inevitably the cross also implied the crown.

Conqueror and Savior, thank You for Your example of no compromise with evil.

Jesus Begins His Ministry

From then on, Jesus began to preach, "Repent of your sins and turn to God, for the Kingdom of Heaven is near" (Matt. 4:17).

The time had come for Jesus to begin His earthly mission. Let's take a look at what He did first: He left Nazareth and went to live in Capernaum. Jesus left His parents' home, never to return there again. He locked the door of the past and threw open the door to the future. This was final, the end of His former life – a decisive moment that comes in all our lives; a time when we must make important decisions without hesitation.

Jesus went to Galilee and there began His ministry. Galilee was the northernmost district of Palestine; a mere fifty miles in length and twenty-five miles wide. In spite of this, Galilee was densely populated and the most fertile part of Palestine. Thus Jesus began His ministry in the most densely populated part of the country.

> Preaching is the primary task of the church.
> BILLY GRAHAM

The name Galilee is from the Greek word *galil*, meaning "circle." The region was inhabited by Phoenicians, Syrians and Samaritans. Galilee was therefore open to new ideas. The trade route of the world, as it was known then, passed through Galilee. The traffic of the entire known world of the time passed through Galilee. A saying of the time was, "Judea is the road to nowhere; Galilee is the road to everywhere!" It was often invaded and controlled by foreigners. History forced Galilee to open its doors to foreigners and therefore also to new ideas and influences. This was also the place destined for the new Teacher with a new doctrine. It was here that Jesus began His mission and delivered His first message from God.

Jesus of Galilee, I thank You that Your message also reached my ears and irrevocably changed my life.

Messenger of God

From then on, Jesus began to preach, "Repent of your sins and turn to God, for the Kingdom of Heaven is near" (Matt. 4:17).

Matthew tried to discover a prophecy of Jesus' work in the Old Testament. He found it in Isaiah 9:2: "The people who walk in darkness will see a great light." He made this prophecy applicable to Jesus, who would be known as the Light of the world. Today's Scripture reads, "From then on, Jesus began to preach." The word "preach" has acquired a negative meaning and is largely connected with boredom.

The word "proclaim" is from the Greek word *kêrrusein,* a king's proclamation. *Kêrux* is the Greek word for *heraut,* the man who brought the message directly from the king.

> Everything God does in our time or will do in eternity is to tell people how much He has loved them from eternity.
>
> JOHN GILL

The *heraut's* voice was a voice of absolute certainty. There was no doubt about his message: no "maybe" or "possibly" or "probably." It was the king's message: as clear as day and just as unmistakable. Goethe said, "Tell me of your certainties: I have enough doubts of my own." Preaching is the proclamation of certainties! You cannot get others to believe in something you don't believe yourself.

Christ's message has authority: He speaks on behalf of a King! The preacher dare not speculate; he must believe in what he proclaims. This was possible because Jesus' message came from a Source outside of Himself. Preaching is not the expression of one person's own opinion; it is God's voice speaking through someone. Jesus' first message is an order: "Turn from your sins!" In other words, "Turn back to God!"

Lord Jesus, grant that all who spread Your message receive it from the Source; and that those who hear it will accept it.

Jesus' Ministry

Jesus traveled throughout the region of Galilee, teaching in the synagogues, preaching everywhere and announcing the Good News about the Kingdom (Matt. 4:23).

This Scripture reading is of great importance because it gives us a summary of the three great activities in Jesus' life:

He proclaimed the gospel, or, as we put it; He preached. Preaching is the proclamation of certainties. This is why Jesus came – to do something about the ignorance of people. He came to tell them the truth about God; things they would never find out on their own. He came to put an end to their guesswork and to show them who God really is.

Jesus preached in the synagogues. There is a difference between preaching and teaching: Preaching is the proclamation of certainties, while teaching is the explanation and importance of those certainties. Jesus came to put right our misunderstanding about God and the kingdom. There are times when people do know the truth, but interpret it incorrectly or come to the wrong conclusions. Jesus came to explain to people the true meaning of religion. He came to heal those who needed to be healed and to take away people's pain. He did not come only to speak, but also to do; to put action to His words.

> The church is the only society on earth that exists for the benefit of non-members.
>
> WILLIAM TEMPLE

Jesus came as a Preacher to clear up all misunderstandings about God. He came as a Teacher to clear up all the confusion. He came as a Healer to heal all pain. We must also proclaim these certainties, and be ready and willing to defend our faith. In addition, we must put our faith into action. In so doing we follow in Jesus' footsteps, as His disciples.

Holy Lord, help me to be Jesus' faithful witness every day.

Jesus Speaks to Fishermen

"Come, follow Me, and I will show you how to fish for people"
(Matt. 4:19).

All the activity in Galilee was centered near the Sea of Galilee. It is thirteen miles in length from north to south and eight miles wide from east to west. Luke never refers to it as *thalassa* (the sea) but always as *limnë* (the lake). It lies 680 feet below sea level. Because it lies in a dip, the surrounding terrain is extremely fertile. It is one of the loveliest lakes in the world.

The lake of Galilee was a particularly popular place to fish. The fishermen of the time mainly used boats and nets. It was in fact these nets that Peter, Andrew, James and John were busy mending when Jesus called them. They probably already knew Jesus and had most likely listened to Him. Now Jesus was asking them to throw in their lot with Him. They were not educated, rich, influential people. They were plain, ordinary people – fishermen: those who had all the qualities that would make them good fishers of people. As fishermen they were *patient*. As fishermen they also had *perseverance* and must never become despondent, but must keep on trying. They had *courage*. Fishers of people must be ready to weather the storms as well as the dangers that arise when the truth is proclaimed. Fishers of people must have *insight*: they must sense when the time is right. The sensible preacher and teacher will never force themselves on people, but always indicate the way to Christ.

> I believe there are far too many accommodating preachers ... Jesus Christ did not say, "Go into the world and tell the world that it is quite right." The gospel is something completely different. In fact, it is directly opposed to the world.
> C. S. LEWIS

Lord Jesus, I clearly heard Your voice. Use me for Your glory.

The Gateway to Happiness

One day as He saw the crowds gathering, Jesus went up the mountainside and sat down. His disciples gathered around Him, and He began to teach them (Matt. 5:1-2).

Jesus trained His disciples to be His ambassadors. In this we have the essence of everything Jesus taught – but also who He was. It is about the only comfort in life and in death: that we belong to Jesus Christ. When Jesus says in Matthew 5:12, "Be happy about it! Be very glad!" He is not talking about something vague that we will find one day in the hereafter, but God's happiness – now, here and every day!

Jesus' teachings were not meant only for His disciples, but also for you and for me in life today, so that we will live in Christ and people will see His image in us. Jesus is the Source of all true happiness, and to be really happy, we must know Jesus.

> Do not let your happiness depend on something you may lose, but only upon the Beloved who will never pass away.
>
> C. S. LEWIS

Christ's happiness is an "unusual" happiness: Kingdom happiness! Our human happiness often depends on chance or a stroke of luck. It's something like winning the lottery and not knowing what to do with it. Human happiness is something life can give us ... and just as suddenly take away again or destroy. The short-sighted person calls it happiness if things go well for a while – then they are cheerful and glad. But this is not what happiness or blessedness means in God's language.

Jesus, Source of true joy, thank You for teaching us what true happiness really means.

Genuine Happiness

One day as He saw the crowds gathering, Jesus went up the mountainside and sat down. His disciples gathered around Him, and He began to teach them (Matt. 5:1-2).

What then is the true meaning of Jesus' happiness or blessing? Firstly, it is indestructible: "No one can rob you of that joy" (John 16:22). Christ's happiness is happiness even in pain and sorrow. It is joy that can never be destroyed by loss, pain or suffering. It is happiness that shines through tears and that cannot be taken away by life or death. It is not determined by our external circumstances: "It is not what I have, but what I am, that determines whether I am happy or unhappy" (Goethe).

> God is more anxious to bestow His blessings on us than we are to receive them.
> St. Augustine

Christ's happiness is lasting happiness born from a walk with God. It is like the depths of the ocean: on the surface it roars and surges; waves crash and break; storms rage and the waters foam – but deep down it is still, calm and undisturbed.

Happiness is not a human achievement, not something we can earn through effort and hard work: It is a gift of God! There are eight gates we must pass through to find God's happiness. We are to console in Christ those who mourn; to be gentle; to satisfy hunger and thirst; to be merciful and to receive mercy from God; to be pure in heart as we walk with God; to be peacemakers; and to be willing to be persecuted for the sake of what is right. If we do all of this, we will have discovered the secret of true happiness.

Holy Teacher, grant that I will pass through the gates of God's happiness and find true joy and blessing.

Unconditional Surrender

"God blesses those who are poor and realize their need for Him,
for the Kingdom of Heaven is theirs" (Matt. 5:3).

This is probably the most important of all the Beatitudes. The main idea is this: Unconditional surrendering to God's will always leads to unprecedented happiness and rich blessings. It is not about wealth or poverty, but about our relationship with God. When we trust God, earthly possessions become less important to us and we grow closer to God and His kingdom.

This Beatitude says to us in effect, "Happy are those who realize their need for God, who trust Him and are obedient to Him." The world says, "Get everything you can, and hold on to what you've got." The Christian says, "He must become more and I must become less!"

> There is no other method of living piously and justly, than that of depending on God.
> JOHN CALVIN

The only people who are without hope, are those who are smug and self-satisfied. The Beatitudes are for those who struggle desperately to draw close to God. They are at their wits end and don't know where to turn. This can happen for any reason: poverty; poor health; unexpected sorrow and suffering; dreams that failed. It relates to real-life issues and problems. It is anything that drives us to God and makes us seek His grace.

We can deal with desperation in more than one way. We can seek help from other people, which brings temporary relief. We can also try to solve our problems on our own. Or we can take our problems and stand before God like beggars, without making any demands because we deserve nothing from God. This is the first gate which we must pass through to receive the true happiness which only God can give.

Holy Father God, thank You that through Your Spirit I can get
to know You better and that I am dependent on Your grace only.

Give Control to Jesus

"God blesses those who are poor and realize their need for Him, for the Kingdom of Heaven is theirs" (Matt. 5:3).

~∽⦿∾~

The modern person finds it very difficult to be dependent. Our independence and self-reliance mean a lot to us. But this self-dependency is an illusion. It is a big lie that Satan plants in our hearts. Just think of the story of the rich fool. His sin was not that he was rich – it's no sin to be rich – his sin was that He didn't take God into account. To pursue independence from God is to waste your life on a mirage in the desert.

Christ says emphatically that God blesses those who realize their need of Him. A new day dawns in our lives when we stop running from this truth, when we realize that we are dependent on God alone!

> There are always uncertainties ahead, but there is always one certainty – God's will is good.
> VERNON PATERSON

Can giving up control of our lives result in happiness? Yes! says Christ. An unparalleled happiness touches your life with mercy and enables you to reach the kingdom of God. It is not an exuberant and sensational, shiny and glittery happiness, decorated with tinsel like the world's kingdom. It is quiet, deep and untouchable peace and happiness.

We discover true happiness in life only when we become totally dependent on God through Jesus Christ. The Holy Spirit wants to lead us through this beautiful gateway: the gateway of unconditional surrender to God and His plan for our lives. Have you told God yet? Have you surrendered? Won't you do it today and receive God's happiness in your life?

Lord my God, I am totally dependent on Your love and grace and I thank You for this.

The Broken Heart

"Blessed and enviably happy are those who mourn, for they shall be comforted" (Matt. 5:4 AMP).

The following words appear above this gateway to God's happiness: "The happiness of the broken heart." God has a holy purpose for all suffering and heartache. He wants to make us better people. Who would understand this better than Christ? Is there a need in your home? Jesus didn't even have anywhere to lay His head. Have your friends disappointed you? His friends denied and betrayed Him. Are you wrestling in prayer with grief that you cannot handle? He wrestled in prayer in Gethsemane, sweating blood. Are you mourning a loved one? He wept at the tomb of His friend Lazarus. Do you feel forsaken, even by God? He wept on the cross in God-forsaken agony. What better consolation than to hear from His mouth, "God blesses those who mourn."

> As gold is purified in the furnace, so the faithful heart is purified by sorrow.
> GUARINI

The poet Robert Browning Hamilton wrote:

"I walked a mile with Pleasure; she chattered all the way; but left me none the wiser for all she had to say. I walked a mile with Sorrow, and ne'er a word said she; But oh! The things I learnt from her when sorrow walked with me."

This is so true: in the darkest night we seek the stars; in our sorrow we are driven to God. The Arabs have a saying: "If you live in the sunshine every day, you will later live in the desert." Fruit trees need rain to grow and certain life lessons can be taught through sorrow. That is why sorrow is a gate we must pass through in order to experience God's happiness.

God of love and grace, thank You that through the Holy Spirit I know that sorrow can be transformed into grace.

Sorrow

"Blessed and enviably happy are those who mourn, for they shall be comforted" (Matt. 5:4 AMP).

Sorrow can do two essential things: 1) It can show us the goodness of our fellow man like nothing else on earth, and 2) It can teach us, more than anything else, God's great comfort and love. Many of us have discovered the fellowship of our fellow man and God in moments of sorrow, which we would never have done otherwise. If we accept it in the right way, new beauty and strength can be born in our hearts.

However, sorrow and grief remain a painful issue in our lives. Therefore it is a wonderful comfort to know that God cares about our sorrow and grief and is involved in our suffering. Didn't His own Son drink a full cup of sorrow, down to the last drop?

> Sorrow looks back;
> worry looks around,
> but faith looks up.
> RALPH WALDO EMERSON

"God blesses those who mourn, for they will be comforted." Surely there is not a human heart in the whole world that hears this Beatitude without being deeply touched. A promise of comfort in sorrow must find its way into every human heart. There is so much grief in the world that we gladly listen to a voice that brings comfort. Grief and sorrow are commonplace.

Every home has its cross to bear and every heart endures pain. And don't forget the secret hurt of many a heart that no one knows of. This is often twice as painful because there is no one to share it with. It is when today's Scripture means so much: God cares! And not only does He care: He will wipe the tears from our eyes with His holy and loving hand.

Thank You, Heavenly Father, that I don't have to go through the valley of grief and pain alone.

Jesus, the Comforter

"Blessed and enviably happy are those who mourn, for they shall be comforted" (Matt. 5:4 AMP).

There is so much hidden sorrow that people try to cover up with a mask, in the hope of hiding it from others, but they are never completely successful. There is the pain of addiction to a habit that is ruining their lives. There is the sadness of a broken marriage; the heartache of estrangement between parents and rebellious, disobedient children. There is the hidden hurt that a person cannot share with anyone because it is shameful.

Then there are those in mourning. Think for a moment of the fearful heart of the person in mourning. Death cannot be bought off, it relentlessly takes a loved one. It leaves our hearts empty, our whole world and our lives are left empty. There comes a day in everyone's life when we weep in the protective isolation of our own sanctuary for loved ones who died

> Earth has no sorrow that heaven cannot heal.
> THOMAS MOORE

too soon. What heavenly music it is then to hear Jesus Himself say, "God blesses those who mourn, for they will be comforted." Small wonder that people turn their faces and tearful eyes to Jesus, the Comforter. He was always prepared to pour balm on the wounds.

The greatest of all human sorrow is born from our sin ... and this He also bore for us. Isaiah prophesied, "Comfort, comfort my people, says your God. Speak tenderly to Jerusalem. Tell her that her sad days are gone and that her sins are pardoned. Yes, the Lord has punished her in full for all of her sins" (Isa. 40:1-2).

We thank and praise You, Lord Jesus, because You understand our sorrow and grief and You paid the price to atone for our sins.

Those Who Mourn

"Blessed and enviably happy are those who mourn, for they shall be comforted" (Matt. 5:4 AMP).

T he phrase "those who mourn" embraces so much: worry about backsliding from the living God; being superficial in serving Him; a lack of godly fruit; hesitating in believing His holy will; our obsession with earthly possessions. Christ brings comfort to all who have learnt through grace that He triumphs over sin. He carried our sin on His shoulders, hung on the cross and became our Savior. "The old has gone, everything has become new!" When we understand the purpose of *our* suffering, we understand the purpose of *His*: Jesus came to comfort all those who mourn.

Remember this: He holds your hand. You have a Mediator who not only died on the cross, but was raised from the dead and ascended to heaven. He will comfort all those who cry out to Him. He never leaves you alone in your need and worries, your troubles and distress.

> Sorrow makes us all children again, destroys all differences in intellect.
> RALPH WALDO EMERSON

He is with you in the fiery furnace, in the depths of the sea, in the valley of the shadow of death. He is with you every day up until the end of the world ... and for all eternity.

Remember, it is not what you lost that counts, but what you kept. The bitter Mara is the transit gate to the heavenly Elim. The Holy Spirit leads you through this gateway. Trust only Him who pours your cup and, with a loving hand, gives it to you to drink. It is the same hand He uses to wipe the tears from your eyes. "God blesses those who mourn, for they will be comforted."

Lord Jesus, thank You that You paid for all my sins and sorrows on the cross.

The Gateway of Gentleness

"God blesses those who are humble, for they will inherit the whole earth" (Matt. 5:5).

～つG＾

Gentleness means friendliness and mildness in your relationship with others. Other definitions of gentleness are kindness, tenderness, timidity, and patience. These are not characteristics that people get excited about. Something about the meaning of the word "gentleness" gives it a negative rather than positive connotation.

People often scornfully say, "He/she is so meek and mild." By implication they are saying that the person is too soft or weak; almost spineless or cowardly. Nowadays people think gentleness doesn't pay if you want to get somewhere in life. We believe "Nice guys come second!" The credo of most people is: I want to get somewhere in life! How I get there doesn't really matter as long as I assert myself on the sports field, in the business world, politics and, sad to say, also in the church and religious circles.

> A gentle word, a kind look, a good-natured smile can work wonders and accomplish miracles.
> WILLIAM HAZLITT

The buzzword of our day is "self-assertion" – looking after my self-image. This is the "law of the jungle": the survival of the fittest! It is to make myself and my interests my first priority, declare myself perfect, deny God and His omnipotence in the process. I can do it myself. I am alone against the world and I must look out for myself. In this way, I assert myself against God and the whole world around me.

Lord Jesus, work in my life through the Holy Spirit, so that I will be gentle like You.

Jesus, the Gentle

"God blesses those who are humble, for they will inherit the whole earth" (Matt. 5:5).

Ever since the time of Adam and Eve in paradise, humans have a tendency towards pride and self-assertiveness. In today's Scripture, Christ instructs us to think in a new way. He Himself was the prototype of gentleness and lowliness. No one was as notable and mighty, and at the same time, as humble as Jesus: He entered Jerusalem on a donkey, and washed the feet of His disciples. His gentleness was not weakness in any way, but the essence of strength.

There is a resemblance between the first and third Beatitude: "God blesses those who realize their need for Him" is a command for humbleness towards God. "God blesses those who are gentle and lowly" encourages humbleness towards others. This means deep and genuine selflessness. One's own interests should not be of vital importance.

> Humility is royalty without a crown.
> SPENCER W. KIMBALL

Gentleness is a sign of contentment. It is the direct opposite of greediness – the "givers" as opposed to the "takers." They understand something of the suffering in the world.

Where does this gentleness come from? How does one obtain it? What is the secret of this happiness? You can be soft-hearted and friendly, unselfish and uncomplaining only when your life is in God's hands. Then you know that God is with you and that He will take care of you. The Holy Spirit wants to lead you towards this. The "new earth" will consist of gentle and humble people. Will you feel at home there? Then allow the Holy Spirit to lead you through this gateway.

Lord Jesus, let me follow Your example and wash the feet of others, instead of getting them to wash mine.

Yearning for What Is Right

"God blesses those who hunger and thirst for justice, for they will be satisfied" (Matt. 5:6).

Very few of us really know what it's like to be hungry and thirsty. The people Jesus spoke to knew only too well. They were genuinely poor. He gave them bread to eat and they knew thirst in its worst form. But the people's hunger couldn't be satisfied by refreshments served with tea; their thirst couldn't be quenched with a cup of coffee or a cooldrink. Rather it was the hunger of the dying; the thirst of someone who would die if he wasn't given something to drink. This is why Jesus so often spoke of the Bread and the Water of Life.

Now Jesus applies this hunger and thirst to our spiritual lives. He comes to us with a serious question and a challenge: "How serious are you to do what is right before God?" Just as badly as the dying need bread and water? How intense is your yearning for righteousness? "As the deer pants for streams of water, so I long for You, O God. " (Ps. 42:1). Many of us have noble ideals for our relationship with God, but when the decisive moment comes we are not willing to make the necessary effort. This, then, is our encouragement. We must be willing to strive for what is right. To make no effort is a sin, but God will satisfy those who make a sincere effort.

> Humans need Jesus Christ as a necessity and not as a luxury.
> JOSEPH PARKER

Where do we find this bread and water? The Holy Spirit leads us to Christ and the Bread and Water of Life. Those who reach out to Jesus will never thirst again. This Beatitude is an invitation to the feast of the Lamb. The host is Jesus Himself and the feast lasts forever, from now until eternity.

Thank You, Redeemer and Savior, that I heard Your knock at the door of my heart, and opened the door to You.

Mercy

"God blesses those who are merciful, for they will be shown mercy" (Matt. 5:7).

This Beatitude teaches us that the gospel is all about people. Christ gave His life because He cares for people – and He expects it from His followers. It is a principle that runs through the entire New Testament. Mercy and compassion literally mean getting under someone's skin and identifying with this person to the extent that eventually you see through their eyes, think with their mind and feel as they do. It is caring about another's need and understanding for other people's circumstances.

The Parable of the Samaritan mentions three types of people: takers, hoarders and givers. The people who attacked the traveler are the takers. Their philosophy is: "Everything that is yours, is mine, I take it!" The hoarders are the priest and the Levite (church people) who saw the man but walked on. Their philosophy in life is: "Everything that's mine is mine, I keep it!" They are afraid to become involved. They block their ears and harden their hearts, fearing that their mercy might cost them something.

> I choose kindness ... I will be kind to the poor, for they are alone. Kind to the rich, for they are afraid. And kind to the unkind, for such is how God treated me.
>
> MAX LUCADO

The Samaritan is the prototype of the giver. His was an act of compassion, mercy and Christian love. These people say: "Everything that is mine is yours. I give it!" He gave unconditionally, like the flower gives its fragrance without expecting anything in return. God smiles on this world through the eyes of such people. Jesus didn't ask if we deserved it when He laid down His life for us. His instruction to us is: Go, and do the same!

Lord Jesus, teach me to have a compassionate heart like You.

The Pure Heart

"God blesses those whose hearts are pure, for they will see God"
(Matt. 5:8).

⌒◯⌒

What does "heart" mean in spiritual terms? It means the core or the deepest point of our lives; the part that is hidden. Because it is hidden, it can be an ugly place: a murky fountain, bubbling with bitter and poisonous water. The deeper we delve into it, the more decay we discover. And this is not true of only the heart that is not born again; the rebirth of our sinful hearts is not completed all at once. Think of David in Psalm 51. No one would have queried his faith in God. Yet look how shamefully he overstepped the mark with Bathsheba. In his deepest being he was a man after God's own heart, yet he was overcome by temptation. A believing heart is by no means a godly, pure or holy heart.

But David didn't give in to self-pity or despair. He took refuge in God. The believing heart perceives its own impurity, but also knows to pray in earnest for purification, expecting complete forgiveness.

> No one is more dangerous than he who imagines himself pure in his heart: for his purity, by definition, is unassailable.
> JAMES BALDWIN

David confessed that he was a leper before God because of his sin, unworthy to be in God's presence – like the lepers who had to live outside the city. David yearned for God to absolve him so that his heart would be pure. We dare not shrug our shoulders and say, "Oh well, all people are sinners." This is not about "all people," but about you personally. It is about your heart. Isn't it time that you and I also prayed David's prayer?

I thank You, Father God, that I am washed clean in the blood of the Lamb.

Whiter Than Snow

"God blesses those whose hearts are pure, for they will see God"
(Matt. 5:8).

Picture in your mind's eye the leper wandering around in the field: he misses his home, his people, the temple of God – *but he is a leper!* We wander about like this on the path of sin, yearning for God's forgiveness and purification. The believing heart not only knows its own impurity, it also prays fervently for forgiveness: "Purify me from my sins, and I will be clean; wash me, and I will be whiter than snow" (Ps. 51:7). When we are faced with the awfulness of our sinful hearts, it drives us to God. We can't erase or forgive our own sin. So, then, to Christ! Give us Christ or we shall die in our distress! And then the miracle happens: God cancels out our debt for Christ's sake. Whiter than snow! Everything unsightly is covered by a white sheet and everything turns white. Christ's righteousness can be likened to this: it descends on us gently, like snowflakes; it covers all our leprous sins; all the areas in our life are purified – heart, soul, thoughts, speech, actions – everything is covered by the snow-white righteousness of Christ: "But if we confess our sins to Him, He is faithful and just to forgive us and to cleanse us from every wrong" (1 John 1:9).

> My strength is as the strength of ten, because my heart is pure.
> SIR GALAHAD TENNYSON

In our own eyes we are polluted sinners. But God sees us through His Son and judges us according to the untarnished holiness that is whiter than snow. So, look away from your sins and fix your hope on Christ. The Holy Spirit wants to lead you through this gateway – the gateway you thought you would never get through. What do you see when your heart is pure? You see God, in all His splendor and majesty and glory!

Wash me, O Holy Spirit, so that I will be whiter than snow.

Peacemakers

"God blesses those who work for peace, for they will be called the children of God" (Matt. 5:9).

⌒ↄᏩ⌒

G od is a God of peace. Christ is called the Prince of Peace. Those who strive to be peacemakers will be called children of God. To be called a peacemaker you must live in peace with God, with yourself and with your fellow humans. Such people know a quiet, inner peace.

Peace is one of the wonderful fruits of the Holy Spirit. To be a peacemaker is an active virtue. They don't isolate themselves in a monastery and meditate on peace; they go out into the world, they are exposed to life and work persistently for peace.

What does the word "peacemaker" mean to us? It is a lifestyle that works for the good of our fellow humans. This peace is not a result of escapism, but of our battle with and victory over our problems. It is a well-trodden path to peace – even if it is accompanied by strife. It is not something passive, but passionately

> Every man and woman is born into the world to do something unique and something distinctive; and if he or she does not do it, it will never be done.
> BEJAMIN E. MAYS

positive. The peacemakers are happy people because they are doing God's work on earth. They try to make the world a better place in which to live, always pulling out weeds of negativity and planting flowers of goodwill. It is the age-old struggle in ourselves: the Spirit against the flesh. But first we must make peace with ourselves. In our inner being there is a struggle between good and bad; light and darkness; life and death. Those who have found inner peace are happy, because their lives belong to God.

Lord Jesus, Prince of Peace, come and live in my heart and reform my life so that I will become a peacemaker.

Work for Peace

"God blesses those who work for peace, for they will be called the children of God" (Matt. 5:9).

Peacemakers are people who first make peace with God. Peacemakers are also those who create healthy relationships between people. Then there are people in the world who are hubs for conflict, trouble and bitterness, and they always cause strife. We find them in every church and community. They sow seeds of dissension, misunderstanding, distrust, and discord.

Two brothers had flourishing wheat farms next to one another. Occasionally they had a bumper crop. The elder brother said, "My brother doesn't have a wife. I'll help him and give him some of my wheat." And every moonlit night he took armfuls of golden wheat, carried it across the fence and put it down on his brother's land. Meanwhile, the younger brother said to himself, "My brother has a wife and family. I'll make life easier and give him some of my wheat." And every moonlit night he crossed the fence and put them on his brother's land. The inevitable finally happened: the two brothers bumped into each other, each with arms piled high with wheat. Tradition has it that the first church on earth was built on that spot.

> If we know no peace, it is because we have forgotten that we belong to one another.
> MOTHER TERESA

This is the litmus test for being a child of God. We must do our best to create the right environment for people to live happily. Peacemakers are willing to stick their necks out for peace, even jeopardizing their personal safety. To be a peacemaker is not an ideal or a dream. In Christ it is a doable reality. It is the Holy Spirit who leads us through this gateway and enables us to be peacemakers.

Holy Spirit of God, use me to be a peacemaker for You.

The Persecuted

"God blesses those who are persecuted for doing right, for the Kingdom of Heaven is theirs. God blesses you when people mock you and persecute you and lie about you and say all sorts of evil things because you are My followers. Be happy about it! Be very glad! For a great reward awaits you in heaven" (Matt. 5:10-12).

The gospel of Jesus Christ is incorruptible and uncompromisingly honest. It speaks of persecution, carrying a cross and suffering. Christ does not mislead us. He didn't come to make life comfortable for us, but to save us for eternal happiness. Think for a moment of the people Jesus is speaking to here: a new faith was surging through the world, and for His followers, their Christianity would mean separation and suffering.

Lies were being spread about Christians. The Roman government feared them because they spoke about a Messiah and refused to recognize the Emperor as God. The persecution of Christians was so bad that they ran out of wood to crucify them.

> Against the persecution of a tyrant, the godly have no remedy but prayer.
> JOHN CALVIN

Christ spoke to the people about the glory of the bloodstained road. We are also called to take up our cross and follow Him: Our Christianity must cost us something. It is proof that we are willing to walk in the footsteps of the prophets and martyrs if need be. It means that we share not only in Christ's victory, but also in His suffering. It encourages our fellow believers. Nobody suffers in vain. Christ confirms that it brings us untold happiness. And Christ is with us because He never forsakes or abandons us. When we pass through this gateway, our reward is indescribably great. Then we receive a double wage: untold happiness on earth, and eternal peace in heaven.

Gracious God, let me never hesitate if I am ridiculed and persecuted for the sake of Your truth.

Salt of the Earth

"You are the salt of the earth. But what good is salt if it has lost its flavor? Can you make it salty again? It will be thrown out and trampled underfoot as worthless" (Matt. 5:13).

These words gave rise to one of the greatest compliments we can give someone: "You are the salt of the earth." In the ancient world, salt was held in high regard. The Greeks saw it as holy (*theion*). The Romans believed that nothing on earth was more useful than salt. In Christ's time, it had three main qualities:

Salt was the symbol of cleanness and purity. The glittering whiteness of salt made this association easy. Salt was one of the most primitive offerings to the idols. For the Christian, salt is the symbol of purity. Christians are to maintain the standards of purity in an impure world.

> The greatest gift we can bestow on others is a good example.
> THOMAS MORELL

Salt was a preservative. It was used to prevent food from going bad and rotting. Salt prevents corruption. If Christians want to be salt for the world, their lives must have a certain antiseptic quality. Christians are instructed to be purifying preservatives in their community.

The greatest and most obvious quality of salt is that it gives flavor. Food without salt is tasteless: Christianity is to life what salt is to food. Yet we often fail in this. Oliver Wendell Holmes said, "I might have entered the ministry if certain clergymen I knew had not looked and acted so much like undertakers." People need to rediscover the lost flavor of Christianity.

Useless Christianity is disastrous. If Christians don't do their duty as Christians, they are heading for disaster.

Holy Spirit of God, help me to be salt to the world around me.

Light of the World

"You are the light of the world. A city on a hill cannot be hidden. Neither do people light a lamp and put it under a bowl. Instead, they put it on its stand, and it gives light to everyone" (Matt. 5:14-15 NIV).

Jesus expects His followers to be like Him. The light that shines from a child of God is reflected light. Christ does not ask us to produce our own light: We must shine with the reflection of His light. It is light that is born from the presence of Christ in the believer's heart. What does Jesus mean by this?

Light can be seen. Before matches were made, lighting a lamp was a problem, so when people left their homes, they put it under a bowl so that it kept burning without being a danger. But the primary purpose of the light was to be seen. Likewise, Christianity is something that must be seen. Our Christianity must not only be visible in the church, but also in our daily life and activities.

> Darkness cannot drive out darkness; only light can do that. Hate cannot drive out hate; only love can do that.
> MARTIN LUTHER KING, JR.

Light is a guide. Lights along the road warn us of cliffs and rockfalls; along the seawall or breakwater lights warn us of the tide. In the same way, Christians must show the right path to others by means of their example and way of life.

A light is often a warning to stop when there is danger ahead. It is sometimes necessary for Christians to warn people of danger. Our warning should not be given in anger or irritation, or with criticism or judgment. With love, it will be effective.

The light that can be seen; that serves as a guide; and that is a warning – this is the light Christ calls us to be.

Light of the world, thank You that I can light my lamp from Yours and in a humble way be a light to others.

Let Your Good Deeds Shine

"In the same way, let your good deeds shine out for all to see, so that everyone will praise your heavenly Father" (Matt. 5:16).

The following are a few important things we must take note of:

When we set an example by the good deeds we do, people notice. "Good" in the Christian sense of the word, mustn't be good only, but also attractive. The tragedy of so many Christian examples is that they have an element of coldness and harshness, without a trace of love. There is goodness that attracts, and goodness that alienates. A Christian's life should make Christianity something special and appealing.

Our exemplary lives and good deeds must not draw attention to ourselves, but to God. Otherwise we are guilty of theatrical exploits. At a conference that Dwight L. Moody attended, there was a group of young people who held a prayer session that lasted all night. The next morning they came across Moody and told him, "Mr. Moody, just look how our faces are glowing!" Moody answered quietly, "Moses didn't know that his face glowed." When a person consciously draws attention to themselves, they are not setting a Christian example.

> Remember as you go about your day that you may be the only Jesus some of your friends, neighbors and family will ever see.
>
> WANDA E. BRUNSTETTER

Christians never think about what they do, but about what God enabled them to do. They never focus people's attention on themselves, but point them in God's direction.

God and Father, help me through Your Spirit to let my light shine to honor You only.

Always Available

"And be sure of this: I am with you always, even to the end of the age" (Matt. 28:20).

One of the most glorious truths of the gospel is that the living Christ, who became human for our sakes, is and always stays with each believer. How comforting this is to know, especially when our hearts are filled with sadness we cannot explain.

Even if some of us struggle to experience this Jesus as a reality in our lives, He is with us wherever we might be – where we get to know Him better, when we praise and worship Him, even where we try to break through our doubts and uncertainties. He tells us Himself to stop battling on our own and to come to Him. He is with us wherever we may go, even in our moments of deepest doubts.

We know, however, that when we grab hold of this gracious offer, we will have to break with all our sins. We cannot live in Christ's presence on our own conditions. The only way we can experience and enjoy His presence is when we obey His will.

> We need never shout across the spaces to an absent God. He is nearer than our own soul, closer than our most secret thoughts.
>
> A. W. TOZER

Without the living Christ as your Savior, you daren't venture into the unknown future. But when He is King of your life, He is always present. And through His Spirit you become increasingly aware of Jesus' presence with every step you take into the future.

I praise and thank You, Lord Jesus, that You are always there for me. You never leave me and never let me down.

February

Love Conquers All

Thank God for this gift – a gift too wonderful for words!
~ 2 Corinthians 9:15

God loves us, not because we are so lovable,
but because He is love.
~ C. S. LEWIS

Unchangeable God and Father,
we thank You that You came to
earth in the form of Your Son;
that through His coming we could receive
a new understanding of who we really are.
We know we are Your children and that
Your eternal arms always support us.
We thank You that Jesus' coming
gave us new insight into life:
that it is no longer pointless and
meaningless because You made it meaningful.
We are grateful for the new insights that His
coming brought about You, our Father. Through Jesus,
You are the Source of all abundance and blessings.
We thank You, Lord Jesus, for passing on to
us new insights about our destination;
You taught us to know and live love in its purest form,
how to love and be loved – and be thankful for that.
We thank You that Your words brought us
a new understanding of our fellow humans,
especially those who live in the twilight zone
of poverty, loneliness and misery.
Thank You that we may reach out to
them in Jesus' name and help relieve their distress.
Send Your Spirit to us and meet all our spiritual needs
from the abundance of Your grace and love.
Holy Jesus, we find peace in obeying Your will,
and in our fellowship with You lies our spiritual strength.
This we pray in Your glorious name.

Amen.

Offensive Words

*"If you are even angry with someone, you are subject to judgment!
If you call someone an idiot, you are in danger of being brought
before the court. And if you curse someone, you are in danger of
the fires of hell"* (Matt. 5:22).

The issue here for Jesus is offensive words. Firstly, there is the
man who says *"raka!"* to his brother; he is harshly judged.
The word *raka* describes a tone of voice. The emphasis is one of
contempt, which Jesus strongly condemns. There is probably no
sin that is more unchristian than contempt. There is the contempt that is born from the pride of birth status, which we call
snobbishness. Secondly, there is the contempt that comes from
acquiring intellectual knowledge. We
dare never look down in contempt
on someone for whom Christ died.

> The greatest remedy for
> anger is a delay.
> SENECA

Then Jesus speaks of the person
who calls his brother *moros* (fool).
This is the man the psalmist speaks of in Psalm 14:1: "Only fools
say in their hearts, 'There is no God'." Such people are moral
fools who live immoral lives and wish in their hearts there is no
God. To call someone a fool was to insult his moral character.
It was to steal his name and reputation and to brand him as a
licentious and immoral person. Therefore Jesus says that the
most serious sin of all is to destroy someone's reputation.

What Jesus is saying here is that murder will always remain a
sin. But it is not only a person's visible deeds that are condemned; their deepest inner thoughts are also judged by God. Those
who harbor ongoing anger, use foul language and destroy a
person's character are all murderers in their hearts.

*Holy Spirit of God, keep me from harboring anger in my heart;
instead, fill me with Christ's love.*

Forbidden Anger

"You have heard that our ancestors were told, 'You must not murder. If you commit murder, you are subject to judgment'. But I say, if you are even angry with someone, you are subject to judgment! If you call someone an idiot, you are in danger of being brought before the court" (Matt. 5:21-22).

Here we have the first example of the new standards set by Jesus. Moses' law said, "You must not murder" (Exod. 20:13). But Christ says that even anger towards your neighbor is forbidden. It is not good enough to just keep from striking someone; you are not to even be angry with them.

Firstly, there is the person who is angry with his neighbor. There are two words in Greek for anger: *thumos,* described as a flame; it is anger that flares up and quickly subsides. Then there is *orge*, the anger that "ages." It is a long-lasting anger that is nursed to keep it hot. This kind of anger must be accounted for before the Judgment seat. Jesus condemns all selfish anger: "Your anger can never make things right in God's sight" (James 1:20). Jesus forbids the anger that broods inside you and refuses to forgive and forget. If we want to obey Christ, all anger needs to go.

> He who angers you conquers you.
> ELIZABETH KENNY

Then Jesus goes on to speak about two cases where anger culminates in harsh words. The Jewish teachers forbade such anger and words. They spoke about "oppression through words" and of the "sin of insult." They had a saying: "Three groups end up in *Gehenna* (perdition) and never come back: the adulterers, those who shame their neighbor in public and those who call their neighbor insulting names." Both anger in a person's heart and anger in a person's speech are forbidden by Christ.

Father God, grant that Your love will keep me from anger towards my fellow humans.

Be Reconciled

"So if you are standing presenting a sacrifice at the altar in the Temple and you suddenly remember that someone has something against you, leave your sacrifice there at the altar. Go and be reconciled to that person. Then come and offer your sacrifice to God" (Matt. 5:23-24).

When Jesus spoke these words, He was reminding the Jews of a principle they knew well. The idea behind sacrifice was quite simple: If someone had done something wrong, the relationship between that person and God was impaired; the sacrifice was meant to put the relationship right again. However, two important things always had to be remembered.

Firstly, the sacrifice was never meant to make up for deliberate sin. If someone sinned unintentionally, then the sacrifice was effective. But if someone sinned deliberately and in a defiant way, then the sacrifice was invalid. Secondly, the sacrifice was a token of true remorse and confession. The main idea was to first put matters right with others before you set matters straight with God.

> The glory of Christianity is to conquer by forgiveness.
> WILLIAM BLAKE

Jesus is very clear about this: we cannot be right with God unless we are right with our fellows; we cannot hope for forgiveness unless we have confessed our sins to both God and to those we have sinned against. Our sacrifice will be to no avail until we have done so. We sometimes wonder why there is a dividing wall between God and us; why our prayers are not answered. The reason could well be that we built the wall ourselves because we are in a tainted relationship with our fellow humans or have wronged someone without doing anything to set it right.

Holy Master, keep me from harboring an unforgiving heart.

Forbidden Desire

"You have heard the commandment that says, 'You must not commit adultery.' But I say, anyone who even looks at a woman with lust has already committed adultery with her in his heart" (Matt. 5:27-28).

Here Jesus gives us the second example of His new standards. The law laid it down: "Do not commit adultery" (Exod. 20:14). The Jewish teachers took adultery so seriously that the punishment was nothing less than death. But Jesus emphasizes the fact that not only is the person who committed the forbidden act guilty before God, but also those with the forbidden thought.

It is essential that we understand what Jesus is saying here. He is not talking about the normal, natural desire that is part of human nature. According to the literal Greek meaning, the person who is condemned is someone who looks at a man or a woman with intentional lust; who deliberately uses his eyes to stimulate desire.

> Adultery is a sin and is opposed to the will of God and to all that is pure in body, mind and heart.
> W. H. Griffith Thomas

"The heart and the eyes are the two agents of sin" is a Jewish proverb. In a world rife with temptation, many things deliberately focus on stimulating lust: books, movies, magazines, advertisements – all of them aimed at stirring up the worst in a person. The people Jesus condemns here are those who intentionally use their eyes to arouse passion, who take a strange kind of pleasure in awakening forbidden things. For the person who is chaste, everything is pure. For the person with the polluted heart, any imagery provokes the worst in them.

Lord Jesus, with my eyes fixed on You, there is no room for lust.

Eliminate Temptation

"So if your eye – even your good eye – causes you to lust, gouge it out and throw it away. It is better for you to lose one part of your body than for your whole body to be thrown into hell" (Matt. 5:29).

Jesus demands something tremendous from us here. He insists that anything that causes us to sin or that tempts us, must be removed from our lives, root and all. Two pictures come to mind: First, a stone hidden on a road that causes a person to stumble. Secondly, there is the image of a pit that has been dug in the ground and covered over. The unwary passerby may stumble and fall to his ruin.

Naturally, Jesus' words must not be taken too literally. What they mean is that anything that tempts you to sin must be mercilessly rooted out. It is a given that thoughts and images of forbidden things are the most difficult to get rid of.

There are two ways of overcoming forbidden thoughts. The first is through Christian action; to fill your life with Christian deeds to such an extent that there is no time or place for immoral thoughts. It makes you forget about yourself completely and sets you free from lustful thoughts. The second is to fill your thoughts with good things. As long as your thoughts are filled with sinful desires they will not be overcome. This can only be achieved by fully involving yourself in Christian actions and Christian thoughts. By sacrificing your life and time for others, you will, by the grace of God, save your own life.

> Little by little, in patience and long-suffering, thou shalt conquer by the help of God, rather than by violence and thine own strength or will.
>
> THOMAS Á KEMPIS

Holy Master, grant that I will be so busy in Your service that there will be no time or place for impure thoughts.

Peace in Our Time

"Come to terms quickly with your accuser while you are on your way traveling with him, lest your accuser hand you over to the judge, and the judge to the guard, and you be put in prison. Truly I say to you, you will not be released until you have paid the last fraction of a penny" (Matt. 5:25-26 AMP).

Here Jesus gives us some very practical advice: Sort out your problems timeously, before they snowball and you end up with even more trouble. He advises people to take care of disagreements before the matter is taken to court. In the ancient world it often happened that two people traveled on the same road to court. Such matters were usually judged by the town's leaders. A time was fixed when the debtor and creditor had to appear before them. If someone was found guilty, they were handed over to the court official whose task it was to see that the debt was paid in full. Jesus' warning can be applied to two situations in life:

> Those who are truly forgiven, truly forgive.
> MARTYN LLOYD-JONES

It could be practical advice. Time and again in life a dispute, if not settled in time, can escalate. Bitterness breeds bitterness. We should be humble and admit that we are at fault, taking the first step towards reconciliation. If this initial step is not taken, bitterness and bad feelings worsen. Secondly, we should set matters straight with people while we are still alive, because we could appear before God at any moment, the final Judge of our deeds.

What Jesus teaches us is that if you wish to experience happiness now, in present times, and in eternity, never allow a broken relationship into your life. Act immediately – tear down the dividing walls and be reconciled.

Holy Father, give me the grace to be the least and to bring about reconciliation.

The Ancient Law

"You have heard the law that says the punishment must match the injury: 'An eye for an eye, and a tooth for a tooth.' But I say, do not resist an evil person! If someone slaps you on the right cheek, offer the other cheek also" (Matt. 5:38-39).

Jesus quotes the oldest law within living memory: an eye for an eye and a tooth for a tooth. This is the law of the jungle – the survival of the fittest. This law was called the *Lex Talionis*. The original purpose was to limit revenge. Instead of taking revenge against injustice by exterminating an entire tribe, the law stipulated that the punishment must be meted out in accordance with the crime. Furthermore, this was not the right of a private individual, but had to be determined by a judge (Exod. 19:18).

This law was never executed literally in any civilized community. The tooth and eye were converted into a monetary value and the transgressor had to pay the equivalent amount. But Jesus erased the idea, because revenge, how limited and controlled it might be, has no place in a Christian's life.

> Don't repay evil for evil. Instead, pay them back with a blessing. That is what God has called you to do, and He will bless you for it.
> 1 PETER 3:9

What Christ says is that no true Christian ever asserts a right. Unfortunately, churches are full of people who cling to their insults and swear to avenge themselves. These people have not even begun to understand what Christianity is all about. Christians don't think of their rights, but of their duties; not of their privileges, but of their responsibilities. Like our role model, Jesus Christ, we must be willing to be insulted and suffer injustice, for the sake of the kingdom of God.

Holy Spirit, lead me to the point where no insult will upset me and revenge will be something that does not even occur to me.

The Right Things, the Wrong Reasons

"Watch out! Don't do your good deeds publicly, to be admired by others, for you will lose the reward from your Father in heaven" (Matt. 6:1).

For the Israelites there were three important tasks, three pillars on which a good life was based: charity (the giving of alms); prayer; and fasting. Jesus in no way wanted to reject these responsibilities. However, what worried Him was that we often do the right things but with the wrong motives.

You can be charitable without actually helping the receiver, demonstrating your own generosity and basking in praise. You may pray in such a way that your prayers are not really directed at God, but are meant to impress others. A person can do good deeds only to be praised, for the sake of personal prestige and to demonstrate to the world how "good" they are.

> Good works will never produce salvation, but salvation should produce good works.
> ANONYMOUS

Jesus teaches us that these things are valid and that they do deserve recognition. He says if you give alms to demonstrate your own generosity, people will admire you – but that is all you'll ever get. If you pray in a way that shows off your devotion, people will think you are devout – and that is all you'll ever get. If everyone knows you are fasting, you will receive their admiration – but that is all you'll ever get. Then you are paid in full. This is why we must seek the reward that only God can give. It is shortsighted to prefer a temporary reward to God's eternal reward.

Lord Jesus, let me do good deeds with the right motive.

How Not to Pray!

"When you pray, don't be like the hypocrites who love to pray publicly where everyone can see them. I tell you the truth, that is all the reward they will ever get" (Matt. 6:5).

Few nations had nobler expectations of prayer than the Israelites, and no nation placed prayer higher on their priority list than they did. "Prayer is vital," the rabbis said, "more important than all good works."

However, certain crucial errors entered the Jewish prayer life. In Jesus' time there was a growing trend towards strictly formal prayer. The Jews prayed according to three prescribed things: The first was the *Shema* that consisted of three short Scriptures. All Jews had to pray the whole *Shema* every morning and evening, and for this reason it ran the risk of becoming an idle repetition of words.

> There is no formalism as dangerous as evangelical formalism.
> J. C. RYLE

The Jewish liturgy also prescribed certain prayers for different occasions. There was scarcely an event or occasion that did not have special prayers: before and after meals; prayers concerning light, the new moon, lightning, comets, rain, storms, the sea, dams and rivers, receiving good news, and entering or leaving a town or city. This had to do with the fact that every event in life was brought to God's attention. But because the prayers were so precisely prescribed, the whole system tended to become very formal. The prayers slipped from the tongue automatically, with little meaning. So, don't view prayer as a formal commitment to ensure God's grace. In the same way, we don't want our quiet time to degenerate into a habit and become a mere formality.

Holy Father, grant that my conversations with You will never degenerate into a formality.

Anytime, Anywhere

"When you pray, don't be like the hypocrites who love to pray publicly on street corners and in the synagogues where everyone can see them" (Matt. 6:5).

Another danger was the tendency to restrict prayer to certain places, especially the synagogue. While it is true that God seems closer to us in certain places, there were some rabbis that went as far as claiming that prayer was only effective if in the temple or synagogue. So it became the custom to go to the temple during the hour of prayer (see Acts 3:1). The danger was that it led to the notion that God is limited to certain places, which could make people forget that the entire earth is God's temple.

> Of all the commitments enjoyed by Christianity, none is more essential and yet more neglected than prayer.
> FRANCOIS FÈNELON

The Jews also tended to pray long prayers – though this tendency is certainly not limited to Jewish people. Many people have the mistaken idea that the length of their prayer determines the quality of their devotion. At the time – and to this day – there is this belief that if we hammer at God's door long enough, He will be forced to listen. Many Christians fall into this trap. In fact, the best kind of worship is found in silence before God.

Jesus emphasizes two things: Firstly, all prayer must be directed at God. Our only thought and desire should be to meet God. Secondly, Jesus reminds us that we are praying to a God of love, who is more willing to answer our prayers than we are to pray. We mustn't think we have to drag His gifts and grace out of Him, but remember that we are speaking to Someone who is only too willing to give.

Father God, teach me through the Holy Spirit to pray to You in spirit and in truth.

Approach God in Solitude

"When you pray, don't babble on and on as people of other religions do. They think their prayers are answered merely by repeating their words again and again" (Matt. 6:7).

The last fault Jesus found with some prayers was that they prayed to be seen by others. Prayer times were at 09:00, 12:00 and 15:00, wherever a person found themselves at the time. So it was quite easy to make sure they were on a busy street corner at these fixed times so that everybody could see how committed they were. It was nothing but play-acting and not genuine prayer at all. To those who were proud, the Jewish prayer system lent itself to showing off.

Jesus laid down two central prayer rules. The first, as previously mentioned, was that all prayer was to be directed at God. Jesus' criticism was aimed at people who didn't pray to God, but to people. You daren't be more concerned about impressing the crowds than meeting with Jesus. Whether it is public or private prayer, the person who prays must have no other thought on their mind and no other desire in their heart other than to meet with God.

> The first rule of right prayer is to have our heart and mind framed as becomes those who are entering into converse with God.
> JOHN CALVIN

Secondly, Jesus insisted that we remember that the God who hears our prayer is a God of love and that He is more than willing to answer our prayers. For this reason Jesus urges us to approach God in solitude so that we exclude all people and thoughts from our prayer time and focus only on God.

Master and Savior, teach me through the Holy Spirit what it is to really pray in faith.

How to Pray

"When you pray, go away by yourself, shut the door behind you, and pray to your Father in private. Then your Father, who sees everything, will reward you" (Matt. 6:6).

Prayer in general should be one of the most intimate things in the lives of God's people. We can only approach it with holy reverence. Prayer fills even those who know nothing about it with awe. When they see someone with hands folded in prayer and head bowed, they involuntarily put their finger to their lips. People always realize that the person is standing before the highest Majesty; they hesitate and are shrouded in respectful silence until the prayer is finished. In a church service it is always the most touching moment when heads are bowed in unison and the entire community kneels before God.

> Prayer is less about changing the world than it is about changing ourselves.
> DAVID J. WOLPE

However, where it is customary for all family members to read the Word of God together, every family member experiences the uplifting, sacred and comforting power of communal prayer. Even when they have grown old, many people still remember their family's prayers.

Let's take a look at the prayer prayed "secretly." Jesus portrays it in a masterly way: "When you pray ... " is how He begins. In the previous verses we read of how the hypocrites and the religious fakes prayed. They deliberately made a public show of prayer. These people received their reward from the public: they were regarded as superbly devoted people, they were called the pillars of the kingdom of God. This was their reward, while God in heaven concealed His face from them. Thus we sense the contrast when Jesus cautions His disciples: "When you pray, go away by yourself, shut the door behind you."

Holy Father, thank You for the gift of prayer.

Quiet Moments with God

"When you pray, go away by yourself, shut the door behind you, and pray to your Father in private" (Matt. 6:6).

⌁ ⟳ ⌁

Perhaps, even nowadays, we can do with the advice Christ gives us – because many of us don't have a place for our quiet time, a quiet room where we can bare our souls to God. It's not about the room, but about the quiet moments we spend alone with God. Life is so demanding these days. We have a hundred responsibilities in and outside the home, as well as our Christian activities and duties. In many houses there is no such thing as a quiet room anymore.

Because of this, it is difficult to concentrate, introspection becomes rare and we don't feel the need to withdraw from the buzz of the world as much, and to find strength in fellowship with God. We know that this results in spiritual impoverishment. We can only stay strong and powerful in our deepest being through solitary fellowship with God. When you are alone behind a closed door to escape from the world with its pressing problems, you should not even leave the door ajar. If you do, you can be sure that the world will follow you and disturb your quiet time.

> Only the prayer which comes from our heart can get to God's heart.
> CHARLES H. SPURGEON

What it boils down to is that we need to have a closed door between us and the world outside. Even the presence of a best friend is a hindrance. If ever anyone knew how to pray it was Jesus, and yet He withdrew from the circle of His most trusted apostles to spend the entire night alone on a solitary mountaintop in prayer with His Father. This is what it means to "shut the door behind you."

Loving Father, thank You for those precious moments of prayer with You behind a closed door.

Pray in Seclusion

"When you pray, go away by yourself. Then your Father, who sees everything, will reward you" (Matt. 6:6).

It is a rich and deep lesson that Jesus teaches us here. First of all it declares that God is not a visible God. He is concealed in the glory of heaven; He is concealed in the sunshine; He is hidden in the wind; He is disguised in the rustling leaves in the treetops. On mountaintops and in valleys, yes, our God is everywhere, but He is a hidden God. This is why He comes behind the closed door to refresh His children's souls. He is God; He is also the Father who knows everything.

> Prayer is not a matter of getting what we want the most. Prayer is a matter of giving ourselves to God and learning His laws, so that He can do through us what He wants the most.
>
> AGNES SANFORD

Pray to your Father in your solitude, because the Father's name is a guarantee that He is listening to your words, your stuttered prayer, your whispers and even to the silent sighing of your heart: "Then your Father, who sees everything, will reward you." The actors praying on the streets find their reward in the reaction of people who call out, "Look how devout they are!" But the solitary person praying in seclusion finds their reward from God. He blesses them in all kinds of ways to show them that their prayers are heard and answered.

Abraham prayed and was given the promise that Sodom and Gomorrah would be spared; Moses prayed and every time it brought a stop to the plagues in Egypt; Elijah prayed and heaven was locked and reopened; Samson prayed and made the temple of Dagon topple down. We can go on giving examples of New Testament prayer heroes. God rewards in royal fashion the person who prays sincerely.

I thank You, Father God, that I never pray to You in vain.

The Quiet Room

"When you pray, go away by yourself, and pray to your Father in private. Then your Father, who sees everything, will reward you" (Matt. 6:6).

God richly rewards secret prayer! Many a woman has a quiet place where she goes first thing in the morning. There she prepares for the day by quietly folding her hands in prayer. How does she manage to keep going? The secret is the "secret" prayer of her quiet time. God never leaves us to fend for ourselves.

We often see this repeated in other situations. Broken by our sins, we fall to our knees and pray for mercy, pleading the blood of Christ that was spilt for the forgiveness of sins. And God rewards us by pouring out His peace – peace that surpasses all understanding. Where do the youth get the strength to survive the battle of the flesh; to be more than conquerors? In the quiet room! Where do we find the grace to keep quiet when we are verbally abused, and when we are slapped on the right cheek, to turn the other one also? In the quiet room!

> He who has learned to pray has learned the greatest secret of a holy and happy life.
> WILLIAM LAW

Why is it that some people struggle so at the death of a loved one, while others reverently lift tearful eyes to heaven, their souls quiet before God? Once again the answer is: in the quiet room! There the person with hands folded in prayer is rewarded by God with strength and courage. We don't have all the answers, but one fact remains: We will always be put to shame by His reward – the abundance of His grace – and then our prayer becomes a song of praise and thankfulness for God's undeserved reward.

Jesus, my Example in prayer, I thank You for the reward You give me in my quiet room.

Conversations with God

"When you pray, don't babble on and on as people of other religions do" (Matt. 6:7).

The Jewish liturgy provided prescribed prayers for all occasions. There is practically not a single aspect of life for which there wasn't a prescribed prayer. The idea was to bring every occurrence in life to God. But because the prayers were so strictly prescribed, the entire system lent itself to formalism. The result was prayers without meaning.

We mustn't see prayer as formal duty, but as an act of humility by which we receive God's undeserved goodness. Our prayers must be new and fresh every day, because this formalism is not only something that threatens Jews. Even our quiet times can degenerate into formal and rigid rituals. The dedicated Jews had fixed times for prayer. Wherever a person happened to be at that specific time, they had to pray. It was possible that some people were sincere and remembered God, or it could have been a mere formality for others, and then the prayer was only words, without giving God a thought.

> There is no man nor church in the world that can come to God in prayer, but by the assistance of the Holy Spirit.
> JOHN BUNYAN

There was also a tendency to link certain prayers to certain places, especially with the synagogue. It is true that there are specific locations where one is more inclined to pray and so it became a habit to go to the temple daily during prayer times. The danger of this custom is that people might start feeling that God is limited to certain holy places, forgetting that the entire earth is God's temple. The problem doesn't develop as a result of the system, but in the people for whom it becomes a habit more than anything else.

Father God, make my conversations with You holy.

Our Father!

"Our Father in heaven ... " (Matt. 6:9).

The word "father" conjures up different feelings for different people: a loving advisor; treasured friend; faithful provider – to name but a few. Then there are those who might say, "If He's anything like my father, I hate Him." Others say that God is the kind of Father they would have wanted. With the disciples, who lived in a patriarchal community, the entire family's life revolved around the father: He provided for the family, protected them and maintained discipline. Jesus illustrated this kind of father in the parable of the Prodigal Son. He didn't stop loving his willful son and he didn't punish him when he returned.

Can God's character be revealed in a word like "father"? There are more than two hundred names for God, yet Jesus chose "Father" because it is the easiest for people to understand. God becomes "Abba" – the affectionate name Hebrew children used to address their fathers. We, as sinners, may call the Holy God, the Consuming Fire, Father. Those who have no hope left, who have no prospects of a heavenly home, may call Him Father.

> Earthly fathers and mothers, husbands, wives, children and earthly friends, are all shadows. But God is the substance.
>
> JONATHAN EDWARDS

What does this say to us? It says that God loves us with an unfathomable love; a love that gave His Son to suffer and die for our sins. The person who understands this is like the little boy standing on the street corner shouting down the street, "The Father is coming! The Father is coming!" He does this not so that the other children must run like terrified chickens, but that they will leave everything: sand castles, mud pies and tricycles, and run towards Him, who stands with open arms.

Father, thank You for the great privilege of calling You Father.

Our Father

"Pray like this: Our Father in heaven ... " (Matt. 6:9).

To whom did Jesus pray? His Father! "Father, forgive them ... "; "Father, I entrust my spirit into Your hands ... " This relationship is there for all of us; all we need do is make it our own. All who accept Him have a heavenly Father. And those who stubbornly refuse? When the Pharisees rejected the truth, Jesus wanted to teach them, so He said, "You are the children of your father the devil, and you love to do the evil things he does" (John 8:44). Through Jesus, God says to His children, "Do not let your hearts be troubled. Trust in God; trust also in Me" (John 14:1).

> He who thinks most of heaven will do most for earth.
> ANONYMOUS

When we pray, "Our Father ... " we acknowledge God as Father and all the marvelous things that go with this. And we do not say only "Father," but "Our Father." With this, Christ unites all His children as spiritual brothers and sisters. In addition to our relationship with God, we also have a relationship with one another. We share our lives with others and it is not always easy, but it is possible, and a precondition in God's household. When we pray, "Our Father ... " we commit ourselves to loving God as well as our fellow humans.

Have you ever said to God: "I don't want to be Your child. I want to be a runaway child. You are not my Father!" Or have you been praying the Lord's Prayer like you learnt it as a child, without understanding? Have you used it as a magic word in the hope that it would make the impossible possible? May God grant that from now on you will say like a trusting child, "My Father, I love You dearly!"

Loving Father God, thank You that I have been able to get to know You and that I can share in the sonship of believers.

The Names of God

"Pray like this: Our Father in heaven ... " (Matt. 6:9).

Yesterday we talked about "Our Father," a loving and compassionate Father, as a good-natured father ought to be. But this Father in heaven is also God. That is His name: a glorious, heavenly, holy name. His name is different and cannot be compared to any other name. His name encompasses all: All-knowing, All-seeing, All-mighty. When Moses asked Him at the burning bush who He was, He answered, "I am who I am."

His name is clearly written across creation: on every dewdrop, every cloud, on every majestic mountain and in every green valley. His name is evident in the order of the universe, but especially in His covenant, in Christ and in the Holy Spirit. We find the very being of the only true God in Christ: "Anyone who has seen Me has seen the Father!" (John 14:9). Other than the evil that loves anonymity and wants to strip us of our identity, God has a name and He has made it known to us: The Holy One, the Almighty, the Eternal: "Holy, holy, holy is the Lord God Almighty, who always was, and is, and is to come" (Rev. 4:8 NIV).

> The name of God is anything by which He makes Himself known to us.
> WESTMINSTER CATECHISM

And what do we, insignificant humans, do with God's name? This name is flung across the globe: in books, by word of mouth, in the media, in films and theaters, on walls and obscure places. In the process the name is violated. We abuse His name and make it hollow, insignificant and meaningless. We don't think about what we say or whose name we misuse. "The Lord sits in majesty in Jerusalem, exalted above all the nations. Let them praise Your great and awesome name. Your name is holy!" (Ps. 99:2-3).

Most Holy God, grant that I will keep Your name holy.

Keep His Name Holy

"Our Father in heaven, may Your name be kept holy" (Matt. 6:9).

We are called to honor the name of God. Yet we use His name as a swear word; sometimes in a crude and coarse manner to shock people, as a stopgap when we're too lazy to think, or to let off steam. This is blatant abuse that will not go unpunished. There is also the subtle misuse of His name with variations like "Jeez" or "Gee" for Jesus. We curse in His name when we want to insult someone. This is shocking slander.

We commit perjury in His name. We agree to speak the truth in the presence of God, but we tell lies and half-truths. We put our hand on the Bible and declare: "The truth, the whole truth and nothing but the truth." Small wonder the church voiced its concern and suggested we do away with the oath, because God is slandered by it. The oath remains, but the Bible is no longer used.

> Even in the church we seem to have lost the vision of the majesty of God.
> JOHN STOTT

We often say God's name without respect or reverence when we worship. Words are simply recited or sung or prayed. Our heart is not in them and they are empty, with no soul. We read the Bible while our thoughts are far away and we sing without spirit. We perform religious rituals purely out of habit.

What then must we do with His name? We must do what is done in heaven: We must keep His name holy; pray reverently to God; praise His name enthusiastically in church; and honor His name in religious ceremonies, Holy Communion, and other events. We must confess His name before people and protect it. Our whole lives must be an answer to the prayer, "May Your name be kept holy."

Holy God, I will do my utmost to honor Your name.

Your Kingdom Come

"May Your Kingdom come soon" (Matt. 6:10).

The first three sentences of the Lord's Prayer are about God: His name, His kingdom and His will. Our text today refers to God's kingdom – a prayer for our modern day, for our world, for our battered country, and for you and me personally. To say, "May Your kingdom come soon" seems a contradiction. Isn't it already God's world, His universe? Of course everything belongs to God. But prayer appears to be contradictory. God doesn't steamroll everything under His rule. We can still choose our "own kingdoms" over His – but the worst happens when we are left to ourselves. When we pray for God's kingdom to come, we pray for faith in God to come: that we and all people may live in faith. For this reason the Heidelberg Catechism prays: "Rule us by Your Word and Spirit in such a way that more and more we submit to You."

> Inside the will of God there is no failure. Outside the will of God there is no success.
> **BERNARD EDINGER**

There is no problem with God's kingdom. The problem lies with us and our submission to it. With this prayer we ask for the downfall and destruction of our self-made kingdoms. It is a liberating prayer, spanning the world in all its facets.

The artist Raphael created an impressive painting of the Madonna – Jesus' mother. He brought it to Dresden as a gift for the king. They looked around in the throne room for the best place to display it; the light had to be just right, the position central in order to display it best. The only option was where the throne stood, but the king said, "Make room for the immortal Raphael!" It sounds appropriate – but it is wrong: God alone deserves the throne. Therefore: "Make room for the kingdom of God!"

Lord, I praise You, that Your kingdom has come in my life.

The Kingdom of God

"May Your Kingdom come soon" (Matt. 6:10).

This prayer calls on us to pray that people would be saved; that they would come to God and acknowledge Him of their own free will. He has already come to us through Christ; He came through His Spirit on the Day of Pentecost; He wants to come to you today. When we pray this prayer, we are absolutely sure that God will answer it. The kingdom of God is coming, through us or in spite of us.

The kingdom of God is one of the central themes of the New Testament. This phrase forms a specific part of Christian literature and doctrine; it is therefore essential that we find clarity in our own hearts about it. Jesus' first public appearance in Galilee, after His wilderness experience, was charged with this theme. Jesus was commissioned to proclaim this kingdom: "I must preach the Good News of the kingdom of God, because that is why I was sent" (Luke 4:43). Christ was the bearer of the Good News of the Kingdom. We can gather from this that the Kingdom on earth is a life or community where God's will is perfectly obeyed – just like in heaven.

> There can be no kingdom of God in the world without the kingdom of God in our hearts.
> ALBERT SCHWEITZER

To be in the kingdom of God is to obey God's will completely. This applies to each of us. It is to devote our heart, our will, our thoughts and our lives completely to God. It is to pray, "Lord, let Your kingdom come – and start with me!" It is to say, "Let Your will be done in my life!" The kingdom of God is where Jesus is. Jesus says Himself in Luke 17:21: "You won't be able to say, 'Here it is!' or 'It's over there!' For the Kingdom of God is among you."

Lord Jesus, thank You that I may find the kingdom of God in You.

Lessons from Jesus

"May Your Kingdom come soon" (Matt. 6:10).

Many people have a problem with the concept of the "kingdom of God." This is because they have a narrow-minded image of His kingdom and fail to see its greatness, its all-encompassing power and majesty. Their walk with the Holy Spirit is limited, because He is the one who teaches us about the Kingdom. So how do we learn about it? Firstly, in Jesus' parables: The Wise and Foolish Girls (Matt. 25); the Seed and the Sower (Matt. 13); the Mustard Seed (Matt. 13); the Marriage Feast (Matt. 22); and many more. Secondly, we learn about His kingdom through His call to conversion, found in the Sermon on the Mount (Matt. 5, 6 and 7). Thirdly, by His rebirth (Jesus' conversation with Nicodemus in John 3). Jesus demonstrated the Kingdom in His life – He lived and died for it.

> Peace does not dwell in outward things, but within the soul.
> FRANCOIS FÈNELON

So how do we become a part of God's kingdom? By acknowledging His kingship over our entire lives and mustering all our strength to work together to expand His kingdom. It can only be done in co-operation with the Holy Spirit: "You will receive power when the Holy Spirit has come upon you. And you will be My witnesses, telling people about Me everywhere" (Acts 1:8). This is what the whole book of Acts is about. You can also become part of God's kingdom by living in His fellowship.

People will see it and know that you belong to the kingdom of God and that you are helping to spread the gospel as far as it is within your power. They will know that God is your King. This is why we pray, "May Your Kingdom come soon."

O God, I pray that Your kingdom may come soon!

The Will of God

"May Your will be done on earth, as it is in heaven" (Matt. 6:10).

This prayer is simultaneously a liberating and a challenging one. It is liberating because it brings us to the believer's acceptance of God's perfect will. It is challenging because one of the most difficult things for humans is to submit ourselves to God. From the start God had a master plan with His creation – and that includes the life of every person. God wants to carry out His plan, but Satan is always trying to subtly sabotage it.

By praying this prayer, we ask no less than the death of our own willfulness – and this means surrendering our lives. With this, we surrender ourselves completely to God. We humans suffer from an almost indestructible, strong and eternal self-love and that is why this is a dangerous prayer: It could cost us our lives. Martin Luther claimed that it was a dangerous prayer, because it meant obedience without talking back. Of course, we are sometimes willing to compromise: a part of His will; half; a quarter; or, in a generous moment, we are prepared to give up nine-tenths of our will.

> The will of God will never take you to where the grace of God will not protect you.
> ANONYMOUS

With this prayer, we ask for the strength to be obedient and devoted to God's will; we ask for the power to resist Satan. Some people do the will of the majority, others say they are their own boss and will do as they please. Who can really meet God's demands? No one! It is impossible for humans. On this broken earth there was only One who could do God's will to perfection: Jesus, the living Christ! "My nourishment comes from doing the will of God, who sent Me, and from finishing His work" (John 4:34).

Holy Father God, let Your perfect will be done in my life.

The Example

"May Your will be done on earth, as it is in heaven" (Matt. 6:10).

⟨❀⟩

Only one person here on earth could do God's will to perfection. He set the example for us in Gethsemane, when He wrestled in prayer and handed over His struggle to God. In and through Christ it is also possible for us.

The kingdom of God starts here on earth, when God's will is done just as perfectly as in heaven. Doing His will is being part of the kingdom of God. Then heaven comes into our hearts; this is why Christ says that the kingdom of God is "in" us. Naturally people say, "Your will be done" in different ways. Some say it in desperate defeat. Then it is no prayer; it is fatalism – blind fate that manipulates people like pawns.

Then there are those who say it with a spirit of bitter rebelliousness. They see God as a strong enemy that no one can defeat. They accept His will, but do it grudgingly and with suppressed anger.

> In His will is our peace.
> DANTE

There are also people who pray this prayer in love and complete trust. Their wish is to do God's will as perfectly as it is done in heaven. These people are sure of God's wisdom and love. They believe that God wants only the best for us. What is God's will for you personally? What is God's will for our country? What is God's will for the world? In so doing, this prayer connects heaven and earth. What we are in fact pleading for is that our willfulness, our stubbornness will make way for service, love, peace and reconciliation. That's why we pray, "May Your will be done on earth, as it is in heaven."

I praise and thank You, Lord Jesus, that You teach me to submit unconditionally to God's will.

The Final Victory

They found that the stone had been rolled away from the entrance. So they went in, but they didn't find the body of the Lord Jesus (Luke 24:2-3).

The things that took place on that first Easter Sunday defied all belief. The entrance to the tomb was safeguarded by a massive stone that could not be moved without a major undertaking and lots of noise. Additionally, the tomb had been officially sealed so that no one could go in or out. To crown it all, soldiers kept guard at the grave throughout the night.

Yet as the day broke after an uneventful night, it was discovered that the stone had been rolled away and that the tomb was empty.

> The empty tomb of Christ has been the cradle of the church.
>
> PRESSENSÉ

No matter what ideas people come up with, nothing in the hundreds of years since the event has provided a satisfactory explanation. It is clear that nothing less than a miracle took place: Jesus' prophecy came to pass and the will of God was fulfilled.

Jesus conquered death – He emerged from the tomb, and is alive for all eternity! Now we can rejoice with Peter: "All praise to God, the Father of our Lord Jesus Christ. It is by His great mercy that we have been born again, because God raised Jesus Christ from the dead" (1 Pet. 1:3).

Resurrected and glorified Lord Jesus, thank You that You won the victory over death and made eternal life possible for me.

Sin

"Forgive us our sins, as we have forgiven those who sin against us" (Matt. 6:12).

We find it extremely difficult to say, "I'm guilty!" or, "Please forgive me!" But this is the only way to be forgiven. It is the bridge we must cross in order to lay our burden of sin at the foot of the cross. But when it concerns our own honor and prestige, the sinful nature of humans is quite devious, as we see when we read about the fall of Adam and Eve in paradise. We read how they tried to put the blame on others: Adam blamed Eve; Eve said the snake tricked her. But Adam even went a step further – he said it was God's fault: "It was the woman You gave me" (Gen. 3:12). But all his inventiveness was to no avail; he was guilty and he knew it.

> When Christ's hands were nailed to the cross, He also nailed our sins to the cross.
> ST. BERNARD OF CLAIRVAUX

Isn't God being unfair when He demands things we are unable to do? Surely God is being unreasonable. And so we convince ourselves that we are victims. We say that God treats us unfairly when He punishes us. Do you remember when you were little, how you went around the corner after being punished and sat there all alone, crying with self-pity – because "nobody loves me"? Even at that early age we knew how to mask our guilt with self-pity. This tactic of playing the victim is as old as humanity. The lazy servant in the Parable of the Talents did it: "I was afraid I would lose your money, so I hid it in the earth. Look, here is your money back" (Matt. 25:24-25). The single coin in his hand was proof, but he was in fact insinuating that he was the one who was wronged and that his master was unreasonable to expect anything more of him.

Lord Jesus, the sin in my life – that is my pain. Relieve it with Your forgiveness.

Willful Disobedience

"Forgive us our sins, as we have forgiven those who sin against us" (Matt. 6:12).

⌒◷⌒

There is, however, a serious short circuit in the logic of us sinners. Nothing is ever as innocent and simple as we would like to think. We cannot escape from being accountable for our sins. God created humans with the ability to obey His will; after all, we were created in His image. But because of our sin, we have destroyed that image. Our problem is not injustice, but the willful disobedience and transgression of God's will.

The sooner we stop justifying or covering up our own faults, the sooner we get to what Christ wants to teach us in this prayer: "Forgive my sins, O God! I have sinned against both heaven and You! O God, have mercy on me, a sinner!" But we don't want to say this, because we still have a few excuses up our sleeve. No, God will certainly not let sin go unpunished. He is angered by sin and will judge it fairly and punish it temporarily and forever.

> Sin is to cast aside the will of God and to live according to one's own will.
> SUNDAR SINGH

Sin stirs up God's fierce wrath and indignation. This statement may seem strange and unacceptable to the modern man. A God of love whose anger is righteous – surely this is unthinkable. People in our day want to create a kindly, harmless image of God: a dear old Father who just looks the other way when we sin. Neither the Old nor the New Testament acknowledges such a God. And because we demote God and water Him down, we don't have an idea of the vileness of sin and we refuse to pray, "Forgive us our sins."

Crucified Lord Jesus, thank You again that You paid my debt of sin. Help me to live in such a way that the world will know what the forgiveness of my sins cost You.

No Compromise

"Forgive us our sins, as we have forgiven those who sin against us" (Matt. 6:12).

Our God is a holy God, and He makes no compromise with sin – He doesn't tolerate it at all! In this day and age, even the idea of punishment is becoming outdated. Children must not be punished anymore because it infringes on their personal rights. But sin remains sin before God and we pay a high price for it.

Now the sinful human grabs at straws: Is God not merciful? He is after all, love. But He is also just and holy! We must not play His holiness off against His love. Of course God is merciful. The fact that we are alive is proof of God's mercy. But His love is by no means weak; it is strong and holy. It gives much but also demands much.

God is merciful – but God is also just! God is just – but God is also merciful! Do you see the difference between the two concepts? Come with me to Golgotha – there the impossible became possible! There the tension was broken when Jesus was broken. There righteousness and mercy flowed into one.

> God has cast our confessed sins into the depths of the sea, and He's even put a 'No Fishing' sign over the spot.
> DWIGHT L. MOODY

Jesus had to die for the sake of God's righteousness. He paid the highest price so that we, the rebels, could be set free. He endured God's wrath so that we could experience His love. He was forsaken by God so that we could know God, never to be forsaken again. He carried our curse so that we might be showered with blessings. The message of Golgotha is: God is righteous! God is love! That is why Jesus teaches us to pray, "Forgive us our sins."

O Lord, I hear Your voice calling, "Oh, come to Me, so that with My precious blood I can set you free."

March

The Heart of the Father

Since we are living by the Spirit, let us follow
the Spirit's leading in every part of our lives.
~ Galatians 5:25

I know the Bible is inspired because it finds me
at greater depths of my being than any other book.
~ SAMUEL TAYLOR COLERIDGE

O Holy Spirit of God,
come now and live forever in my heart and in my thoughts.
Be the inspiration, through the Word,
for all my thoughts and deeds.
Take possession of my imagination and grant
that all my thoughts may be in line with the Word.
Take possession of the deepest core of my will,
and through Your Word, control my life in its totality.
God-given Word, be with me in my silence and in my words,
when I work and when I relax, in the freshness of the morning
and also the melancholy of the night.
Grant me the grace, Spirit of the Word, to delight
in the mystery of Your pronouncements.
Make my heart an altar and pour the
purifying fire of Your love into it.
Spirit of the Word, be with me today in everything I do.
Don't let me deny friendliness and courtesy to those around
me, for I know I'm being true to the
Word in the way I treat others.
O Holy Spirit, be with me when I
read and study the Word today.
Grant that it would refresh my spirit
so that I will keep on seeking in it
the pure, and the good, and the true.
Lord Jesus, You broke the bread there at the lake,
break every day Your Bread of Life for me, O Lord.

Amen.

Forgiveness Received and Given

"If you forgive those who sin against you, your heavenly Father will forgive you. But if you refuse to forgive others, your Father will not forgive your sins" (Matt. 6:14-15).

The Lord's Prayer has an important condition: In order to be forgiven, we need to forgive. Those who forgive others have all had the same experience – they have been forgiven. Helmut Thielicke says that forgiveness is like a relay race. We must always receive the baton of forgiveness first and then pass it on again. Anyone who breaks the rules of the race is disqualified. We must receive the baton of forgiveness from God's hand and then go out into the world, passing it on to everyone, and yes, even to our enemies.

Forgiveness remains a struggle that runs counter to our ego, pride and self-assertiveness. If we refuse it, we burn the bridge that we ourselves have to cross in order to find forgiveness. Christ puts a very high premium on forgiveness. He not only preached it, but also practiced it. When He was nailed to the cross,

> It is always the case that when a Christian looks back, he is looking at the forgiveness of sins.
>
> KARL BARTH

He prayed for those who had nailed Him to it: "Father, forgive them, for they don't know what they are doing" (Luke 23:34). Peter wanted to know how many times a person had to forgive The Rabbis taught that you had to forgive three times and then no more. Peter was generous in his self-satisfaction and was prepared to forgive up to seven times. Then Jesus brought him back to earth: not seven times, but seventy times seven times! For Christ there are no limits. In order to be forgiven, you must forgive!

God of love and mercy, I praise You that all my sins have been erased. Give me the ability to forgive others like You forgave me.

Hand in Hand

"Forgive us our sins, as we have forgiven those who sin against us" (Matt. 6:12).

We must forgive to be forgiven. Those who refuse to forgive cannot lay claim to God's forgiveness. Godly and human forgiveness go hand in hand. Why? Because we owe God infinitely more than a human being could ever owe us. Christ told the parable of the man who was in great debt, but because of his stirring pleas, he received forgiveness from a loving and merciful king. Soon afterwards, he had a fellow officer put in prison because the man owed him a few coins. Nothing that any person owes us can be compared to what we owe God – and yet we treat our earthly debtors so poorly. We can do nothing to pay our debt of sin, but Christ paid all our debts so that we could go free as ransomed people.

> Forgiveness of sins is the very heart of Christianity, and yet it is a mighty dangerous thing to preach.
> MARTIN LUTHER

We need to learn to forget. As long as we remember a wrong and feed it in our mind, there is no way we will forgive. We often say, "I'll never forget what so-and-so did to me." And then the offense grows out of all proportion in our imagination and we make it even more difficult to forgive. There is also the clumsy remark, "I'll forgive but never forget." This is not forgiveness, just a lame excuse to nurture the grievance.

We need to learn to love. We can't love someone and refuse to forgive that person. Love clears all stumbling blocks and makes communication possible. Love connects us to God – He who forgave us in love so that we could forgive others. Of course it is not easy to forgive. It cost God His Son to forgive us.

Holy Father, I stand in awe of Your ability to forgive. Help me to follow Your example and forgive others.

Protection from Sin

"Don't let us yield to temptation, but rescue us from the evil one" (Matt. 6:13).

～⌇～

Temptation puts us right in the midst of sin. The devil *tempts* us to bring out the worst in us, while the Lord *tests* us to bring out the best. No one is safeguarded from temptation. This prayer is a plea that God would help us resist temptation; that He would give us the strength to pass the test. In today's Scripture, we see that Satan went as far as tempting even Jesus. But Christ was victorious and that is why we should stay close to Jesus.

Temptation can come from outside: friends who want to lead us astray; avarice; ambition; pride. But temptation can also come from within. It is possible that we have a weak spot in our spiritual life. How does one resist temptation? Through self-respect and integrity. If you lose that, life is hardly worth living. James Garfield, the 20th U.S. president, was requested to do something dishonest that would mean great financial gain. He was told, "No one will ever know!" His answer was, "President Garfield will know and I must live with him. And, naturally, God will know." We are often saved from sin by the pain in a mother or father's eyes. Think of the sorrow in Jesus' eyes when Peter denied Him.

> You don't drown by falling in the water; you drown by staying there.
> EDWIN L. COLE

There is also the living presence of Jesus Christ. This is also our strength – the fact that He is always with us. He was tempted just like we are and He triumphed. Prayer is of the utmost importance. We can't stumble when we're on our knees.

Lord Jesus, give me the strength to resist temptation through the inspiration that Your actions bring.

Longing for Home

"A man had two sons" (Luke 15:11).

W e have a place called "home" and we often want to return there when life gets tough. It is a deep longing for a place and surroundings of yesteryear.

King Constantine of Greece, who was in exile in England for many years, was willing to formally renounce his kingship if he could only go back "home" as an ordinary citizen.

We read in Psalm 137 of the Israelite prisoners of war pining for their country in Babylon: "Beside the rivers of Babylon, we sat and wept as we thought of Jerusalem" (Ps. 137:1). People have an inborn and everlasting attachment to "home," which cannot be blotted out. We read in 2 Samuel 23:15: "David remarked longingly to his men, 'Oh, how I would love some of that good water from the well by the gate in Bethlehem.'" David was fleeing for his life from Saul's rage and was hiding in caves and forests. He saw Bethlehem from the top of a mountain – his hometown where he was born and raised, where he looked after sheep as a young boy and drew water from the well thousands of times.

> Three things are necessary for the salvation of man: to know what he ought to believe; to know what he ought to desire; and to know what he ought to do.
> THOMAS AQUINAS

All of us have these pangs of nostalgia for the place of our youth. And this is the way it is with God, the loving Father. We can go as far away from Him as we like, but our hearts always bring us back to Him. We have a longing for God and the longer we stay away from Him, the stronger this wistfulness becomes.

Praise the Lord because He is good! His love is everlasting! Thank You, Loving Father, that You put eternity in my heart and that You are home to me.

The Parable of the Prodigal Son

May the enemies of my lord the king and all who rise up to harm you be like that young man (2 Sam. 18:32 NIV).

⟨ ༄ ⟩

The Lord Jesus told the Parable of the Loving Father and the Prodigal Son with three groups of people in mind:

- His disciples that He wanted to equip for their task.
- Tax collectors and sinners who came to listen to Jesus' words. They were the strays from faraway lands who had an overpowering longing to return to the Father's house.
- The Pharisees and Scribes – the conceited church leaders of the time, whose rules and laws made it practically impossible for the repentant sinner to become part of the church.

We must also keep in mind that there were two sons in the Parable of the Prodigal Son; that in the final analysis, both were in fact rebels. We have all sinned and none of us deserve God's grace and love. One son openly rebelled against his father. The other stayed home with the soul of a slave, a hypocrite, and nursed the viper of secret revolt deep in his heart.

> I was not born to be free. I was born to adore and obey.
> C. S. Lewis

Rebellion against authority is a tragic, though common, human behavior. How many parents have called out with broken hearts while wringing their hands, "O my son Absalom! My son, my son!" (2 Sam. 18:33). Sadly, it often happens that tight-lipped children with spiked shoes and hard hearts trample love and authority underfoot, disregarding the discipline and caring of their parents' home. They leave to find the freedom of a life they planned and dreamed of – not realizing that it is an illusion.

Holy and loving Father, make me strong when Satan incites me to rebel. Thank You that I am welcome in the Father's house.

Two Sons

"A man had two sons" (Luke 15:11)

At first this is all we know about the older son. The older boy stayed home: an obedient, hardworking and loyal son. But he was without love and joy. He was hemmed in by the limitations of the father's house, but he stayed because he felt it was his duty. He was also the eldest, the firstborn. According to tradition he had a certain status in the household:

- He would receive a double share of the inheritance.
- At his father's death, he would be the head of the household.
- He has a lot of influence even while his father is still alive.
- He has a say in everything as the future owner.

Then the younger son left home. Perhaps it was because of the premature arrogance of his older brother, rather than rebellion against his father. Perhaps the older brother acted as if he was the father and as if his word carried as much weight as their father's. It could be that the older brother deprived his brother of joy in the home by constantly laying down the law.

> The church is the great lost and found department.
>
> ROBERT SHORT

Eternity will one day reveal how many people turned away from the church of Christ by the unloving behavior of "older brothers" who judge people as if they are God. The younger brother chose to see something of the world and to enjoy his inheritance, without having to be accountable to his older brother all the time. Dear older brother, make room for loving the younger brother if you don't want to share in the responsibility for his fall.

Heavenly Father God, help me to minister love and friendliness to all Your children.

Rebellion against Authority

"The younger son told his father, 'I want my share of your estate now before you die'" (Luke 15:12).

There is an almost unbearable sadness about unthankful children. It is an inexplicable situation that can only be traced back to humanity's original sin. Why would you want to tear yourself loose from the Father's arms?

- Because of the inability to understand a parent's unfathomable love. Children accept this privilege as a right, until they stand at the gravestone with tears in their eyes, and then it is too late. Or until they become parents and experience this situation themselves. There is a lack of gratitude for the privilege of being in the Father's house – a place where you belong.
- There are also the so-called irritations and grievances about things in the home. The child doesn't say, "Thank you for raising me, clothing me, caring for me, and teaching me." No, he comes with the ruthless demands.

> Obedience is the only virtue which plants the other virtues in the mind, and cares for them when they are planted.
>
> St. Gregory the Great

He refuses to be a slave any longer and to submit to authority. "I'm not a baby anymore; I'm an adult with common sense and I can think for myself. I know what's good for me. And in any case: old people don't keep up with the times. Their opinions are old-fashioned and outdated – behind the times! Why can't I plan my own life, do my own thing for a change?

And so the irritations and complaints multiply until breaking-point is reached. The child repeats these accusations so often that he starts believing them, against his own better judgment.

Hold me tight, Lord Jesus, especially when the devil has made me blind and deaf to the wealth of love I undeservedly receive.

Yearning for [the Illusion of] Freedom

"I want my share of your estate" (Luke 15:12).

───✧───

The restrictive but loving protection of the parental home is suddenly seen as slavery. Like so many before and after him, the boy now suddenly believes unerringly in freedom:

- Freedom of thought, even if it means rejecting his father and his home – as long as his thinking is not restricted!
- Freedom of action: To go where he pleases, when he wants and how he wants; to make friends with whomever he chooses; to spend his time as he sees fit.

Suddenly everything at home restricts his freedom: he is not allowed to stay out late; he may not visit questionable places; he is expected to go to church; to take part in family devotions; and read the Bible and pray before he goes to bed. "This is enough to drive one up the wall. All my friends do what they want. I'm going to find freedom. I want my share of the estate. I'm leaving."

> Why did God give free will to human beings? Because free will, though it makes evil possible, is also the only thing that makes possible any love or joy or goodness worth having.
>
> C. S. Lewis

How dismal is the picture of the person who strayed from God. Maybe your religion is painful slavery to you. Perhaps you are already leaving the house of your heavenly Father. There is hope for you! Christ died so that the gates of paradise can be opened again for you. You *can* go back to paradise, to the Father's house, to happiness and love and true freedom. Christ died so that you could live safely and securely in the Father's house.

Loving and faithful Father, I thank You for the anchors in my life that keep me secure in Your love. I find freedom and joy in You only.

Breaking Free

"I want my share of your estate now" (Luke 15:12).

⟨ ᛞᏩ ⟩

O ur estrangement from God follows a definite and recogniz-
able pattern:

First we are anchored in the Father's house; then gradual
resistance grows; this is followed by the inevitable break.

At first there is just a hidden, unspoken motive: dissatisfaction,
growing irritation and the feeling of (supposedly) being
deprived of freedom. This inevitably leads to an undisguised
act of rebellion: "I want my share of your estate now."

It is only the grace of God that could have prevented the boy
from getting his belongings and leaving. But the father allowed
him to go. Shouldn't he have been more assertive? Shouldn't he
have put the young rebel in his place?

Why does he let the boy get his own
way? Because the father wanted his
son to stay at home by choice. True love
doesn't force anybody. This breaking
away from the father's house didn't
happen suddenly and unexpectedly
one day. No, it brooded in the boy's heart for a long time.

> None are more helplessly
> enslaved than those who
> falsely believe they are free.
> JOHANN WOLFGANG VON
> GOETHE

So the sparks of excitement about the foreign land without
limits ignited an inextinguishable fire in his heart. Now he was
going to break free, once and for all! Free from the stifling, soul-
destroying routine. And then the day dawned when the young
man could finally leave. He was not planning a short journey. His
journey was specifically to a "distant land." He took everything
he owned with him. It had to be a clean and irreversible break.
This would make it easier to be daring and live a life without
limits. All that remained was decadence!

Savior and Redeemer, send Your Holy Spirit to keep me safe.
Thank You for Your protective love.

Free and Independent

"A few days later this younger son packed all his belongings and moved to a distant land" (Luke 15:13).

The father's intention was certainly not to chain his son to him; to pressurize him – and least of all, to see him deeply unhappy. They most probably spoke about these things: "But, son, try to understand; we don't want to boss you around or smother you. We love you dearly and don't want you to get hurt. We have never wanted to push you or live your life for you. Look at people who have broken loose from their anchors. They eat the bitter fruits of frustration and failure. They are hurting themselves and their parents, and causing much sorrow."

We can just imagine the boy's angry answer: "But Dad, do you think I'm as bad as these other young people you're talking about? I won't allow myself to be dragged into things. I also want to be free and independent." "But, son, you are free! You can come and go as you wish in this house. You can share in everything we have here. Real freedom also has to obey some rules."

> A man's worst difficulties begin when he is able to do as he likes.
> THOMAS H. HUXLEY

Then the boy's argument becomes heated: "This is the problem, Dad. I don't want to be here anymore. I can stand on my own two feet and think for myself. I want to eat and drink and be merry, because tomorrow I could be lying in the graveyard – and what have I had of my life then? I'm finished with this house! I'm leaving!" And then it happened: the boy packed his belongings and left. He had broken with his father's house forever! Or had he?

Loving Father God, help me to resist the tempting whispers of Satan and to remain true to You, my Father and Refuge. Protect me so that I won't stray from You because of my stubbornness.

Leaving

"A few days later this younger son packed all his belongings and moved to a distant land, and there he wasted all his money on wild living" (Luke 15:13).

The road stretched out before him, winding its way to a hill on the horizon. Dazed by the enchantment of the great life awaiting him, he walked towards his new future, cheerful and excited. Behind him in the doorway stood the boy's father, his eyes misty, his heart about to break. It is inevitable that there will be rules in the home, but the son must accept this as a sign of protective love, not as a yoke or burden. But his youngest son rejected this love: he left his father's house and took the broad road or the "highway to hell" (see Matt. 7:13). Stand still and look back. Someone is standing there in the doorway, with outstretched arms. Look, His hands are pierced, His eyes plead with you and He softly calls your name. Won't you turn back before it's too late? Can a child really choose to leave the parental home? Yes, it happens! Some have already chosen their own road and tried to cut God out of their lives.

> There are two freedoms – the false, where a man is free to do what he likes; the true, where he is free to do what he ought.
> Charles Kingsley

Their eyes are on the world's bright lights. Their anchors come loose one by one: They don't read the Bible anymore; they don't pray; they seldom, if ever, go to church; they can't stand the company of believing Christians. Turn back before you have gone too far: Whoever wants to follow their own way will sometimes mistake wildfire for stars; and if the glimmer of light fascinates them, they are easily lured from the right path.

Hold me, O Father, in Your love, so that I don't cut myself loose from You and land up in the vortex of estrangement.

The Grass Is Greener

" ... There he wasted all his money on wild living" (Luke 15:13).

The road away from God leads downhill: first you walk, then you break into trot, then you run, and from there it becomes a fast track to self-destruction. A person's estrangement from God always follows a definite line. First the anchors are broken loose by rebellion. This is followed by a revolt and undisguised resistance to love: "I want my share of your estate now" (Luke 15:12). Then there is the final break with everything precious and wholesome, leaving the Father's house.

The son is now a world citizen. He tore himself from the narrow-mindedness of his hometown, while here in the big city he can enjoy life fully. How ashamed he would be if his friends were to meet his simple, small-town parents with their religion and integrity. He must give his old man his due: he wasn't stingy. In this way, the son spends his days in blissful oblivion – and squanders all his money.

> Salvation is God's way of making us real.
> ST. AUGUSTINE

This "distant land" is not always geographically far; it is not necessarily measured in hundreds of miles. And it is not always possessions that are squandered, but the spiritual inheritance that God gave us. Lost sons are not only those who are guilty of sin, but also those who are gradually sinking deeper and deeper into the quagmire of immorality; moving farther and farther away from God – those who subtly, secretly and cleverly deny or shun the Father's love.

Father of love and compassion, it is good to be near You. Thank You that You hold me with a hand of love.

Disillusionment

"About the time his money ran out, a great famine swept over the land, and he began to starve" (Luke 15:14).

There was a young man in the Old Testament who also left for a far and foreign land of shadowy darkness and twilight zones. His name was Samson, which, when translated, means "sunshine." He was called by God to save his people and free them from their oppressors. He was a Nazarene: set aside for God. He allowed himself a strange freedom and ate forbidden fruit. In lust, he fell for the wiles of treacherous Delilah. Where do we find him in the end? Bound by the chains of the enemy, his eyes gouged out, stripped of his immense strength, without his people – and his God. Samson's strength did not lie in his powerful build or muscular arms; not even in his Nazarene vow! Samson's strength lay in his obedience and love for God. When he lost that, he lost everything.

> We find freedom when we find God; we lose it when we lose Him.
> PAUL E. SCHERER

And so the boy of our parable found the "freedom" he yearned for. "But," he started asking himself, "am I really free?" While he was chasing pleasure and revelry, he didn't have much time to think. He sighed secretly at times.

Now a vague wistfulness takes hold of his heart. For the first time he thinks: "I wonder how things are at home? I don't belong here; these are not my kind of people; not my kind of life." He can't do it anymore. This isn't freedom. If only he could get away from all this. The gnawing loneliness and longing for home consumes him, and he's running out of money at an alarming rate.

Loving Father, grant that I will remain safely in Your house forever and ever.

Famine!

"About the time his money ran out, a great famine swept over the land, and he began to starve" (Luke 15:14).

Instead of going home in desperation, the young man chooses to work as a slave for a farmer. There the boy sits, among the pigs! The advocate of freedom! In the land of his dreams he is now humiliated; he has become a slave, looking after pigs, and even the food they eat doesn't look so bad. He is without money, without friends, without food, and has lost all self-respect.

Sin is a ruthless taskmaster. It will settle for nothing less than total humiliation and destruction. The worst thing that could happen to a young Jewish man was to look after pigs.

> There is no more urgent and critical question than that of your personal relationship with God and your eternal salvation.
> BILLY GRAHAM

He is brought to a standstill for the first time and thinks seriously. His mind is clear for the first time in a long while. He simply doesn't have money anymore to party. Now a question burns in his heart: How did it happen? He thinks back to what he used to be: a young nobleman from a respected family; well-dressed, physically healthy; with possessions and a wealthy upbringing. But it has all been squandered. He is alone in his humiliation.

He has no money left! How is it possible that he could have spent a fortune in such a short time? he wonders. To make things worse, there is a famine in the land. The life that he longed for, and pursued while there was so much at stake, is gone. Now the last thing he thinks about is the freedom he wanted at all costs. It was all nothing but a false venture.

"As the deer longs for streams of water, so I long for You, O God" (Ps. 42:1).

Coming to His Senses

"When he finally came to his senses, he said to himself, 'At home even the hired servants have food enough to spare'" (Luke 15:17).

This young man had to go through deep waters of wretchedness before he came to realize that his only hope was to go back to his father's house. While wandering through the streets of the city, after being thrown out of his luxurious apartment, he often thought of and longed for home. So it came about that he went to see a pig farmer. He stood at the door of the farmer's house like a beggar, eyes downcast, clothes in tatters and shoes worn, asking the farmer to be a slave. Life broke him: the proud neck that wouldn't bow before his father was now bowed before a stranger, begging for work. Dad had said in one of his "sermons" that what you sow in life you will reap. And in his life he sowed weeds that were growing so profusely they threatened to strangle him. What was he thinking when he left his father's house and broke his heart in the process?

> Salvation is a work of God for man, rather than a work of man for God.
> LEWIS SPERRY CHAFER

For the first time he starts thinking about the nature of freedom. He had fooled himself and what he took to be freedom evaporated so quickly. A ridiculous farce, this is what the freedom of the world is; an illusion, fabricated by the devil. Even his father's day laborers were better off than he was in this land of slavery. They got more bread than they could eat – and he was starving! "There is only one way out of the depths of my despair: the road back home!"

Thank You, Savior and Redeemer, that no one can sink so deep in the quagmire of sin that You cannot save them.

Dreaming of Home

"Here I am, dying of hunger!" (Luke 15:17).

It is interesting that the father's house is always in the disillusioned lost son's thoughts. This is the wonder of God's grace: not even a far and foreign land can erase the image of the father's house. Sin cannot destroy the longing for God. The desertion of a child cannot diminish a parent's love for them. What a discovery: battered and humiliated by sin, the child still misses home. Or perhaps *because* of it! With the ruins of his life around him, amid the remnants of his failed life, the lost son remembers a parental home and the love of a father's heart. The longing becomes unbearable because he knows he has a father who loves him and is waiting for him to return.

> Fight to escape from your own cleverness. If you do, then you will find salvation and uprightness through Jesus Christ our Lord.
>
> JOHN CLIMACUS

What will he do? It is as if the angels of heaven are holding their breath ... and then they break into a song of praise. The Father's love has triumphed. The son in the distant land says with determination, "I will get up and go to my father. Ragged and dirty as I am, I will go home. I will ask him to forgive me."

Perhaps you are in a crisis hour in your life. The longing for God has been awakened in your heart and laid bare. Then get up! The Father is waiting for you. No, much more – He is coming to meet you! He is coming towards you, in Jesus Christ, with outstretched arms. The Father calls, "Come, My child, come home! When you hear My voice today, don't harden your heart. Come, come home!" Then get up and say clearly, "Loving Father, I'm coming. I'm coming home!"

I praise, glorify and thank You, Lord Jesus, that through You, I am able to know the Father's house and the Father's loving heart.

Going Home

"I will go home to my father" (Luke 15:18).

The road back to God always demands a decision from us. The lost son made his decision. He was going home; he would leave the distant land; he was going home where he belonged! But listen to this: the road back to the Father's home is not only a decision; not merely nostalgia; not just a wish. The road "back home" is an act: an unmistakable and decisive act! It is always wonderful to go home. Ask the exile from Ceylon, or the hostel student going home for the holidays; or the lost son from the distant land of sin and shame. Home! What emotional connotations this word has; how poignant the sacred memories!

We also come "home" to God – home from sin and shame! We do this every time we repent. But it requires determined action and effort. Remorse is not just a feeling – it is action. We must get up every time we are knocked down by the wretchedness and humiliation of sin; out of despair and heartache; loneliness and longing; self-pity and self-reproach. And we must do it straight away.

> Because no man is excluded from calling upon God, the gate of salvation is set open unto all men. Neither is there any other thing which keeps us from entering in, save only our own unbelief.
>
> JOHN CALVIN

Take note of the boy's words: "I will go home to my father." You must get up and go, with a prayer in your heart: "I've broken the bonds that tied me, Lord, I'm coming back! You will heal me and cleanse me, O Lord, I'm coming to You!"

Savior and Friend, thank You for the work of the Holy Spirit in my life, that leads me back to You.

A Heart That Is Humbled

"I will go home to my father and say ... " (Luke 15:18).

The young man in our story is going on another journey. This time it is in the opposite direction: back home! How different it is from the first one. To rise above your misery with good intentions in your heart is easy, but to actually undertake the journey – that is not so easy. The devil sees to that. The world is much better at welcoming you than letting you go.

"Nothing can stop me now. I'm going home!" The lost son continues walking. His feet hurt and his clothes are in tatters, and shame overcomes him. Then the surroundings start to look familiar. This is his world; the place where he was born and spent his innocent childhood days. He knows some farmhouses along the way. Some families invite him in and give him a meal and a place to sleep. They know his father.

> I have never ceased to wash in that fountain that was opened for sin and uncleanness, or to cast myself upon the tender mercy of my reconciled God.
> CHARLES SIMEON

Then there are others who turn their backs on him: "The little so-and-so. Now he knows which side his bread is buttered. Now that he's messed up his life, he wants to come home. He is not even ashamed of dragging the family name through the mud. If I were his father I would have known what to do with him." The closer he gets to the house, the more difficult every step becomes. How can he arrive on the farm looking like this: in rags and tatters? He won't fight for his "rights" anymore, but humbly ask to be taken on as a hired hand. He will confess: "Father, I have sinned against both heaven and you, and I am no longer worthy of being called your son" (Luke 15:18-19).

I praise Your Holy name, O loving Father God, that by virtue of Christ, I have a Father's house and a Father's heart to return to.

The Father's House

"While he was still a long way off, his father saw him coming"
(Luke 15:20).

〜⟡〜

We might as well say it again: it is never easy to get up and tackle the journey back to the Father's house. People will make it difficult for you. Like the Prodigal Son's brother, church-goers and others will make you feel unwelcome. There will be those who will remind you of your sinfulness. Even a preacher may say hurtful things at times. But one thing is certain: you don't ever have to doubt the Father's warm welcome. So carry on walking and head straight home!

And so we see the lost son coming over the last hill, heart pounding. Only one refrain repeats itself: I'm going home! Then he reaches the last rise – and there he sees the father's house in all its glory. He is crying unashamedly now. And then – is it possible? – he sees his father, and he is coming to meet him!

> Our worst days are never so bad that you are beyond the reach of God's grace. And your best days are never so good that you are beyond the need of God's grace.
> JERRY BRIDGES

Do you know that last rise in the road? Golgotha! That's what they call that hill. "The Father is coming to meet me," you say. "But I see a cross standing there." Yes, my friend, God comes to meet His children in this way. "For God so loved the world that He gave His only Son, so that everyone who believes in Him will not perish but have eternal life" (John 3:16).

"And while he was still a long way off, his father saw him coming. Filled with love and compassion, he ran to his son, embraced him, and kissed him" (Luke 15:20). Come, let us kneel before the Father in amazement. Let us thank God for the wonder of being able to go home.

Thank You, Lord, that You always take back Your children.

The Hallelujah Chorus!

"His son said to him, 'Father, I have sinned against both heaven and you, and I am no longer worthy of being called your son'" (Luke 15:21).

Have you perhaps listened with complete abandon to Handel's *Messiah?* It is an experience you should allow yourself every time you reflect on the homecoming of the Prodigal Son. The *Messiah* is a description of Jesus Christ's life in music and song. The symphony is deeply moving. First there is the announcement of His coming to this sin-torn world. Then follows the wonder of His birth, His life and His work. The tragedy of His bitter suffering, crucifixion and death is next. Finally, the whole rendition reaches a climax with the magnificence of the mighty *Hallelujah Chorus.* To hear ten thousand Welsh artists/vocalists singing this is an unforgettable spiritual experience that is out of this world. We are now at the *Hallelujah Chorus.* Let's read it as it is given in God's Word: "But his father said to the servants, 'Quick! Bring the finest robe in the house and put it on him. Get a ring for his finger, and sandals for his feet. And kill the calf we have been fattening. We must celebrate with a feast, for this son of mine was dead and has now returned to life. He was lost, but now he is found'" (Luke 15:22-24).

> Grace is the gift of Christ, who exposes the gulf which separates God and man and, by exposing it, bridges it.
> KARL BARTH

So, deep in confession I sorrowfully repeat the words: "Father, I have sinned against both heaven and you, and I am no longer worthy of being called Your son" (Luke 15:21). At the cross He saved my soul and gave me the gift of His life!

"Praise the LORD! Give thanks to the LORD, for He is good! His faithful love endures forever" (Ps. 106:1).

A Loving Father

"Filled with love and compassion, he ran to his son, embraced him, and kissed him" (Luke 15:20).

⌒⟲⌒

The title of this parable could just as well have been "The Parable of the Loving Father." The lost son is not the hero. This parable tells us more about the love of the father than about the wayward child. And so the Prodigal Son comes home and truly becomes a child of the father again, in every sense of the word. We are never what God meant us to be – truly children of God – before we come home to God. God's grace is indescribably wonderful. The father undoubtedly heard about his son's immoral life in the distant land. That is why he said, "This son of mine was dead and has now returned to life" (Luke 15:24). We can't deceive God. He knows everything about us: the foul sins we openly commit, and the concealed and secret sins we nurture. And yet, in spite of it all, He still comes to meet us; despite the rags and dirt and broken body.

> To confess your sins to God is not to tell anything [God] doesn't already know. Until you confess them, however, they are the abyss between you. When you confess them, they become the bridge.
>
> FREDERICK BUECHNER

We said God knows all about us. If He knows everything, why does He want His children to confess their sins? Is it really necessary that the sobbing child must say to his father, "Father, I have sinned against both heaven and you"? Yes, my friend, we dare not cover up anything. Confession of guilt is necessary. Confession of sins is also confession of faith. It is liberating and purifying. We can't just come back home from the far land of sin and slip in through the back door as if nothing happened – we must come in at the front door of confession of sin.

Merciful and loving Father, thank You for the freedom and healing sincere confession brings.

Confession of Guilt

"Father, I have sinned against both heaven and you, and I am no longer worthy of being called your son" (Luke 15:18).

Confession of guilt was the decisive proof that the son's attitude had changed completely. He didn't come home to get more money; have some homemade food or to persuade his elder brother to go back with him. No, he had finally come home to stay and to live a life of thankfulness and obedience.

This is why confession is necessary, because this is the turning point of becoming a child in the parents' home again. Listen to the first words this boy said when he arrived home: "Father!" What right did he have to use this word? Even if we come back home as lost sons and daughters, we may still say "Father." What a wonderful privilege.

Confession is the first step to repentance.
ENGLISH PROVERB

The unfaithfulness of a child does not destroy the love of a caring father. Even if we are unfaithful – God remains faithful. The father of the lost son still acknowledged him as his son and allowed him to confess his guilt.

The boy admitted his guilt – but he wasn't allowed to say foolish and unnecessary things. Confession of guilt is good for the soul; don't let anything rob you of the opportunity to do so. Come, cry unashamedly in your Father's arms. Tears of remorse are pleasing to God. God does not leave us there in the dark. Presently a new day will break!

O Father God; You welcome us back from the distant land of sin in the name of Christ. Thank You for the privilege of being able to call You "Father."

Celebration

*"We must celebrate with a feast, for this son of mine was dead
and has now returned to life" (Luke 15:23-24).*

Take note of how this father treats the remorseful son who
confesses his guilt so readily. It is as if he is not even aware
of his son's ragged, filthy condition. He embraces him. He holds
him in his arms and says, "We must celebrate." Then spontaneous festivities break out. The father says in no uncertain terms:
"This is the son of the father's house! And in this house it will be
celebrated with a feast!"

It is as if the father says: "Take away every sign of his old,
sinful life; of his fall and humiliation; of his hunger and longing:
Bring a new robe!" Somewhere lies a
bundle of discarded rags. The dirty
clothes have been taken away and
there his son stands, dressed in the
best clothes: "All these things are
gone forever. And the one sitting on
the throne said, 'Look, I am making
everything new!'" (Rev. 21:4-5).

> Do you believe the Lord
> will call a poor sinner, and
> then cast him out? No! His
> word stands forever, "Him
> that cometh unto Me I will
> in no wise cast out."
> DWIGHT L. MOODY

"Put a ring on his finger! From
now on he will walk with me and work with me in the vineyard.
His sonship has been restored. Let the festival bells ring! Now
the fattened calf can be slaughtered. Let us celebrate!"

The wayward son was invited to the feast as the guest of
honor. His remorse and confession of guilt were his entrance
ticket: "But if we confess our sins to Him, He is faithful and just
to forgive us and to cleanse us from all wickedness" (1 John 1:9).

*My heart breaks into a thankful song of praise, my Savior and my
Redeemer, that I may share in this glorious celebration because
of what You did for me, Jesus my Lord. Grant that my life would
reflect this festive joy.*

Son or Slave?

"Please take me on as a hired servant" (Luke 15:19).

Christ wanted to teach us a specific lesson through this parable. When we have been raised by the grace of God from a spiritual death, when we come home to the Father's house from a life of sin, we do not return to slavery, living as hired hands.

Is there joy in your heart because you have come home? Do you know the joy of the lost son who found the right road again? This joy isn't found in external circumstances. While Paul was in prison, he wrote a letter to the young congregation in Philippi. He didn't write about the cold, damp dungeon. He wrote about joy! It is seen in his letter like a golden thread: "Always be full of joy in the Lord. I say it again – rejoice!" (Phil. 4:4).

> You are the heir to the Kingdom. Prosperity is your birth right and you hold the key to more abundance in every area of your life than you can possibly imagine.
> HENRI NOUWEN

In the name of our loving Father, don't wrap yourself in a cloak of sorrow any longer. Take off the rags and tatters of gloom and despondency. God Himself will give you the best festive robe that has been purified by the blood of the Lamb: "They have washed their robes in the blood of the Lamb and made them white. That is why they stand in front of God's throne and serve Him day and night in His Temple. And He who sits on the throne will give them shelter. They will never again be hungry or thirsty; they will never be scorched by the heat of the sun. For the Lamb on the throne will be their Shepherd. He will lead them to the springs of life-giving water. And God will wipe every tear from their eyes" (Rev. 7:14-17).

I have received indescribable amazing grace from You, O Lord. I am a runaway child, back in the Father's home.

Anger That Consumes

"The older brother was angry and wouldn't go in" (Luke 15:28).

The older son's anger was now ablaze: "There's no way I'm living under the same roof as him;" "I refuse to accept or acknowledge him as my brother;" "I refuse to forgive his lousy behavior;" "I refuse to believe that his return is sincere and lasting;" "I refuse to believe that his confession of guilt is genuine." "I ... I ... I!" The servants share in the joyful festivities, but the older son refuses to set foot in the house. He is a good-looking farm boy, with suntanned face and arms, hands calloused from hard work, legs tired from walking in the service of the father. He is an obedient son and a respected churchgoer: but without love!

> The person, who knows he is forgiven, forgives.
> Martyn Lloyd-Jones

There is a fundamental rule in God's household: "'You must love the Lord your God with all your heart, all your soul, and all your mind.' This is the first and greatest commandment. A second is equally important: 'Love your neighbor as yourself'" (Matt. 22:37-39). There is no substitute for love.

Listen to this: "If I have the gift of prophesy and can fathom all mysteries and all knowledge ... but have not love, I am nothing" (1 Cor. 13:2 NIV). Love forgives everything! Because whoever loves, learnt from the Source of Love to pray: "And forgive us our sins, as we have forgiven those who sin against us" (Matt. 6:12). If there is no love, only hate, envy and jealousy remain. The older brother refuses to go in: he remains standing outside with his burning anger and unforgiving heart – and is consumed by it.

Father God of love and grace, help me to forgive just as abundantly as You forgive me and to make the road back to the Father's house easy for sinners, through a loving Christ-like attitude.

Spiritual Pride

"All these years I've slaved for you and never once refused to do a single thing you told me to" (Luke 15:29).

The word "sabotage" is derived from the French word *sabot*. A *sabot* is a wooden shoe that factory workers wore to protect against the wet and cold concrete floor. If the workers wanted an undeserved day off, one of them would put his wooden shoe in the machinery and the whole factory came to a standstill, hence the word "sabotage."

A father's immortal love won back a lost son from the clutches of sin – and now he faces the danger of losing an honorable son. How sly the devil is in his onslaughts on the children of God! But this father has infinite patience. He goes out to his son where he stands outside the house, sullen and cross, consumed by anger, refusing to come in. The father speaks to him kindly. Just as he refrained from reproaching the younger son for his wicked and lavish life in the distant land, he speaks kindly to his eldest son.

> Never cease loving a person, and never give up hope, for even the prodigal son could be saved.
> SØREN KIERKEGAARD

Then the storm breaks. Lightning flashes in the older son's eyes; his voice is like thunder. The icy winds of bottled-up jealousy and hatred reach gale force. Where does the older son start in this unjust and violent tirade? He starts with himself! "I have worked hard all these years. My hands are calloused from working for you ... for the church. I give my tithe. I go to church; I read the Bible and I pray regularly." I ... I ... I! It is as if he has earned his place in the father's house! "All these years I've worked hard for you."

Lord Jesus, You know everything, You know that I love You!

The Soul of a Slave

*"All these years I've slaved for you and never once refused to do
a single thing you told me to" (Luke 15:29).*

L et us pay close attention to the older son's reproaches: "And
in all that time you never gave me even one young goat for a
feast with my friends" (Luke 15:29). He is not aware of his privileges: He is secure in his father's house; he is given food and
clothes; he has a loving father who lets him share in his abundance. With tunnel vision he focuses on a goat, while all of his
father's livestock is at his disposal.

First the older son tells his father how good he has been, then he
tells his father how wicked his brother is. He starts by saying, "Yet
when this son of yours comes back ... " Not "my brother." He even
lies about him, saying that he was spending his inheritance on
prostitutes. His violent outburst car-
ries on: what a no-good wanton boy
his brother is and it is for him their
father has had their finest calf slaughtered. The older brother doesn't even
get one young goat and look what
his brother gets.

> The greatest happiness in
> life is the conviction that
> we are loved – loved for
> ourselves, or rather, loved
> in spite of ourselves.
> VICTOR HUGO

Why doesn't his father leave him
outside in the cold? He'll only spoil the fun if he goes inside. This
is how all of us would react. But just hold it there. Shouldn't we
rather ask prayerfully: "Lord, could this be me?" Sometimes we
work for the Kingdom because we feel forced to, like slaves that
find no joy in it. We do it just to curry God's favor. Answer honestly
today before God: Do you look for happiness in a circle of a few
handpicked friends? How deeply we sadden our heavenly Father
with our lack of love!

*Lord Jesus Christ, let me rejoice with the angels over one sinner
who is saved. Help me to serve You with integrity.*

Lack of Brotherly Love

"Yet when this son of yours comes back after squandering your money on prostitutes, you celebrate by killing the fattened calf!" (Luke 15:30).

We can imagine how this older brother had to comfort his father when the younger brother left, when the heartbroken father stood staring toward the hills where his son disappeared, longing for him: "Come now, Father, the work must go on. He is not worth worrying about. He would not have made it anyway; his heart was never in farming. As far as I'm concerned, Dad, the farther away he goes, the better."

This parable reminds us of the one about the Pharisee and the Tax Collector! Both of them went to the temple to pray. Jesus had those in mind who were convinced they were right with God, and looked down on others (see Luke 18:9). The Pharisee was striking a pose before God and witnessing (not praying!). "I thank You, God, that I am not a sinner like everyone else – I don't cheat, I don't sin, and I don't commit adultery. I'm certainly not like that tax collector! I fast twice a week, and I give You a tenth of my income" (see Luke 18:11-12). Nowhere does he mention a love for God or for his neighbor.

> Grace is the free, underserved goodness and favor of God to mankind.
> MATTHEW HENRY

Don't we all display a bit of the Pharisee underneath? Aren't we often guilty of a serious lack of love like the older brother? Come, let's make the sincere prayer of our hearts today the words of the remorseful tax collector: "O God, be merciful to me, for I am a sinner" (Luke 18:13).

Everything, O Father, is grace and undeserved favor. Help me through the Spirit to seek genuine love.

This Son of Yours!

"Yet when this son of yours comes back, you celebrate by killing the fattened calf!" (Luke 15:30).

On the happy day that the lost son came home, we find the zealous older brother hard at work. He was working in the fields and didn't know what was happening at the house.

By evening he returned home – to the sounds of celebration. He was surprised. What was happening? Song and merriment in their house? Impossible! Since that little troublemaker left home there had never been a sign or sound of joy.

As the firstborn he found it unacceptable that something was going on, and that he was not told anything about it. How dare his father ignore him like this! He had to find out what was happening. So, did he go to his father like a good-natured son and ask him? No, he called a servant. "What is going on here?" he asked the hired man. Even this servant shared the father's joy; his eyes lit up as he told the story.

> You will find as you look back upon your life, that the moments when you really lived are the moments when you have done things in the spirit of love.
> HENRY DRUMMOND

Beside himself with joy, the servant said, "Your brother is back … We are celebrating because of his safe return" (Luke 15:27). One would expect a brother to rush into the house after hearing this good news, and embrace his brother; that he would be glad for his father and join in the festivities. Unfortunately this is not what happened: "The older brother was angry and wouldn't go in" (Luke 15:28).

Father of grace and forgiveness, fill my heart with Your abundant love, so that my lost brothers and sisters will be just as precious to me as they are to You.

Homecoming

"We had to celebrate this happy day. For your brother was dead and has come back to life! He was lost, but now he is found!" (Luke 15:32).

How deeply we sadden our heavenly Father with our lovelessness! We not only sadden the Father. Think of the younger brother – he must have been deeply hurt by his brother's bitter words. My friend, let's be honest with one another: it is no disgrace to be a churchgoer; it is no disgrace to work faithfully for your church; it is no disgrace to lead a virtuous and faithful life; to read the Bible and to pray regularly. On the contrary: this is the wonder of God's grace in your life. But then your attitude towards your brothers and sisters must also be right, in particular towards those who have strayed: The unmarried daughter who is expecting a child; that person whose imprisonment is of his own doing; the drug pusher. What do we know about their bitter struggle and heartache, the painful humiliations they suffer, the heartbreaking suffering and misery in their hearts and homes?

> We must learn to regard people less in the light of what they do or omit to do, and more in the light of what they suffer.
> DIETRICH BONHOEFFER

We see people drowning in their misery, coming loose from their anchors and sliding away on the slippery road of sin. Do we lift a finger in Christian compassion and love, or offer a supporting hand? Or do we say with great relief: "Thank You, Father, that it's not me." Isn't it more convenient to deny our Christian duty by excusing ourselves, thinking we would rather not be involved?

Loving Father, thank You that You taught me that I am not only my brother's keeper, but that I am also my brother's brother.

Unconditional Love

"His father said to him, 'Look, dear son, you have always stayed by me, and everything I have is yours'" (Luke 15:31).

Child of the heavenly Father, His house is also your house; His farm is also your farm; His possessions are also your possessions – and all His children are your brothers and sisters. Just remember: we are all sinners. What we read in 1 John 1:8 is quite clear: "If we claim we have no sin, we are only fooling ourselves and not living in the truth."

In spite of his shameful, rebellious behavior, the older son is still called "son" by the father. This is love speaking. Why won't this child realize his wealth? He has a share in everything the father owns. He has the privilege of being near his father at all times. The father's treasury is always open to him. How terrible is the evil of ingratitude and lovelessness – especially in those who ought to know better and behave differently. They haven't yet attended the training school of love; they can't put the law of love into practice. They cannot rejoice with the angels when a lost sinner comes home.

> God weighs more with how much love a man works, than how much he does.
> THOMAS Á KEMPIS

Can you and I say in all honesty that we are free from spiritual pride, from submissive religiosity and from the sin of lovelessness? The Father has spoken to us during this past month and He speaks to us in all earnestness. He begs us to come in and be part of the festive joy for lost sinners who have found their way back home. Come, kneel in the brightly lit banquet hall of the Father's house. Firmly take the hand of your younger brother and embrace him like your Father embraces you.

God of unfathomable love, teach me to follow Your example and to love unconditionally.

April

Christian Love

Though He was God, He did not think of
equality with God as something to cling to. Instead,
He gave up His divine privileges, He took the humble
position of a slave and was born as a human being.
~ Philippians 2:6-7

I, the Eternal Wisdom, was mocked as a fool in a white garment
before Herod, My fair body was rent and torn without mercy by the
rude stripes of whips, My lovely face was drenched in spittle and
blood, and in this condition I was ... led forth with My cross to death.
~ HENRY SUSO

Eternal God and Father of our Lord Jesus Christ,
It was love that made You send Your Son to this sinful world to
set us free. It cost Him a humanly impossible price:
He had to become the Man of Sorrows
so that we could have access to heaven;
He had to cast off His godly majesty to
make us children of the King;
He descended to earth in poverty so that
we could be given the richness of forgiveness;
He gave His love unconditionally so that
we could pass this love on to others;
He set the perfect example by His life and suffering,
so that we could follow Him every day of our lives.
He died a shameful death on a brutal cross,
so that we may be saved and forgiven,
and have eternal life.
He was raised from death triumphantly
so that we could become part of His
triumphal procession through the ages.
Lord Jesus, Man of Sorrows,
make me willing to accept the challenges of being Your child
and to live or die as Your faithful witness.
Thank You that those who share in Your cross,
also share in Your crown!
Thank You that those who suffer with
You will also live with You.
For Jesus' sake.

Amen.

A Song of Praise!

"For Yours is the kingdom and the power and the glory forever. Amen" (Matt. 6:13 AMP).

～◯C～

The original manuscripts of the Bible didn't have this doxology or song of praise. A doxology is a response or answer to the words of the liturgy. It is thought that one of the early monks, who wrote down this prayer by hand, was so touched by it that he spontaneously wrote and added this addendum. We also feel like this after meditating on Christ's words for weeks on end, and because of the rich blessing we receive from this prayer.

We learned that we may call Him Father; that His name is holy; that His kingdom is coming; that His will is perfect; that He gives us our daily bread; that He forgives our sins; that He enables us to forgive others; that He protects us against temptation; and that He delivers us from evil!

> Praising God is one of the highest and purest acts of religion. In prayer we act like men; in praise we act like angels.
>
> THOMAS WATSON

We are infinitely thankful when we take a look at the road by which we came. An unthankful Christian is an unsaved Christian because gratitude is the outcome of rebirth, conversion and salvation. I want to please my Savior in my thankfulness. I want to listen when He speaks to me through His Word. I want to speak to Him in prayer and listen to Him when the Holy Spirit whispers. I want to witness for Him: "You will receive power when the Holy Spirit comes upon you. And you will be my witnesses, telling people about Me everywhere" (Acts 1:8). If we consider all of God's acts of grace, we feel led to kneel down before Him and rejoice.

Praise the Lord, O my soul, and everything in me, praise His holy name!

How Not to Fast

"When you fast, don't make it obvious, as the hypocrites do, who try to look miserable and disheveled so people will admire them for their fasting. I tell you the truth, this is the only reward they will ever get" (Matt. 6:16).

Fasting is an essential part of many Eastern religions. The Jews in Jesus' time had only one compulsory day of fasting, on the Day of Atonement (see Lev. 16:31). But they still made much of individual fasts. Fasting was connected with mourning for the deceased. They also mourned in remorse for sin. It was the outward proof of inner sorrow for sin. Fasting was sometimes also in preparation for a revelation. Moses fasted on the mountain for forty days and forty nights before he met God (see Exod. 24:15). Jesus fasted before He was tempted by Satan (see Matt. 4:3). Sometimes fasting was an appeal to God: for rain or a successful harvest.

> Fasting is a divine corrective to the pride of the human heart. It is a discipline of the body with a tendency to humble the soul.
>
> ARTHUR WALLIS

In the Jewish tradition there were three main ideas in people's thoughts: Fasting was a deliberate effort to attract God's attention; it showed that the person's remorse was sincere; and the fast was also intercessory – that God would deliver the nation from slavery. These methods of fasting resulted in certain dangers. The greatest of these was that a person might be motivated to fast as proof of their superior holiness. Then it became an intentional demonstration, not to God but to those who noticed them. It was no longer an act of humility, but of spiritual pride.

Father God, let Your Holy Spirit guide me to know when I should fast to draw closer to You.

When You Fast

"When you fast, comb your hair and wash your face. Then no one will notice that you are fasting, except your Father, who knows what you do in private. And your Father, who sees everything, will reward you" (Matt. 6:17-18).

E ven though Jesus condemned the wrong way of fasting, His words imply that there is a good form of fasting. There are many reasons for this. Fasting is good for a person's health. Fasting is good for self-discipline. We easily become self-sufficient because we can buy everything we need. Fasting can prevent us from becoming slaves to habit; we fast to prove that our habits aren't our masters. Fasting proves to us that we can do without certain things. The fewer things we regard as necessary, the more independent we will be, otherwise we fall prey to the luxuries of life. Fasting gives us the ability to walk past a tempting display window and yet keep ourselves from buying useless items we can easily do without.

> Fasting is a letting go of all things that is seen and temporal. Fasting helps express, deepen, confirm the resolution that we are ready to sacrifice anything, even ourselves to attain what we seek for the kingdom of God.
> ANDREW MURRAY

Fasting makes us appreciate things more. Sometimes things in life are so rare that we really enjoy them. Fasting retains the excitement of life by keeping things fresh and new. It would be good for us to fast in our own way and according to our own needs, so that the godly joy of the world can be our pride and not a collar around our necks.

God of the holy fast, grant that I won't look somber and be hypocritical when I fast.

Our Daily Bread

"Give us today our daily bread" (Matt. 6:11 NIV).

Bread is the symbol of all our human needs: food, clothing, housing, health; also of the wisdom we need to earn our bread in the modern world. In this prayer we plead that God will provide for us on a temporary basis. Bread is also the symbol of our eternal needs. That's why Jesus said, "I am the Bread of Life." We must receive the Bread of Life from His hand every day because it is essential to us. Every time we take Communion, we are reminded that His body was broken for us, just like the grain of wheat is crushed to provide us with bread. With this prayer we also ask God to meet our spiritual needs.

God doesn't give manna from heaven anymore, but He gives His blessings in nature; the skills to process raw materials, to plant an own orchard so that we can enjoy our bread. Yet God doesn't spoil His children. Take note: "Give us *today* our *daily* bread." This means that we are totally dependent on God from day to day. We ask every day and He gives every day! God doesn't give us everything we need all at once; neither does He give us everything we want.

> God's gifts put man's best dreams to shame.
> ELIZABETH BARRETT BROWNING

When we pray for our daily bread it's not a materialistic prayer to surround ourselves with all of life's luxuries. It humbles us to pray from day to day ... and to thank God every day. We plough, sow, fertilize, harvest, transport, cook and serve before there is food on the table. But it still remains God's gift to us. When we say "Give us today ... " we admit our deep dependence on God. We ask for His rain, His sunshine, His growth.

Heavenly Father, I thank You for Your caring love from day to day.

Deliver Us from Evil

"Don't let us yield to temptation, but rescue us from the evil one" (Matt. 6:13).

❧ ❦ ❧

So does this prayer mean that the evil one has the last word after all the glorious things that have been said about God and His kingdom? Our Father; His kingdom; His will; His provision in all our needs; forgiveness received and given. Is evil worming its way into the agenda again? Isn't it time that we are led to green pastures and peaceful waters? Are we finding ourselves on the battlefield again, among weapons of destruction? No, definitely not! With this prayer we simply acknowledge that Satan is a powerful enemy and we must be saved from him. This prayer is not a salute to Satan, but rather a proclamation of his downfall: We can be saved from him!

The basic question of Catechism is: What must I do to be comforted and blessed in life and death? The answer is: I must know how great my wretchedness and sins are and how I can be saved from them; and I must

> The blood of Jesus washes away our past and the name of Jesus opens up our future.
> JESSE DUPLANTIS

know how thankful I should be to God for my salvation. How am I to be saved? By acknowledging the magnitude of my sin? No, this cannot save me. Knowing that I am seriously ill does not make me well. Having medicine won't heal me: it is only when I take that medicine that healing is possible. Knowledge of sin without the knowledge of salvation leads to despair.

Salvation means being set free from the chains of Satan and sin. Jesus Christ made this salvation possible by His life, death and resurrection. He set us free and broke the chains that bound us.

Loving Savior and Redeemer, thank You that You broke the chains in my life and set me free.

Don't Put It Off

"Don't let us yield to temptation, but rescue us from the evil one" (Matt. 6:13).

In order to be blessed and content in life and death, we need to be sure that Jesus has saved us personally from the debt, punishment and domination of sin. God asks everyone who prays this prayer, "What do you know about salvation?" Time is running out – also your time of grace! Every day that you continue living in sin, there is less hope for you. Taking your time to make sure of your salvation can cost you eternal life. If you keep putting it off, you are saying to Satan, "Here is my immortal soul; take it for safekeeping until I come and claim it from you. And if I never turn up to claim it, well, then take me with you into the eternal misery of perdition."

> One of the most fundamental marks of true repentance is a disposition to see our sins as God sees them.
>
> CHARLES SIMEON

"But if we confess our sins to Him, He is faithful and just to forgive us and to cleanse us from all wickedness" (1 John 1:9). Make sure that your sins have been forgiven. Repeat after Paul, "Oh, what a miserable person I am! Who will free me from this life that is dominated by sin and death? Thank God! The answer is in Jesus Christ our Lord" (Rom. 7:24-25).

If we belong to Christ we are not in the last instance destined for evil, but on our way to our Savior who delivers us from evil, Jesus Christ; to the green pastures and peaceful waters; at a new dawn in our lives. This is what we plead for when we pray, "Deliver us from evil."

Just give me Jesus, who was crucified for me!

Anchored in the Father's House

All who are led by the Spirit of God are children of God (Rom. 8:14).

Do you wonder about the disruption and confusion in to-day's world? There is an answer: We have lost our homing instinct; we have become "world citizens." As a result, many people have lost direction. The relationships in our lives are not coincidence. There is a reason the verse says, "A man had two sons." It is a silhouette of our connectedness with God. The devoted child of God sometimes longs for heaven with the same deep longing that we have for our birthplace. Our birthplace implies our parents' home, our childhood memories, our brothers and sisters. No wonder the first commandment that deals with human relationships starts with "Honor your father and mother" (Exod. 20:12). He who understands the wonder of parenthood also understands the wonder of God's loving Fatherhood, and of being a child of God.

> There is nothing we can do to make God love us more ... and nothing we can do to make God love us less.
> PHILIP YANCEY

Being lost is being without God; without anchors or connectedness; unattached and unrestrained – this is perdition itself! Salvation is being inextricably anchored in God and confessing: "I know to whom I am entrusted." This is eternal life! This is heaven.

And so our earthly attachments grow into eternal anchors. We don't come from nowhere and we're not on our way nowhere. We are attached to our Father for now and all eternity. His Word teaches me: "See how very much our heavenly Father loves us, for He calls us His children, and that is what we are" (1 John 3:1).

Loving Father, I humbly thank You for the anchors You brought into my life so that I wasn't shipwrecked on the ocean of life.

Guard Your Mouth

Take control of what I say, O Lord, and guard my lips (Ps. 141:3).

We struggled for two long years to get an estranged member of the church back in the congregation. When he eventually hesitantly walked into church on a Sunday morning, two members of the church council approached him in the foyer – with the specific purpose of welcoming him. One of the members cracked a rather insensitive joke: "What has the Southeaster blown into church today? Judgment Day must be close!" Quite understandably, our church-estranged friend turned around on the spot and went home. It took seven more months to convince him to come back to church again.

> To reach something good it is very useful to have gone astray, and thus acquire experience.
> ST. TERESA OF AVILA

Jesus told three parables in response to negative remarks by the Pharisees and scribes. The Lost Sheep was one out of a hundred; the Lost Coin, one out of ten; and the Lost Son, one out of two. The whole debate reached a dramatic climax when Jesus told them about the older son in the parable of the Lost Son: about the attitude of church people; people who are safely in the Father's house, but who refuse to be glad when a sinner repents and is saved.

As the story unfolds, the listener becomes part of the events. It could have been me; it could have happened to me – I could have been the elder or younger brother. It is as if Jesus wanted to say to all of us, "Do you see now how easily a person can be lost? Do you see how moving it is when a lost sinner is saved by caring, enduring and persevering love?"

Good Master, protect me from the danger of getting lost in the Father's backyard because of a lack of love.

Jesus Clears the Temple

"Get these things out of here. Stop turning My Father's house into a marketplace!" (John 2:16).

⁘

Also this act of clearing the Temple had to take place because it was done by the promised Messiah (see Mal. 3:1-4). Jesus had good reasons for clearing the Temple. The idea of Jesus with a whip in His hand is astounding. What caused this flare-up of anger in the Temple courts?

The Passover celebration was the largest feast of all the Jewish feasts. It was every Jew's ideal to celebrate at least one Passover Feast in Jerusalem in his lifetime. There was also a certain tax that every Jew had to pay: Temple tax! It was towards the upkeep of the Temple and its sacrifices. This tax had to be paid in shekels or Jewish money, and this brought money changers to Jerusalem that exchanged foreign money for Jewish shekels – at an exorbitant profit. What infuriated Jesus was that the pilgrims who came for the Passover, and who couldn't afford the tax, were cheated into paying large amounts for the Jewish money. It was a shameless public exploitation that was done in the name of religion.

> Worship that pleases God comes from an obedient heart.
> ANONYMOUS

Apart from the money lenders, merchants were also selling cattle, sheep and doves. A visit to the Temple required a sacrifice. The pilgrims wanted to bring a thanks offering for their safe journey to Jerusalem. The law stipulated that the animal to be sacrificed had to be without blemish, and pure. This too became an unashamed exploitation at the expense of the poor, humble pilgrims. This is what drove Jesus to burning anger. It was impossible for Jesus to stand by and passively watch the poor worshipers being exploited.

Holy Father God, grant that my worship will always be pure; free from earthly customs.

The Lord's Temple

"Get these things out of here. Stop turning My Father's house into a marketplace!" (John 2:16).

⌒◯⌒

Jesus acted drastically because His Father's house had been desecrated. There was worship in the Temple without respect and deference. Respect is an instinctive attitude and worship without reverence is an evil thing: It is worship that does not realize or acknowledge God's holiness; it is worship that has become a formality. We dare not use the house of God for anything other than worship in spirit and in truth.

There could also be another reason for Jesus' conduct. Mark makes an interesting addition in the description of Christ's words: "The Scriptures declare, 'My Temple will be called a house of prayer for all nations'" (Mark 11:17). The Temple consisted of a succession of courts which led to the center of the Temple: the Holy of Holies. There was the court of the Gentiles; then the court of the women; then the court of the Israelites; and then the court of the priests. The Gentiles were

> What greater calamity can fall upon a nation than the loss of worship.
> RALPH WALDO EMERSON

allowed only in the court of the Gentiles and therefore the selling took place in that court, because it was the farthest a Gentile could enter into the Temple to meditate, pray and make contact with God. But the Temple authorities and Jewish merchants made a marketplace of the court of the Gentiles. Because of the deafening noise there, no one could really worship and thus it excluded the Gentiles from God's presence. Let us remember Jesus' anger towards those who made it impossible for Gentiles or the serious seeker to have contact with God.

Lord, grant that I will follow Your example and always be willing to share Your love with Gentiles and seekers.

A Night Visitor

There was a man named Nicodemus, a Jewish religious leader who was a Pharisee. After dark one evening, he came to speak with Jesus (John 3:1-2).

Most of the time Jesus was surrounded by ordinary people, but now we see Him in contact with one of the aristocrats of Jerusalem. Nicodemus was undoubtedly rich, because when Jesus died, he bought His body and anointed it with expensive myrrh and aloe. He was also a Pharisee. In a certain sense they were the best people in the whole country.

Nicodemus was a ruler among the Jews; an *archom*. This means that he was a member of the Sanhedrin. The Sanhedrin was a court of seventy members and to the Jews it was the highest court. Naturally their power under Roman dominance was very limited, but it was still extensive. They had spiritual jurisdiction over every Jew in the entire world and one of their main tasks was to investigate and evaluate anyone who was suspected of being a false prophet. Thus it is amazing that Nicodemus wanted to speak to Jesus.

> There is no more urgent and critical question in life than that of your personal relationship with God and your eternal salvation.
> BILLY GRAHAM

Nicodemus belonged to one of the most esteemed families in Jerusalem. Why would a Jewish aristocrat come to this homeless Prophet who was once a carpenter in Nazareth? It was a miracle that Nicodemus got the better of his prejudices and came to Jesus for advice and that at night. Nicodemus was a confused man who enjoyed all the esteem, but who lacked something important in his life. Most likely he hoped to find the Light in the darkness of night.

Thank You, Lord Jesus, that You enter each our lives in such a special manner.

Being Born Again

"Rabbi," he said, "we all know that God has sent You to teach us. Your miraculous signs are evidence that God is with You" (John 3:2).

Nicodemus' conversation with Jesus started with his statement that one couldn't help but be impressed by the signs and wonders that Jesus performed. Jesus' answer was that the signs and wonders were not so important; the most important thing was the change in a person's inner being, and that could only be described as a new birth. When Jesus said that one must be born again, Nicodemus misunderstood Him. Jesus meant that to be born again you had to undergo such a radical change that it looked like a new birth. The process is not only a human achievement but is brought about by the grace and omnipotence of God.

> Before an individual can be saved, he must first learn that he cannot save himself.
> M. R. DeHaan

This idea of rebirth runs through the entire New Testament (see 1 Pet. 1:3; 1 Pet. 1:22; James 1:18; Titus 3:5; Rom. 6:11; 2 Cor. 5:17; Gal. 5:16; Eph. 4:22-24; Heb. 5:12-14). This is exactly what happened when a heathen became converted to Judaism: He became a new person in all respects and therefore Jesus could assume that Nicodemus understood the concept.

So what does rebirth mean to us? It embraces a few important things: It concerns the kingdom of God that cannot be entered unless rebirth has taken place; the fact that we cannot be God's children without being born again; and the idea of being children of God as well as having eternal life. The fact is that rebirth is an unavoidable prerequisite of becoming children of God.

Your grace, Heavenly Father, is immeasurable; because of this sinners can become Your children.

Keep Prayer Sincere

"When you pray, don't be like the hypocrites who love to pray publicly on street corners and in the synagogues where everyone can see them" (Matt. 6:5).

No nation ever had higher ideals for prayer than the Israelites; no religion gave higher priority to prayer than they did. The rabbis said, "Great is prayer, greater than all our good works." But certain mistakes slipped into their prayer life.

It started with the tendency of prayer to become quite formal. This meant it could very easily become the idle repetition of words that people mumbled mechanically. (Christians can hardly criticize this approach. It happens before many Christian meals when grace is said.)

Something every Jew had to repeat every day was called the *Shemoneh 'esreh.* This means "the Eighteen." It consisted of eighteen prayers and was, and still is, an essential part of the service in the synagogue. With time, another prayer was added to make it nineteen, but the original name stayed. The prayers are short and to the point. No church has a nicer liturgy than the *Shemoneh 'esreh.* The law was that every Jew had to repeat it three times a day: mornings, afternoons and evenings. Unfortunately it became nothing more than habit. There was even a summary that could be prayed if a person was pressed for time. Thus prayer became an artificial repetition, not only for the Jews, but for Christians also.

> Every great movement of God can be traced to a kneeling figure.
> DWIGHT L. MOODY

Holy Father, grant that Your Spirit will lead me so that I will always speak to You meaningfully in prayer.

Words of Truth

"Make them holy by Your truth; teach them Your Word, which is truth" (John 17:17).

Jesus prays that His disciples will be made holy by their devotion to the truth. The word that is translated as "made holy" means "set apart for a special task or sacred use." When God called Jeremiah, He said to him: "I knew you before I formed you in your mother's womb. Before you were born I set you apart and appointed you as my prophet to the nations" (Jer. 1:5). When God established the priesthood in Israel, Moses had to make the sons of Aaron holy because they were set apart for a special task: to serve as His priests (see Exod. 28:41).

But this is not the only meaning of "holy". It also means to equip someone with the qualities of mind, heart and character that are necessary for the task they have to carry out. If someone wants to serve God, they need to possess something of God's goodness and God's wisdom. Those who want to serve a holy God, must be holy themselves. So God not only chooses people and sets them apart for a special task, He also equips them with the qualities they will need to carry out that specific task.

> The value of life lies not in the length of days, but in the use we make of them.
> MICHEL DE MONTAIGNE

We must always remember that God chose us and made us holy, specifically for His service. Our special task is to love and obey Him and encourage others to do the same. We must also always remember that God doesn't simply leave us to our own devices to carry out the great task in our own strength, but that in His grace, He equips us for the task – if we are willing to place our lives in His hands.

Father God, I unconditionally place my life in Your care, so that You can make me holy.

Christian Love

"You have heard that the law says, 'Love your neighbor, and hate your enemy.' But I say, love your enemies! Pray for those who persecute you!" (Matt. 5:43-44).

～⟩⟨～

What does Jesus mean by saying we must love our enemies? The Greek language is rich in synonyms. There are four different words for love. There is the noun *storge* with the accompanying verb *stergein*. These words are used for the love of family. They describe the love of a parent for a child and a child for its parents: family love.

There is the noun *eros* with its accompanying verb *eran*. These words describe the love of a young man for a young lady. Passion is always involved and so is sexual love. There is nothing essentially bad about these words; they simply describe passionate human love. However, as time went by, they were degraded to mean lust rather than love, and they are used nowhere in the New Testament.

There is the noun *philia* with the accompanying verb *philein*. This is the warmest and best word for love. It describes true love and attraction. It describes what a person feels for his most intimate, closest and most faithful friend. It can mean to cherish or to kiss, and it is the highest form of love.

> All God can give us is His love; and this love becomes tangible – a burning of the soul –it sets us on fire to the point of forgetting ourselves.
> BROTHER ROGER

Finally there is *agapè* with the accompanying *agapan*. *Agapè* is the word used in our Scripture verse. Its meaning is "unconquerable good-heartedness." If we feel agapè for someone, it means that irrespective of how that person treats us, we will never allow any bitterness in our hearts. We will want only what's best for them.

We praise You, Lord Jesus, for we have learnt the true meaning of the word love.

The True Meaning of *Agapè*

"I say, love your enemies! Pray for those who persecute you!"
(Matt. 5:44).

Jesus never said to love our enemies with the same love we have for our loved ones. It would be totally impossible and it wouldn't be right. The essence of the word is different. This is quite another kind of love. For example, our love for our loved ones is different; we can't help loving them. Then there is love that we describe as falling in love. We don't have to go and look for this love. It comes to us and it is born from the emotions in the heart. But in the case of our enemies, love is not only something from the heart; it also includes something of the will. It is not something that comes spontaneously; we must will ourselves to do it. It is a victory and triumph over what comes to us instinctively.

> Love of God is the root, love of our neighbor the fruit of the Tree of Life. Neither can exist without the other, but the one is cause and the other effect.
>
> WILLIAM TEMPLE

Agapè doesn't mean the feeling of the heart, that which we cannot help and which is born without us asking for it. It is through determination of the mind that we want to demonstrate unconquerable good to those who wish to harm us. *Agapè* is the ability to love those we don't like and who don't like us. We can only have *agapè* if Christ enables us to overcome our natural tendency towards anger and bitterness.

So it is clear and explicit that the last thing *agapè* or Christian love means is to allow others to do exactly as they please. This means that Christian discipline and punishment should not be aimed at vengeance, but at healing.

Holy Spirit of God, cultivate in me the ability to love my enemies with Christian love.

Love Is the Foundation

"If you love only those who love you, what reward is there for that? Even corrupt tax collectors do that much" (Matt. 5:46).

We must take note that Jesus laid down love as the basis of all our personal relationships with our family and neighbors, and people with whom we share our daily life. Jesus gave this command and we need to apply it to ourselves in the first instance.

We must also take note that it is a command which is only possible for Christians. Only the grace of Jesus Christ can enable us to demonstrate goodwill in our personal relationships. It is only when Christ reigns in our hearts that bitterness dies and His love sprouts. It is often said that our world would be perfect if people would live according to the principles of the Sermon on the Mount, but the simple fact is that no one can do that without Jesus Christ's help. We need Christ to enable us to obey His instructions.

> Darkness cannot drive out darkness; only light can do that. Hate cannot drive out hate; only love can do that.
> MARTIN LUTHER KING, JR.

Perhaps the most important thing is to take note that this command not only allows people to do to us what they want to; we must also do something for them. We are told to pray for them. No one is able to pray for others and hate them at the same time. When we take ourselves, and the person we actually feel like hating, to God, something always happens. We cannot go on hating someone in the presence of God. The surest way of killing bitterness is to pray for the person that we are sorely tempted to hate.

Jesus, Source of true love, grant that I will love my enemies in obedience to Your command.

How to Pray

"But when you pray, go away by yourself, shut the door behind you, and pray to your Father in private. Then your Father, who sees everything, will reward you" (Matt. 6:6).

There was undoubtedly a tendency among the Jews in Jesus' time towards long prayers, but it wasn't a tendency limited to the Jews only. In eighteenth century worship in Scotland, dedication was measured by the length of the prayer. Rabbi Levi claimed that the prayers of people who prayed long prayers were answered. There has always been, and still is a kind of subconscious idea that if you keep on hammering at God's door long enough, He will answer. Yet it is said that a person's words before God should be few. It is easy to confuse talkativeness with devoutness.

> Where there is much prayer, there will be much of the Holy Spirit; where there is much of the Spirit, there will be ever-increasing prayer.
> ANDREW MURRAY

It also happened that many Jews prayed to be seen by people. Their method of praying made arrogance easy. These Jews made sure they were standing on busy street corners during prayer times, or on the stairs of the synagogue. It is easier to put on an act than pray sincerely.

Jesus is laying down two important rules here. All prayer must be dedicated to God. The Jews prayed for an audience, not to God. Many preachers are still more concerned about impressing the congregation than making contact with God. The other rule is that we will always remember that the God we pray to is a God of love that is more willing to listen than we are to pray. So it's all right for us to go to God with simply a sigh on our lips and in our hearts: "Your will be done!"

O, Holy Spirit, teach me how and what to pray.

Genuine Treasures

"Don't store up treasures here on earth, where moths eat them and rust destroys them, and where thieves break in and steal. Store your treasures in heaven, where moths and rust cannot destroy, and thieves do not break in and steal. Wherever your treasure is, there the desires of your heart will also be" (Matt. 6:19-21).

Jesus says people must avoid the things that can be spoilt by moths and rust. In the East, the clothes a person owned made up a large part of that person's riches. But Jesus says it is foolish to set your heart on these things, because the moths can get to them where they are safely stored away and destroy their beauty and value. Possessions like these have no lasting value.

Jesus goes on to say that things should be avoided that can be spoilt by rust. The word translated here as rust is *bròsis.* The literal meaning is to eat away, but it isn't used anywhere in connection with rust. In the East many people's wealth consisted of wheat and grain that were stored in large storehouses. They had a problem with worms that would literally eat away at their wealth. Rats, mice and worms could get into the granaries and eat the grain. There was no permanency in these possessions.

> The man who has God for his treasure has all things in One.
> A. W. TOZER

Jesus also says that we must not store our treasures where thieves can break in and steal them. The walls of most of the houses in Palestine were made of baked clay. Thieves could easily break in and steal by making holes in the wall. There is no permanent value in treasures that can be stolen by thieves.

Holy Jesus, I cling to the most permanent truth of all; to You, Eternal Life.

Treasures in Heaven

"Store your treasures in heaven, where moths and rust cannot destroy, and thieves do not break in and steal. Wherever your treasure is, there the desires of your heart will also be" (Matt. 6:20-21).

The Hebrews were very familiar with the expression "treasures in heaven." It meant especially two things to them.

They believed that the good deeds someone did on earth, became a treasure in heaven. Jesus said that possessions selfishly hoarded, would be lost, but that which was given to others in goodwill, would become a treasure in heaven. The early Christian church lovingly took care of the poor and the sick. They believed: What we keep, we lose; and what we give, becomes a treasure for us in heaven.

The Israelites believed that a shroud had no pockets. The only thing people could take from this world at their death was themselves. Everything that was precious to people here on earth, would mean nothing to them in the hereafter; it only made them unwilling to leave this world. If people's eyes were fixed on eternity during their stay on earth, the things of the world would have little meaning for them and they would leave this world with joy because their eyes were always focused on the things of God.

> The truest end of life, is to find the life that doesn't end.
> ANONYMOUS

Jesus never said that this world was unimportant, but He emphasized over and over again that its worth was not in itself, but in where it would ultimately lead to. This world is not the end of life, it is just a phase on the road to eternity. Our eyes must constantly be fixed on the final goal: eternal life.

Grant, Holy Lord Jesus, that my treasures will not be on earth, but in heaven.

Forbidden Worries

"That is why I tell you not to worry about everyday life – whether you have enough food and drink, or enough clothes to wear. Isn't life more than food, and your body more than clothing?" (Matt. 6:25).

We must make very sure that we understand what Jesus forbids here and what He commands. Jesus doesn't forbid sensible and careful planning in advance, which is a very good thing to do. Jesus never believed in a lackadaisical attitude. What He forbids here is anxiousness and fear that suck the joy out of life. Jesus is teaching us the lesson of careful planning for the future. He uses different lines of reasoning to illustrate His point.

He starts by pointing out to us in verse 25 that God gave us life, and since He gave us life we can trust Him in all things. God gave us our bodies and we shouldn't be so concerned about what to wear. God will make sure we receive the things that enrich and support life. Then Jesus talks about the birds (Matt. 6:26). They aren't concerned about life, and storing up things for an unknown future, and yet their lives carry on. The point Jesus makes here is not that birds don't work, but that they don't worry about everyday life.

> Never try to carry tomorrow's burdens with today's grace.
> ANONYMOUS

Jesus goes on to point out in verse 27 that worrying is pointless in any event. It can't add a single moment to your life, so worrying is really useless and serves no purpose at all. In verses 28-30, Jesus talks about the beauty of the flowers that adorn the hills of Palestine. He reasons that if God gives the flowers such beauty, the human being, who is the crown of His creation, will be given much more.

Lord Jesus, keep me from every tendency to worry.

Live Day by Day

"For the pagans run after all these things, and your heavenly Father knows that you need them. But seek first His kingdom and His righteousness, and all these things will be given to you as well." (Matt. 6:32-33).

N ow Jesus raises a fundamental argument against worrying. Worry is a character trait inherent in the pagans who do not know God. Worry is in fact a lack of trust in God. One might understand that the pagans feel this way because they believe in an unpredictable god, but it should not be part of the lives of those who call God their Father, and who believe in His love.

Jesus mentions two ways in which to put a stop to worrying. The first is to concentrate on the kingdom of God. Jesus was convinced that worry is banned once God becomes the dominant force in our lives. The second way to overcome worrying is to concentrate on doing and accepting God's will.

> Worry does not empty tomorrow of its sorrow. It empties today of its strength.
>
> CORRIE TEN BOOM

Actually Jesus is saying that worry can be overcome once we discover the art of living one day at a time. We read in Matthew 6:34, "So don't worry about tomorrow, for tomorrow will bring its own worries. Today's trouble is enough for today." If we take each day as it comes and carry out every task required of us, then all the days will be good. It is Jesus' command and advice that we deal with the demands of every day as they come, without worrying about the unknown future and things that might never happen.

Grant, Father God, that I will live each day as it comes, because You want me to.

Don't Judge

"Do not judge others, and you will not be judged" (Matt. 7:1).

There are mainly three reasons why one person cannot judge another:

Firstly, we don't have all the facts. To know all is to understand all. We don't know what temptations they have to grapple with. We must understand their background, and know what temptations they have to resist before we can judge. If we know what a person is going through, we will be sympathetic rather than judgmental.

Secondly, it is practically impossible to be impartial in our judgment of others. Time and again we see people's instinctive, unreasonable reactions. Only the perfectly impartial person has the right to judge, and absolute impartiality is not part of human nature. Thus only God can judge.

> If you judge people, you have no time to love them.
> MOTHER TERESA

Lastly, Jesus gives the biggest reason why we cannot judge others: No human being is good enough to judge another. Jesus sketches the picture of the man with the beam in his own eye, but he is set on removing the splinter from his neighbor's eye. Only people without any faults have the right to talk about the faults of others. We are so ready to criticize: the referee from our seat in the stadium; the sinner from our seat in church. Those who criticize most, usually do the least. We have enough to put right in our own lives; we don't have the time to correct other people's lives. Let's work at our own faults and leave those of others to God.

Gracious Father, keep me from recklessly judging others.

The Character of Prayer

"Keep on asking, and you will receive what you ask for. Keep on seeking, and you will find. Keep on knocking, and the door will be opened to you" (Matt. 7:7).

Anyone who prays would like to know what kind of God they are praying to. They want to know in what kind of atmosphere their prayers are heard. Do they pray to such a kind-hearted God that He is more willing to give than they are to receive? Jesus was born into a nation that loved prayer and He learnt to cherish prayer. In this part Jesus gives us the Christian principle for prayer.

Jesus' examples are carefully chosen. Matthew mentions two and Luke adds another one: If children ask for bread, would their father give them a stone? If they ask for a fish, would he give them a snake; or a scorpion if they ask for an egg? Small stones on the seashore looked just like small loaves of bread. The snake mentioned here probably refers to an eel that was forbidden food according to Leviticus 11:12. A scorpion looks very much like an egg when it is falling asleep, but is deadly when it wakes up.

> Our prayers are answered not when we are given what we ask but when we are challenged to be what we can be.
>
> MORRIS ALDER

God will never refuse to listen to our prayers, or ridicule them. The lesson here is that God will always hear our prayers, but He will answer them in His way. His way is the way of perfect wisdom and perfect love. Jesus says we must persevere in prayer because the test of our sincerity lies in this. God will always answer our prayers in the way He sees fit: in wisdom and in love. We must just continue praying to God.

Thank You, Heavenly Father, that You hear my prayers and answer in Your way.

Christian Ethics

"Do to others whatever you would like them to do to you. This is the essence of all that is taught in the law and the prophets" (Matt. 7:12).

In this Scripture verse Jesus addresses what is probably the most universally important issue. The Sermon on the Mount reaches its climax with this command. What Jesus says here is referred to as the cornerstone of everything He ever said. It is the summit of social ethic and the greatest of all ethical teachings.

It is possible to quote rabbinical parallels for almost everything Jesus said in the Sermon on the Mount; but there is no parallel for what He said here. It was something that had never been said before. It was a new doctrine, a new view of life and the commitments that go with life.

It is easy to find parallels of it in the negative form in the Jewish teachings, but there is no equal for the positive form in which Jesus expresses it. The old doctrine was: That which is hateful to you, *you must not do* to others. In its negative form this principle is practically the basis of all ethical teachings, but no one except Jesus ever stated it in the positive form. Many said, "Don't do to others what you wouldn't want them to do to you." But nobody had ever said, *"Do to others* what you would like them to do to you." Therefore Jesus demands much more from us than the negative expression of this statement. It is easier not to do things than to actively become involved in doing something for your neighbor. The new attitude Jesus is calling for here makes life beautiful and caring.

> Our Lord does not care so much for the importance of our works as for the love with which they are done.
> St. Teresa of Avila

Lord Jesus, grant that my life will be adorned with the resolution to do only good to my neighbor.

A Call to Count the Cost

One of the teachers of religious law said to Him, "Teacher, I will follow You wherever You go" (Matt. 8:19).

Matthew probably included this incident in the chapter on miracles because he saw a miracle in it. A teacher of religious law wanted to follow Jesus! And he gave Jesus the highest title of honor, "Teacher." This in itself was a miracle: A Scribe giving Jesus this title and wishing to follow Him while Jesus stood for the abolishment of all the narrow-minded legalism that the theology of the teachers of religious law was built on.

After the teacher of religious law had spoken these words, Jesus told him that foxes had dens to live in and birds had nests, but the Son of God didn't even have a place to lay His head. It is as if Jesus was saying to him: First think about what you are doing before you follow Me. First count the cost. Jesus didn't want followers that got carried away in an emotional moment. Jesus talked about taking up a cross (Matt. 10:38); loving Him more than family (Luke 14:26); giving everything away to the poor (Matt. 19:21). What Jesus was in fact asking was: Do you love Me enough to pay the price of discipleship?

> There are no crown wearers in heaven, who were not cross bearers on earth.
> CHARLES H. SPURGEON

Everywhere in life we are confronted with demands: students must be willing to learn; athletes must deny themselves many things and be willing to train very hard. All of this is not to put a damper on enthusiasm. However, it is quite clear that if a person's enthusiasm doesn't count the cost of whatever it is that he's letting himself in for, the venture will be a failure right from the start. We dare not teach people that Christ's path is an easy path. Jesus never said it would be an easy path.

Holy Master, help me to follow wherever You lead me.

Jesus Calms the Storm

Jesus responded, "Why are you afraid? You have so little faith!" Then He got up and rebuked the wind and waves, and suddenly there was a great calm (Matt. 8:26).

Violent storms are common on the Sea of Galilee due to the location of the lake. Sudden storms occur with destructive force, so that the existing calmness can be transformed into a raging storm within minutes.

But this story is about far more than the calming of the storm on the Sea of Galilee. It was important to the disciples in the year AD 28, but it is just as important to us today. This incident tells us that wherever in life Jesus Christ is, there the storms of life are calmed.

When the cold, bleak winds of sorrow blow around us, there is calmness in the comforting presence of Jesus. When the hot winds of passion blow, we find security and peace in Jesus' presence. When gale-force winds of doubt threaten to uproot the foundations of our faith, there is peaceful safety with Jesus Christ. For every storm that shakes the human heart, there is peace with Jesus.

> He came in complete human form to meet a universal need in a way that is adequate for all times and places and is without parallel or substitute.
> H. D. LEWIS

The meaning and lesson of this event illustrate to us that when the storms of life shake our souls, Jesus is there, and in His presence the raging storm turns into peace that no storm can rob us of.

We praise You, Lord Jesus, for the peace and calm that You bring into our lives.

Serve Where Needed

When Jesus heard this, He said, "Healthy people don't need a doctor – sick people do." Then He added, "Now go and learn the meaning of this Scripture: 'I want you to show mercy, not offer sacrifices.' For I have come to call not those who think they are righteous, but those who know they are sinners" (Matt. 9:12-13).

Here Jesus says to the teachers of religious law: When you celebrate, you invite only the devout and the self-righteous; when I celebrate I invite those who are aware of their sin and who need God most. The orthodox teachers of religious law upheld the law down to the last detail. Then there were other people who didn't uphold the rules of the law. This second group was called "people of the land" and the orthodox Scribes were forbidden to go on a journey with them; to do business with them; to give them anything or to receive anything from them; to receive them as guests or to visit them.

> By a man's reaction to Jesus Christ, that man stands revealed.
> WILLIAM BARCLAY

But it was particularly the sinners who needed Jesus, and that is why He mingled with them. When He said He didn't come to invite the righteous, but sinners, He didn't mean there were people that were so good they didn't need Him; and He was by no means insinuating that He wasn't interested in good people. What Jesus did mean was that He didn't come for people who were so smug and self-satisfied that they felt they needed no one's help. He came for the sake of people who were aware of their sin and desperate for a Savior.

Jesus emphasizes the fact that only those who knew how much they needed Him could accept His invitation.

Savior and Redeemer, I heard Your voice and thankfully accepted Your salvation.

The Test of Faith

They [the two blind men] went right into the house where He was staying and Jesus asked them, "Do you believe I can make you see?" "Yes, Lord," they told Him, "we do." Then He touched their eyes and said, "Because of your faith, it will happen" (Matt. 9:28-29).

Blindness was shockingly common in Palestine, partly because of the glow of the bright eastern sun on unprotected eyes, and partly because the people had no idea of the importance of hygiene and cleanliness.

These two blind men addressed Jesus as "Son of David." The crowds always called Jesus this, because the return of the Son of David would be the Messiah who would lead His people to freedom and victory. Jesus didn't reply to their plea straight away because He wanted to test the sincerity of their faith. He wanted to be alone with them and that's why they came into the house with Him. It is easy to make a decision in the midst of a milling crowd of emotional people. After being part of the throngs, it is necessary that we return to solitude with Jesus. What we do as part of a crowd is not important to Christ, but rather what we do when we are alone with Jesus.

> The life of faith is continually renewed victory over doubt, a continually renewed grasp of meaning in the midst of meaninglessness.
>
> LESSLIE NEWBIGIN

Jesus asked these two blind men one question only, "Do you believe I can make you see?" This is essential for any miracle to take place. We must put our lives in Jesus' hands and confess, "Yes, Lord ... we do." Then the miracle is performed.

Risen and Living Savior, I know that if we believe, everything is possible for You.

The Harvest Must Be Gathered

"The harvest is great, but the workers are few. So pray to the Lord who is in charge of the harvest; ask Him to send more workers into His fields" (Matt. 9:37-38).

This is one of the most important things Jesus ever said. When He and the orthodox spiritual leaders of His time looked at the crowds of ordinary people, they looked at them in different ways. The Pharisees saw them as chaff that was blown away by the wind and burnt. Jesus saw them as a harvest that had to be gathered. The Pharisees wanted to see sinners destroyed; Jesus in His great love, died for the salvation of sinners.

This is also one of the great Christian truths and one of the greatest challenges for Christians. The harvest will never be gathered unless there are people who harvest the crop. This is one of the burning truths of the Christian faith: Jesus needs people. While He was on earth, His voice didn't reach that many people.

> Jesus Christ didn't commit the Bible to an advertising agency; He commissioned disciples. And He didn't commit them to pass out tracts; He said they would be His witnesses.
>
> JOE BAYLY

He never left Palestine and there was a waiting world outside its borders. To this day He wants people to hear the good news of the gospel, but it will never be heard if people don't spread it.

Prayer is not enough. We can pray every day that the kingdom of God will come, but prayer without works is dead. It was Christ's dream for each person to be a missionary or a harvester. If the harvest of humankind is ever to be reaped, there will have to be people who do it. Somewhere there is someone who we must lead to God.

Lord, I am willing to gather the harvest and lead people to You.

May

A New Life

"Just as you can hear the wind but can't tell where
it comes from or where it is going, so you can't
explain how people are born of the Spirit."
~ John 3:8

All I have seen teaches me to trust
the Creator for all I have not seen.
~ RALPH WALDO EMERSON

Holy God, Holy Spirit,
we worship You as the Giver of new life.
Blow through my life, O Spirit. Cleanse me of all
contamination and impure thoughts,
a lack of love, selfishness and intolerance.
O Spirit, blow like a gentle breeze
through the hearts of all who are sad.
You are the Comforter promised
by the Savior to all who are despondent.
Support those who are in danger of snapping under their grief;
give them new courage for life.
O Spirit, blow through the hearts
of those who have broken loose from You
and have become slaves of sin (see Rom. 6:20).
Make their hearts repentant and let
the wonder of rebirth take place in them.
O Spirit, blow through Your church
and bring a God-willed revival.
Change congregations from sleeping
quarters to buzzing factories
where we work for You because we love You.
Let us take Sunday's life into everyday life and every place.
O Spirit, blow through our land
and its leaders and all its people.
Work powerfully so that there will
be reconciliation, tolerance and peace.
Let God's name be glorified, Christ's attitude live in us,
and let Your fruit, the fruit of the Spirit,
become visible in our lives.
Be to all of us, O Holy Spirit,
the life-breath of the true Christian life.
In the name of our Risen Savior, Jesus the Living Christ.

Amen.

An Unavoidable Encounter

Jesus had to go through Samaria on the way. Eventually He came to the Samaritan village of Sychar (John 4:4-5).

In today's Scripture we see that Jesus' path of grace crosses that of a needy sinner. Jesus was in Judea and had to go to Galilee. He could either take the road along the Rift Valley from the Jordan, which was the easier and more pleasant route. Or He could take the difficult road through the land of the Samaritans – a journey of at least six days through the land of the hostile Samaritans. But Jesus "had to go" through Samaria, because He needed to tell the people of God's love. Nobody has sunk so deep into sin that God cannot save them. The Good News is for *all* people. The gospel is universal but also individual! Jesus came to seek and to save *everybody* who is lost.

> Christians are not men and women who are hoping for salvation, but those who have experienced it.
>
> M. LLOYD-JONES

There was a very unhappy woman in Samaria who was in deep spiritual need; wrestling with her own distinctive, dark problem. She had probably heard about the Prophet but had never met Him personally. She couldn't go to Him, but He could go to her, to the scene of her sinful life. This demonstrates Christ's love that seeks out these people, like God went looking for Adam and Eve in paradise. With this Jesus says to us, "Look! I stand at the door and knock. If you hear My voice and open the door, I will come in, and we will share a meal together as friends" (Rev. 3:20). Perhaps you have heard a lot *about* Jesus; but have you had a Damascus Road meeting with Him, like Paul? Jesus is coming to meet with you, and call you to come "home."

Grant, Lord Jesus, that I will hear Your soft and tender voice, and respond to it.

A Samaritan Woman

A Samaritan woman came to draw water (John 4:7).

W ho was this woman of Sychar who Jesus encountered at the well? Everybody knew her. She was a woman of ill repute. She already had five husbands and was living with a sixth man. She had unrealistic and high expectations of life, experienced one spiritual failure after the other and sank to the lowest level of sin. As a social outcast, she walked a lonely road in the community. This is the way she lived until the day Jesus Christ passed through Samaria, met her and came to her rescue.

There was something that only she and Jesus knew about her: she was deeply unhappy with her sinful life. Jesus knew that in spite of her devil-may-care attitude, she was very unhappy. She had tried to hide this with a show of bravado. But now, here with Jesus, a desperate plea was wrung from her heart. She realized with excitement: The Lord knows all about me! Also about the sorrow sin is causing me. Jesus knew something that only He knew about her and He wanted to share it with her. She could be saved! And so can you and I! God does not find pleasure in the death of the sinner. God hates sin but He loves the sinner. Jesus didn't say to her: Your sin doesn't matter. No, He told her that He could free her from the chains of sin. He could make her pure by His blood. He could change her sensual thirst to spiritual thirst.

> Salvation is entirely the result of the sovereign will and election of God and nothing to do with us at all.
> ANONYMOUS

If Jesus crosses your path today, remember: He knows about your sin, but He also knows about your thirst for salvation. Don't miss the opportunity: Jesus of Nazareth is passing through.

Thank You, Lord, for my encounter with You and for Your saving grace.

The Feud

She said to Jesus, "You are a Jew, and I am a Samaritan woman. Why are You asking me for a drink?" (John 4:9).

In Christ's time Palestine was 120 miles from north to south, or from Dan to Beersheba. It was divided into three main parts: Galilee in the north; Judea in the south, and Samaria between the two. Jesus was spreading the gospel, and because He didn't want to get caught up in dogmatic issues about baptism, He decided to leave Judea and go to Galilee – and consequently, the greatest part of His ministry took place there. The strife between the Jews and the Samaritans was a long and bitter one, which started in 720 BC when the Assyrians invaded the land and looted the kingdom of Samaria. They exiled the inhabitants to Media where they assimilated into the people of Babylon. They colonized Samaria with Babylonians. The Samaritans, who stayed behind in the country, intermarried with the strangers from Babylon. According to Jewish tradition, this was an unforgivable crime.

> Christ came to save all through His own Person.
> IRENAEUS

With time, a similar invasion took place in the southern kingdom of Judea. Their capital, Jerusalem, was ravaged and the Jews were exiled to Babylon. There they jealously guarded their identity and never intermarried. In Ezra and Nehemiah's time, the Persian king Kores allowed the Jews to return to their land and to Jerusalem. They immediately started rebuilding the Temple. The Samaritans offered to help them, but their offer was declined with contempt and they were told they would desecrate the Temple. This is where the bitterness between the Jews and Samaritans was born. This bitter feud lasted 400 years until Jesus appeared on the scene and came to the rescue.

Holy Lord Jesus, I praise Your name as the liberator of every people and language and every nation's sinners.

Worship in Spirit and in Truth

"For God is Spirit, so those who worship Him must worship in spirit and in truth" (John 4:24).

~∽⌒∾~

At the well Jesus asked the woman to give Him water. She was surprised that a Jewish man would ask a Samaritan for water. Jesus' reply is our Scripture for today. Here we have to do with a lonely woman weighed down by a dreadful burden of sin. Jesus led her to awareness of her eternal thirst for the water that gives life – in other words, being born again.

Once we are born again, we see politics and religion in perspective and understand that "God is Spirit, so those who worship Him must worship in spirit and in truth" (John 4:24). Worship is inherent in the heart of each of God's creations. God sows the seed of eternity in our hearts. A believer's highest fulfillment is found in worshiping and glorifying God. Even worshiping a rock, or a totem pole, a mountain or a river or a tree stump – all of this can serve the purpose of giving expression to the inborn need in our hearts to worship God.

> The perfect church service would be one we were almost unaware of; our attention would have been on God.
>
> C. S. Lewis

All people worship: in the rain-drenched forests of Central Africa; in the American prairie. But worship is no guarantee of salvation. It is not *whether* we worship, but *how* and *who* we worship. Outward forms of worship, holy relics and sacred places merely serve the purpose of helping us in our search for God. They may never become the main issue and never ever take God's place. God must be worshiped in spirit and truth.

You are holy, O God, purer than the sunlight. Thank You that I may worship You in spirit and in truth.

True Worship

"For God is Spirit, so those who worship Him must worship in spirit and in truth" (John 4:24).

The sacraments are merely instrumental in helping us in our worship in spirit and in truth. They help us to purposefully draw near to God. Jesus had already spoken to this woman about her thirst, her sinful life and her eternal thirst. Before leaving her, He spoke about true worship. He started by saying to her, "God is Spirit." He is a creative, re-creative, living and life-giving Spirit. Therefore we must not try to localize Him: not in Jerusalem or in Gerizim. The woman wanted to know where to worship, but Christ replied that it didn't matter, as long as we worship God in the right way. He is not a God only on Sundays: He is a God for every day and every place.

We are not permitted to personalize God: God is Spirit. Neither the Pope nor Mother Mary is God. Neither is Luther or Calvin. People often link worship to certain people, an insult to God. When we worship, the question is not who is on the pulpit, but whether God is present. If God is there, even a prison cell can become a temple.

> Worship is the highest and noblest activity of which man, by the grace of God, is capable.
>
> John Stott

Tradition is good and right, but it may never become the main consideration in our worship. It must not be allowed to create a rigidity in us that makes us hesitant to change. God's Spirit is alive and continuously re-creating. New times often require new methods of worship. This Samaritan woman prided herself on the fact that she worshiped where her forefathers worshiped, and yet it didn't make any difference to her own sinful life. Our place of worship must always be close to God to make our worship meaningful.

Spirit of God, purify my worship so that it is what it should be.

Grace for All

"For God is Spirit, so those who worship Him must worship in spirit and in truth" (John 4:24).

W hat Jesus is indirectly saying is that holy things don't necessarily make holy people. We can kneel down before holy things and be very far removed from God. It is possible to be religious and at the same time sinful and unsaved. The woman at the well was intensely interested in the theological issues of her time, but she went on living in sin.

Her theology was orthodox and she had very definite and unusually rigid views on it. But her real relationship with God added up to nothing. Before we can know Christ in the power of His resurrection, we must meet Him personally and be born again. Then, and only then, can we worship Him in spirit and in truth. Whether it is in a church, in a kitchen or in nature – there must be absolute truth in our worship.

Salvation is God's way of making us real people.
St. Augustine

When the body is on its knees, the heart must also kneel before God. When we shut our eyes to the world, we must see only God. When we speak before God, our words must be honest and sincere. When we make promises, they must be promises that cannot be broken, unbreakable vows to God Himself.

Worship must be honest, pure and sincere: like the beggar knocking at the door of a benefactor; like a sinner begging for mercy; like a child sobbing in remorse before his parents. Then we can confess in sincerity, "You are the Messiah! You are my Savior! My Redeemer that ransomed me with Your precious blood; that came to change my eternal thirst into Pentecostal fullness!"

I praise Your name, O Creator God, who rules over everything. Thank You for Your grace for sinners – and also for me.

Unnecessary Ignorance

"If you only knew the gift God has for you and who you are speaking to" (John 4:10).

W e live in an age of unprecedented knowledge, and according to experts it doubles every five years. We know all about the earth and scrutinize outer space. Yet in many cases there is unbelievable ignorance about the eternal salvation of our immortal souls. So many voices come to us – inviting, flattering and challenging voices – causing chaos and confusion in our minds. But above all these voices, the voice of the Man from Nazareth is heard. It is the voice of Jesus Christ, the Son of God, inviting us, "Come to Me and I will give you the Water of Life!"

> Everyone needs to be saved, however great, however illustrious. We are all sinners. We are all born in sin.
>
> M. LLOYD-JONES

There is no excuse for ignorance about Jesus Christ; there should be no confusion about His voice and no uncertainty about what He wants to say to us. The woman at the well was at a crisis in her life. She was ignorant about Jesus Christ. Who is this Man? Woman of Samaria, if only you knew Who He was and what He could do for you!

Deep in our hearts, we all seek this knowledge of salvation that is in Jesus Christ. We look for certainty, but often, because we think there is still plenty of time, we postpone surrendering ourselves to Him. This is eternal life: that we know Jesus as Savior; and this is the eternal curse: that we don't want to know Him. We hear God speaking to us, we know it is God; we know that He is wrestling with us about our immortal souls, but we refuse to listen to Him.

Thank You for the patience You have had with me, Savior and Redeemer. I heard Your voice and answered.

Salvation through Christ

"If you only knew the gift God has for you and who you are speaking to" (John 4:10).

When the Holy Spirit of God begins working in our conscience, we hear God speak to us. We instinctively know it is God and we know that He is wrestling with us. Our blunted consciences are shaken back to life and we become aware of the wrong in our lives. We feel the necessity of change, and know we dare not carry on living as we are. God speaks to us, yet often we are unwilling to answer Him.

We see the steep road and the narrow gate and we refuse to give God a positive answer. We are willing to listen but not to do. We have no real remorse or sorrow about our sin. That is why Christ says to us, "If only you knew ... " If only you knew who is talking to you and what He wants to give you! He offers you the Water of Life – free!

> Lord my God, You have formed and reformed me.
> Anselm

This woman's sensual thirst was unquenchable, but Christ could quench the thirst of her soul. He gives streams and rivers in the desert. He calls: "If anyone is thirsty, let him come to Me." Christ gives us Living Water that cleanses us from our sins and grants us forgiveness. How this woman yearned to be purified!

Christ's Living Water makes us fruitful in His service: to live for Him, to work and to witness for Him. If only you knew how much He loves you! How badly He wants to set you free and save you. Look up at the cross and see His pierced hands and feet, and know for sure that He loves you deeply.

Lord Jesus, You laid down Your life for me. I found shelter and salvation in Your wonderful protection. Praise the Lord!

Life-Giving Refreshment

"Anyone who drinks this water will soon become thirsty again. But those who drink the water I give will never be thirsty again. It becomes a fresh, bubbling spring within them, giving them eternal life" (John 4:13-14).

~ ❦ ~

Zechariah 13:1 contains a profound message: "On that day a fountain will be opened, a fountain to cleanse them from all their sins and impurity." This is the source of Living Water: It flows through the entire world, giving life. This woman came to fetch water from the well of Jacob. But God had intended the spiritual water of salvation for her.

When a jeweler places a gemstone in a crown, he makes a black hollow into which the gem must be set, because a jewel glitters best against a black background. It is the same with the precious jewel of God's grace: It glitters best in a sinner's black heart. The Samaritan woman is proof of this. And how long it took Jesus to open her eyes! When He spoke of the Living Water, she kept on about the excellent qualities of the water. Thus Jesus used the well as point of departure to tell her about the Living Water.

> For you have been born again, not of perishable seed, but of imperishable, through the living and enduring Word of God.
> 1 PETER 1:23

First Jesus spoke of the worthiness of the well and then about its inadequacy, replacing it with the fountain of Living Water. May the purifying water of this fountain flow through your heart, so that your thirst is quenched. We will briefly pause at all these stages and listen for what God the Spirit wants to say to us. May He make us willing to hear and obey so that we can share in the Living Water.

My soul thirsts for You, O God, for the living God. Thank You for the Living Water that I may receive from You free of charge.

Those Who Thirst

"Anyone who drinks this water will soon become thirsty again. But those who drink the water I give will never be thirsty again. It becomes a fresh, bubbling spring within them, giving them eternal life" (John 4:13-14).

Many of us are like this woman at the well. When we read or hear about the Living Water that Christ gives, it is like a foreign language, because we don't know Jesus personally.

We all have treasured memories of the past in our hearts. Perhaps our parents were devout and religious, but the world has sucked us in. There's so much pressure, so many cares and worries. The world becomes appealing and we have gradually become estranged from God. And are we at peace? No, we always thirst for something higher and better.

> Only in Jesus Christ do we have assurance of salvation, forgiveness of sins, entrance into God's family, and the guarantee of heaven forever when we die.
> LUIS PALAU

With fondness we remember how our parents used to read the Bible, prayed together and attended church. Our memories make it seem like we were close to the gates of heaven. What a privilege to have such precious memories. Do you also sometimes think of earlier times and yearn for a better life? Draw often and draw much from the deep and holy well of the memories of your youth. It refreshes and invigorates – even if it also brings shame because we have strayed so far from the Lord of your youth. But we must know that we will not gain eternal life by doing this. Vague memories can never give us what the living Christ wants to give us through His Holy Spirit. Stand up and make the change!

Only You, Lord Jesus, can satisfy the burning thirst in my life.

The Fountain of Living Water

"Anyone who drinks this water will soon become thirsty again. But those who drink the water I give will never be thirsty again. It becomes a fresh, bubbling spring within them, giving them eternal life" (John 4:13-14).

Let's take a look at Jacob's well and its inability to provide perfect fulfillment. The Samaritan woman wanted to know where Jesus would get the water to quench her thirst. Surely He was not better than the patriarch Jacob? She was perplexed and started noticing something mysterious about Jesus. He explains to her that there is a big difference between the water in the well and the Water of Life. He pointed to the well of Jacob and said, "Anyone who drinks this water will soon become thirsty again." The woman knew this from personal experience. And at this point Jesus steered the conversation to the spiritual. He pointed out the marked contrast between temporarily satisfying the thirst of the physical body, and eternally quenching the thirst of the soul. "Please, Sir," the woman said, "give me this water!" (John 4:15).

> Salvation comes by way of a cross and a crucified Christ.
> ANDREW MURRAY

Christ went to a lot of trouble to make the woman realize that she needed more than what human hands could give her. Faith is a personal matter between you and the Lord. The devoutness of your father cannot stand in for you. You must have personal faith. Jacob left a great legacy for his descendants, but he couldn't satisfy the need of their souls. There is only one well that will never disappoint us: Jesus Christ gives us the Living Water! Thus the Fountain of Living Water replaces Jacob's well. Christ invites you today to take that life-giving refreshment.

Redeemer and Savior, with deep gratitude I receive the Water of Life.

An Unsettling Command

"Go and get your husband," Jesus told her (John 4:16).

Christianity also brings about substantial domestic responsibilities. The Holy Spirit flows like a pure stream into the most intimate relationship between individuals. Our thirst for love can only be satisfied by the Fountain of Living Water. Jesus led the Samaritan woman to this unavoidable truth. She cried out in her consuming need, "Please, Sir ... give me this water!" And Jesus answered with an unsettling command: "Go and get your husband."

The Lord forced her to face up to reality. Playing hide-and-seek in her spiritual need would be of no help: the truth had to become known! Jesus wanted to lead her to a point where she admitted her guilt, her immorality and her licentious life. The Lord gave her the order to get her husband, not because He didn't know the true state of affairs, but because He wanted to give her an opportunity to confess.

> The love we shared
> died in the early morning
> light, and we buried her
> cold and pale; tender
> spring grass and fragrant
> early-year's ground covers
> her, without mourning by
> wreathe or flower.
>
> ELISABETH EYBERS

How about it? Will you as a young man or young woman bring the one you love, the one you have a relationship with, and stand in God's light? Or will you be ashamed to come before God with your relationship because it is dark and ominous and will not pass the test of light? Is it just a sensual and light flirtation; a relationship of the flesh that drives you to the pleasure of the moment and then leaves you with a life of self-reproach and a guilt-ridden conscience?

Holy Spirit of God, You alone can purify and cleanse my relationships. Thank You that You did it for me.

True Love

"You aren't even married to the man you're living with now"
(John 4:18).

Is your engagement really a time of preparation; a time of re-flection, introspection, planning and prayer? Do you realize that this unbreakable bond stands firm, above all else? You are not yet married and the fruit of marriage is still forbidden fruit for you. You must be so careful during this period to make sure that you can stand before God intact. When you are in love, physical attraction turns people into a pair of electrically charged wires. Young friend, prayerfully ask God for that fountain's Living Water that will keep you pure so that, on your wedding day, the whiteness of the wedding dress and the bouquets displayed in God's house will not be a mockery.

Go and get your husband! Go and get your wife and come and stand before God! It is disturbing that three out of every five marriages in our country end in divorce. Separation

Lord, we Thy presence seek; may ours this blessing be; give us a pure and lowly heart, a temple meet for Thee.
JOHN KEBLE

has become fashionable and a mere formality. Extramarital re-lationships and immorality are the order of the day. Free love has become fashionable for many. A lack of love, intolerance, unpleasant arguments are the cross in many a home and the sorrow of many a heart. The consulting rooms of marriage coun-cilors and psychologists in 90% of cases are filled with people with marital problems.

Thank You loving Father, that Your Spirit teaches me true love so that my marriage is protected.

Relationships Made Pure

Love each other with genuine affection, and take delight in honoring each other (Rom. 12:10).

Let us not forget to thank God for the large number of families where the marriage is still intact: where it is still the mystical union of two people who are bound together by pure love; homes in which a woman's nobility and a man's honor are still recognized. In general, however, all marriages start poetically and then gradually decline and become prosaic: suddenly the color in the marriage fades and a drab dullness moves into the house to live there.

Caresses turn into cruel arguments that flare up at the slightest provocation. One partner walks all over the other one's love with self-righteous and egotistical spiked shoes, and tramples it underfoot. All that is left of the brightly burning flame of the love of the wedding day is a little pile of smoldering ashes. Why? Why does it happen that something that started so beautiful often goes to rack and ruin? Because the human being forgets that marriage is from God.

> My strength is as the strength of ten, because my heart is pure.
> ALFRED LORD TENNYSON

What was proclaimed to you on your wedding day? Perhaps you didn't even hear it in the romanticism of the moment. It's only human. Listen to it now: Thus the gospel cautions us to honor this holy state of matrimony as an institution that is not grounded on the discretion of the person God created, but on those whom the favor of God our Creator rests.

Holy Spirit of God, purify my love and all my human relationships to become like God expects them to be.

The Great Discovery

Then Jesus told her, "I AM the Messiah!" (John 4:26).

Asobering revelation now dawns on the woman at the well: It was quite possible to be in contact with the Lord for years and still not have made the Great Discovery. It was an eye-opener to realize that she had been so ignorant about God's indescribable gift.

The Scriptures so often speak of this brilliant, illuminating moment of recognition. For example, Job thought he was a godly man because he could defend God and his faith. Then God revealed Himself to Job and he confessed, "I had only heard about You before, but now I have seen You with my own eyes. I take back everything I said, and I sit in dust and ashes to show my repentance" (Job 42:5-6). When Isaiah saw God in the Temple, his reaction was, "It's all over! I am doomed, for I am a sinful man. Yet I have seen the King, the LORD of Heaven's Armies!" (Isa. 6:5).

> God's ultimate purpose is birth. He is not content until He brings His Son to birth in us.
> MEISTER ECKHART

This type of meeting not only makes us aware of our own weaknesses, but also of our inability to save ourselves. Only Christ can save us – this is as clear as day. In our own strength we are doomed to fail. God has a wonderful plan with our lives; we only have to become aware of it, like the sinful woman at the well did. The Lord does not necessarily use competent people; He equips those He uses. Then this former ignorance becomes a song of jubilation; a song of incredible joy: "Blessed assurance, Jesus is mine!" The ignorance of the past makes room for a great discovery.

Redeemer and Master, thank You that You touched also my unworthy life and made me God's child.

Rebirth

Then Jesus told her, "I AM the Messiah!" (John 4:26).

Our meeting with Christ doesn't only make a difference to our past, but also the present. The Samaritan woman came to the realization of her immediate salvation. We are not saved only from past sins, or for heaven one day. In God's household there is also a glorious present tense. This woman discovered Jesus in her present life – and when someone discovers Jesus, it has immediate consequences, and the burning question arises: What do I do with Jesus?

I can reject Him, like the people of Israel. They demanded that He be crucified. This is true throughout history: Cain rejected the Lord and knew no rest; Pharaoh rejected Him and died disastrously; Judas rejected Him and experienced eternal night; Agrippa rejected Him and his life was one tragedy upon the other. We are either subjects or we are not; we are either saved or lost, and on our way to heaven or perdition.

> True conversion will involve the mind, the affection, and the will.
> BILLY GRAHAM

We can accept Jesus in faith as our personal Savior, as the fulfillment of our thirst for God. As of today our lives will never be the same. The discovery of Jesus also has something to do with our future. Our future happiness is very closely connected to Jesus of Nazareth. The Samaritan woman's ignorance was transformed into the knowledge of salvation. Her life, which dishonored God, was transformed and purified. The old things passed away and everything became new. Are you still walking in the night of sin? Jesus of Nazareth is passing by so that it need never be night for you again.

Thank You, Lord Jesus, that You have given everyone who accepted You the right to be children of God.

A Witness of Grace

Many Samaritans from the village believed in Jesus because the woman had said, "He told me everything I ever did!" (John 4:39).

There are some things in life that others can't do for you. Believing in Jesus Christ is something only you can do. Your lamp won't burn on another person's oil; the foolish girls in the parable proved this to us. We must each have our own oil. The Samaritan woman said to the people of Sychar, "Come and see a man who told me everything I ever did! Could He possibly be the Messiah?" Of course she knew it was the Messiah: He saved her! He satisfied her thirst and healed her.

It's not that she didn't believe in Him. It's because she knew that a person must meet Him personally. But her words were so convincing and her life so changed that they had to believe. A witness for Christ is a person whose words and deeds complement each other meaningfully. And when this happens, the world wants to meet Christ. What

> Man of Sorrows!
> what a name for the
> Son of God, who came
> ruined sinners to reclaim!
> Hallelujah, what a Savior!
> PHILIP PAUL BLISS

they saw in the woman awakened a strange longing in them. If He could do that for her, He could do it for them too.

People often live among God's children all their lives, but their hearts are never involved. Which parent would not die for their children? – but they can't! One person can't divide their own salvation into parts and give some of it to others. We are always cast back on God. "Is anyone thirsty? Come and drink – even if you have no money!" (Isa. 55:1), Anyone who is thirsty may come. May you and I say, with the people of Sychar, "He is indeed the Savior of the world!" (John 4:42).

I praise You, Savior and Redeemer, because I know from personal experience that You are the Savior of the world.

An Essential Oneness

"The Father and I are One" (John 10:30).

Sometimes a husband and wife develop such a deep understanding of each other that people say they are perfect. This kind of harmony is often seen in the workplace or on the sports field. Many people wish to achieve this kind of harmony. The people in Christ's time wondered who He was. Instead of telling them that He was truly the Messiah, He said that He and the Father were one.

The Father and Son are one in the sense that they co-operate perfectly to achieve their purpose. Father and Son are also one in their goals, and have the same nature. When Jesus was on earth, He was so perfectly in tune with the Father that it was possible for people to know God by looking at Jesus and understanding who He was.

> God is revealed to us as Father, Son and Holy Spirit each with distinct personal attributes, but without division of nature, essence or being.
>
> JAMES P. BOYCE

Jesus wishes for you to also be one with Him. He wants you to be united to God to such an extent that you understand His purpose, that you obey His commands and help advance His kingdom. He wishes that you will "breathe the same air" and will be filled with the Holy Spirit who is also one with Him. Strangely enough, all this does not mean your own personality will be at any disadvantage or disappear – on the contrary, it will be renewed, deepened and strengthened.

Get your thoughts in line with God's thoughts. Allow His attitude to rule in your life; let His thoughts live in you and allow His heart to beat through yours. What Jesus wants to say to us is that He wishes to reconcile and unite us with God. It is essential that we experience this.

Lord Jesus, let me live in oneness with You!

God's Man of Action

"Don't believe Me unless I carry out My Father's work. But if I do His work, believe in the evidence of the miraculous works I have done, even if you don't believe Me. Then you will know and understand that the Father is in Me, and I am in the Father" (John 10:37-38).

For most people, it's what others do, not say, that counts. When Jesus spoke He spoke with authority, but when the people asked Him who He was, He pointed them to the things He did. He asked them to take note of His deeds. These deeds were acts of compassion, healing and miracles. Jesus was far more than simply a traveling Teacher who spoke about God and His kingdom. Jesus didn't perform miracles because He wanted to impress people. Everything He did was God's deeds. Christ was God's man in action.

You and I are also called to do more than just talk. As a disciple of Christ you must be where the action is. Make no mistake: It is good to talk about God and for God, but it is better, more powerful and more impressive to do deeds that prove you are a God-directed person. Deeds done with compassion and kind-heartedness reflect Jesus' deeds. Charity that costs you something is the way in which Christian disciples prove that they are God's people in action. Don't let your religion stagnate; do something and become a doer of the Word and not just an idle hearer, fooling yourself.

> A man who has to be convinced to act before he acts is not a man of action.
> GEORGE CLEMENCEAU

Lord Jesus, help me not to be satisfied with only speaking about You. Show me what I should do.

Meeting Problems Halfway

"Let's go back to Judea" (John 11:7).

Most people have a problem with time management and making sure everything is done. The experts say the answer is to do what needs to be done now, immediately. The problem is that there are just so many things to be done. We need a priority list.

Jesus Christ knew the value of doing things that had to be done straight away. When He decided to go back to Judea, to heal Lazarus, His disciples tried to stop Him: "Only a few days ago the people in Judea were trying to stone You. Are You going there again?" He knew He would be on earth for a certain time only. It would be better to do what needed to be done straight away, even if it meant taking risks. The light of God shone through the mighty works of Jesus, and it never shone more brightly than when He returned to Judea and raised Lazarus from the dead. Don't postpone the things God wants you to do today.

> Today, our very survival depends on our ability to stay awake, to adjust to new ideas, to remain vigilant and to face the challenge of change.
> MARTIN LUTHER KING, JR.

Jesus said that there are twelve hours of daylight in which to do the Lord's work. In saying this He implies that where He is, there will be Light and Life. If we live without Christ, we are spiritually asleep. When Christ touches us, He wakes us from the sleep of the dead. He brings us life and lets His Spirit live in us. Many of His children are spiritually lulled to sleep without being aware of it. If this is true of you, this is a wake-up call from God. Don't let your spiritual discipline become slack – this is the surest way to fall asleep.

Awake, O sleeper, rise up from the dead, and Christ will give you light (Eph. 5:14).

Jesus Takes Action

Jesus was still angry as He arrived at the tomb, a cave with a stone rolled across its entrance. "Roll the stone aside," Jesus told them (John 11:38-39).

༒

All of us go through crises at times. Then we don't know what to do. We are confused and unable to make decisions. Such crises often cause arguments, conflict and indecisiveness in families. Many of the problems that arise could have been prevented if only there was someone who could take control, make decisions and do what had to be done.

Martha and Mary needed someone who could take control and decide on the best course of action. The sorrow of the sisters, the fact that Jesus didn't arrive in time, the presence of all the visitors, as well as the loss of Lazarus, all contributed towards a terribly sad situation. The sisters said to Jesus, "Lord, if only You had been here, my brother would not have died" (John 11:21). Amid all this confusion Jesus takes control and performs a mighty act.

> If you keep doing what you've always done, you'll always get what you've always gotten.
> JOHN C. MAXWELL

Whatever your circumstances, allow Jesus to take control and let the omnipotence of God take over. If you feel like your whole life is falling apart, call on Him to handle the situation for you. If you have repeatedly made mistakes and caused even more trouble, take everything to Jesus in prayer and ask Him to resolve it. If conflict is making things worse, call Jesus. He is not only "Gentle Jesus meek and mild"; He is strong, decisive and has the ability to handle and solve any problem. When you give the problems in your life to Him, you must also give yourself to Him.

Lord Jesus, take control of my life, my heart and my thoughts, and lead me out of the chaos I've created.

The Voice of the Almighty

Jesus looked up to heaven and said, "Father, thank You for hearing Me. You always hear Me, but I said it out loud for the sake of all these people standing here, so that they will believe You sent Me." Then Jesus shouted, "Lazarus, come out!" (John 11:41-43).

J esus not only took over authority of the village of Bethel where the people mourned Lazarus' death. After they had rolled the gravestone aside, Jesus commanded the deceased Lazarus to come out of the grave. In the story of Creation, God spoke and life, human life, came into being at His command. Now Jesus Christ, the Son of God, had called a dead man back to life. There is no aspect of life or death that is not controlled by Him. He called fishermen to leave their nets and follow Him – and they did just that. He ordered evil spirits to leave a man controlled by demons – and they obeyed Him. He commanded the wind and the waves to calm down, and they did. Now He ordered a dead man to come back to life and His order was obeyed.

> I asked God for all things, that I might enjoy life. God gave life, that I might enjoy all things.
>
> ANONYMOUS

Christ commands you and me to come out of our graves of sin and disobedience. He calls us from the darkness of evil to the Light of His glorious omnipotence and undeserved goodness. He speaks to us at the grave of our despondency, despair and depression, and offers us a new day of hope, happiness and peace.

Will you come out in answer to His almighty voice, or will you choose to stay where you are?

Lord Jesus, I hear Your mighty voice and at Your command I will let go of the destructive things that control my life and find life in You once more.

Let Him Go

The dead man [Lazarus] came out, his hands and feet bound in gravecloths, his face wrapped in a headcloth. Jesus told them, "Unwrap him and let him go!" (John 11:44).

The world we live in today is a world riddled with suffering, sickness and death. The story of Lazarus is therefore good news for us. It tells us that suffering and sadness don't have the last word. God the Father and Jesus Christ, His Son, have the final say. This does not mean that death does not exist; we as human beings suffer and die. We are not immortal. But there is One above us and out of our physical reach, whose ways and omnipotence are far beyond our understanding. He is the Lord of Life and He conquered death. In the final instance your life is in His hands because He holds the power of life and death, and also the future, in His almighty hands.

> It's only after we've lost everything that we're free to do anything.
> CHUCK PALAHNIUK

Always remember to distinguish between Lazarus being raised from death and Jesus' resurrection. Lazarus was raised from the dead to continue his normal lifespan like all other people. When Jesus was resurrected at Easter, He was transformed, transfigured and empowered. Death had no authority over Him.

Jesus offers you His life-giving presence. Put the grave of your sins, depression, selfishness and despair behind you. When you have done that, allow Jesus to set you free from former bad habits, thoughts, attitudes and memories that bind you to the past. Jesus commands you to let them go and to enjoy His fullness, abundance, peace, joy, faith and love.

Holy Master, set me free from the past so that I may live in Your abundance and power.

Christ's Triumphal March

Thank God! He has made us His captives and continues to lead us along in Christ's triumphal procession. Now He uses us to spread the knowledge of Christ everywhere, like a sweet perfume (2 Cor. 2:14).

In contrast to what some believers suggest, the Christian life can have its moments of depression and defeat. Such times can have devastating results if followers of Christ allow them to cloud their spiritual view. When the songs of praise have stopped and the consciousness of Christ's presence has waned, we often reach a point where our faith becomes weak.

Regardless of how dark and difficult the present moment may be, keep your eyes focused on Jesus Christ and always remember that in His power, you will overcome your weakness, and victory will eventually be yours. Remember that Christ is sufficient for you. Therefore don't depend on your feelings or emotions, but on the belief that He will hold on to you.

> From the cradle to the grave man's greatest objective is to obtain peace of mind and spiritual security. This is only to be found in Jesus Christ.
>
> MARK TWAIN

Be grateful that your faith doesn't depend on how you feel. It depends on what you believe about Jesus Christ. If you believe that He is what He says He is – the Son of God, that He lives today and that your future is in His omnipotent hands – then you can share in the grace of His victory. You have already overcome the power that seeks to oppress and defeat you. Lift up your heart, remember to whom you belong and live triumphantly in His strength. Thus, by the grace of God, you can become a companion of Christ in God's triumph through the ages.

Lord, thank You that my discipleship doesn't depend on my emotions, but on You.

An Excellent Example

"I have given you an example to follow. Do as I have done to you. I tell you the truth, slaves are not greater than their master. Nor is the messenger more important than the one who sends the message" (John 13:15-16).

It is always to our advantage to follow a good example. Sometimes a sportsman will say, "So-and-so was my role model." Children will pattern their lives on their parents', or a specific teacher's, or even an older sibling's. You might have done it yourself when you were young and inexperienced.

Jesus is the perfect example for all of us to follow on our spiritual journey to eternity. He is an example to us in His relationship and walk with God. He lived a rich, prayer-filled life. He also set us an example in His strict adherence to certain aspects of public worship. He was in the synagogue regularly. To this day we can still visit the remains of one of the synagogues in Capernaum where He worshiped. He was the perfect illustration of compassion and mercy. When He saw the crowd of five thousand people who came to listen to Him, He felt sorry for them because they looked like sheep without a shepherd (see Mark 6:34).

> Example is the school of mankind, and they will learn at no other.
> EDMUND BURKE

He showed us how to die: trusting God and without any fear of what awaited Him in the future. He ensured that His actions corresponded with His words in a meaningful way. No one ever accused Jesus of being a Pharisee. What He taught others, He put into practice in His own life. You can work through the Gospels and look for other opportunities and examples He gave us. Study and reflect on these and then go and live them.

Holy Master, grant me the courage and the strength to follow where You lead me.

Who Is Jesus?

"I tell you this beforehand, so that when it happens you will believe that I AM the Messiah" (John 13:19).

People have different ideas about who Jesus really is. Some think He was just a Jewish prophet. There are those who think He was an exceptionally friendly and generous man. Others see Him as a brilliant worker of miracles. Some regarded Him as a dangerous rebel, while others don't care who He is.

It was important to Jesus that His disciples wouldn't for a moment doubt that He was the God of heaven and earth who came to our world in the form of a human being. He was a unique person: the Only Son of God! He also had to convince them that His suffering was part of the salvation plan. Jesus' betrayal and death would lead to His resurrection and transfiguration. For this reason they needed to remain faithful to Him throughout the entire Way of Suffering that He had to endure.

> Jesus was God spelling Himself out in language humanity could understand.
> S. D. GORDON

It is of the utmost importance to you and to me that we have absolute clarity about who Jesus is to us today. You must be sure in your own heart and mind that He is your Lord, your Savior and your Guide. You must know for certain that He is more than just a teacher of good thoughts, and far more than just an example of a holy life. He is the Son of God who died for you, who was raised from the dead and who lives today. He loves you deeply and will be your true Friend forever. Do you need to adapt your understanding of who Jesus truly is? Do it now, before it is too late.

Lord Jesus, make my faith stronger each day and help me to share my faith with others.

Where Authority Really Lies

"I tell you the truth, slaves are not greater than their master. Nor is the messenger more important than the one who sends the message" (John 13:16).

It is often said of exceptional people that they are very capable and yet not full of themselves. To be full of ourselves prevents us from seeing ourselves and our achievements in a realistic light. It also hampers our ability to see God in His greatness and glory. Just before He washed His disciples' feet, Jesus told them that greatness lay in serving others.

He also explained to them that He, Jesus, was greater than all of them. By carrying out the duties of a slave, He showed them that they were His servants and that they should not pride themselves on the prominence they were given. Neither should they pride themselves on their future role as leaders of the Christian communities they would form. The word *messenger* in our Scripture could just as well be translated as apostle. Jesus was sending the disciples out to be apostles.

> Humility is a grace in the soul. It is indescribable wealth, a name and a gift from God.
> JOHN CLIMACUS

Whichever position you might hold; in the business world, industry, politics, the church or any professional position, never become too full of yourself and start admiring yourself. No matter how important you might be, always see Jesus as your role model and keep yourself from standing in anyone's way, otherwise they might miss seeing Jesus in your actions. Constantly think of ways in which you can be of service in His kingdom and how you can devote yourself to new methods of serving others. Make sure that you are doing all of this in sincere love for Christ.

Lord, make me satisfied to be only Your humble servant.

Ordinary People

I know those I have chosen. But this is to fulfill the Scripture: "He who shares My bread has lifted up his heel against Me" (John 13:18 NIV).

It is often assumed that God chooses only godly and important people for His service. Some of us may think that the nobler a person is, the better God can use him. We read about religious people who lived exemplary lives and we think if we could be like them, Christ could use us to do powerful work for His kingdom. However, the truth is that Jesus often uses unimportant people to be His servants. There are those who are strong, but others are weak. Some are good, but others have dubious characters: Jacob was a deceiver; Moses was a murderer; David was a mixture of good and bad.

> A Christian is a perfectly free lord of all, subject to none. A Christian is a perfectly dutiful servant of all, subject of all, subject to all.
> MARTIN LUTHER

Jesus chose a strange group of individuals to be His apostles. He knew full well what was in store for them. He took the disciples just the way they were, with all their shortcomings and flaws. Jesus built these people into a team that would go out into the world and be His envoys to people from all nationalities, ages and educations.

You don't have to be perfect for God to use you. But if you are willing to submit to His authority and go wherever He might send you, He will cover your weakness and vulnerability with His strength and love. This is what the undeserved goodness in God's very being is all about. Remember that nobody is too weak or too insignificant for Jesus to use.

Holy Master, use me to Your glory, in spite of my weaknesses or strong points.

The Importance of the Messenger

"Anyone who welcomes My messenger is welcoming Me, and anyone who welcomes Me is welcoming the Father who sent Me" (John 13:20).

⌒∽⌒

One of the strange characteristics of the Christian faith is that it is passed on from one person to another, and from generation to generation. In Jesus' time some of the disciples had obvious weaknesses, while others spread the Gospel for many years. In spite of these discrepancies and problems, God continued using vulnerable people.

In today's Scripture, Jesus was on the verge of sending His disciples out into the world. They would witness for Him to the ends of the earth. The people they witnessed to would never meet Jesus – thus the apostles were very important to God in the planning of His kingdom. They went out to tell people about Jesus and His love for sinners. They would tell people about God who loved the world so much that He sacrificed His own Son to save those who believe in Him. God's power and omnipotence were so great that Jesus knew people would survive the weaknesses and imperfections of His messengers.

> You cannot see faith, but you can see the footprints of the faithful. We must leave behind "faithful footprints" for others to follow.
> DENNIS ANDERSON

Receive and tolerate God's messengers as well as the message they bring you. Accept them not for who they are, but for the sake of Him who brings them to you and in whose place they stand. God does not necessarily call the capable, but He equips those He calls.

Lord Jesus, stand by Your messengers so that they will make the truth clear, both by their words and deeds.

Distress at Betrayal

Now Jesus was deeply troubled, and He exclaimed, "I tell you the truth, one of you will betray Me!" (John 13:21).

Only Jesus knows the anguish we experience. In the Upper Room, surrounded by His closest friends and enjoying a solemn meal with them, Jesus was in "great anguish." Instead of passing through life without any storms, Jesus experienced a good many difficult moments. There were people who were His enemies and wanted to set a trap for Him. Furthermore, He was in constant conflict with the spiritual leaders of His time. His disciples and most other people found it difficult to understand what He was doing. And on top of that, one of His closest friends was a traitor.

> Love takes off masks that we fear we cannot live without and now we cannot live within.
> JAMES BALDWIN

Jesus dealt with His problems in the profound faith that He stood in the center of God's will. Therefore, also let your faith thrive in difficult circumstances. Because Jesus knew anguish, He knows how to deal with yours. You can rest assured that you will get through the troubled times and emerge on the other side a spiritually stronger person.

Don't do what Judas did and try to wear a mask that makes you look like a better person than you really are. You might deceive others, but you won't get away with it where Jesus is concerned. Where you think you fall short, be honest with yourself. Ask advice from someone in the Ministry, or a Christian friend. Do everything in your power to right the wrongs. Don't ever, like Judas, be guilty of play-acting under the guise of Christianity.

Lord Jesus, You know my heart. Enable me to be an honest disciple without wearing a mask of betrayal.

The New Commandment

"I am giving you a new commandment: Love each other. Just as I have loved you, you should love each other. Your love for one another will prove to the world that you are My disciples" (John 13:34-35).

In this world with its lack of love, so many things are said about love. It is the main theme of a myriad of songs; in fact, most songs are about love. Jesus gives us this commandment in a very interesting and ironic situation. The disciples had just entered the Upper Room, arguing about who was the most important. Jesus had to show them what true love was. This was also when Judas started putting his horrific act of betrayal into operation; a most unloving act. The only love that was present here would be revealed in Jesus' surrender of Himself, which was an unequalled act of love. Christ could already see the cross. It was the world's greatest act of love. Jesus would soon leave them, making it even more important for them to stand united like never before. Only by love for one another could they put an end to comparisons, jealousy, power struggles and back-stabbing.

> What's earth with all its art, verse, music, worth compared with love, found, gained and kept?
> Robert Browning

This has always been the road Christ commanded us to follow as Christian brothers and sisters – that we love one another. In the eyes of the world, our inability to do just that is the worst betrayal of Jesus Christ. Take a look at your own Christian community or church group and ask yourself how much mutual love is shared among the members. Then ask yourself how much you contribute towards spreading Jesus' love among your fellow believers. Could a revival of Christian love begin with you?

God of love and grace, help me to love others rather than wanting others to love me.

June

His Kingdom Is Forever

"Don't cling to Me," Jesus said, "for I haven't
yet ascended to the Father. But go find My brothers
and tell them that I am ascending to My Father
and your Father, My God and your God."
~ John 20:17

There is no human power that can
replace the power of the Spirit.
~ LEWI PETHRUS

Blessed God and Father of our Lord Jesus Christ,
and through Him our Father:
You have existed from the beginning and
sent Your Spirit to Your children.
Let Your Spirit work powerfully in us
so that He will lead our thoughts in truth;
Keep our eyes from seeing things that displease You,
and make our hands zealous in Your service,
and our feet willing to take Your gospel to all of humanity.
Let Your Spirit take control of our lives so
that we will be victorious in Your power:
that we will be wise in Your wisdom
and compassionate in Your love.
O Spirit of God, teach us the truth of the Word
and keep us on the right road. Make us receptive to
new truths and bold to take action for Your kingdom.
Keep us faithful in the face of resistance and persecution
and let Your Spirit guide us to do what is right in
Your eyes. Make us faithful witnesses of Your truth
and willing messengers of the Good News.
We surrender ourselves fully to You so that
You may equip us for the task; so that we will
work unconditionally for Your kingdom to come.
Fill us, O Spirit of God, so that Your
blessing will flow through us
to those who are in search of You.
We pray this in the name of Jesus, our Savior and Redeemer.

Amen.

Trust

"Go back to John and tell him what you have heard and seen – the blind see, the lame walk, the lepers are cured, the deaf hear, the dead are raised to life, and the Good News is being preached to the poor. And tell him: "God blesses those who do not turn away because of Me" (Matt. 11:4-6).

✦◯◯✦

Throughout Matthew 11, we hear the emphasis in Jesus' voice change. Jesus emphasizes six different aspects here.

John's career ended in disaster. He never watered down the truth and he couldn't stand evil. Because he offended Herod Antipas, he was thrown in jail. It must have been terrible for John who loved the freedom of wide open spaces. At first he was sure that Jesus was the Messiah who had been sent. But a dying man cannot endure any uncertainty and so John sent his disciples to ask Jesus, "Are you the Messiah we've been expecting, or should we keep looking for someone else?" (Matt. 11:3). In Jesus' answer we hear the emphasis on absolute trust and confidence: "Go back to John and tell him what you have heard and seen." It was the litmus test: the test of actions and results. Jesus is the only person who could be tested by His deeds and not just His words.

> He is the greatest influence in the world today. There is ... a fifth gospel being written – the work of Jesus Christ in the hearts and lives of men and nations.
>
> W. H. Griffith Thomas

The miracles that Jesus mentions to John are miracles He performs to this day: He opens the eyes of those who are blind; He guides those who lost their way back onto the right path; those who were deaf to the voice of their conscience start listening again; those who were dead in their sin, are raised to a new life in Christ. Here Jesus places the accent on trust in His deeds.

Jesus, help me to transform my words into deeds through my actions of love.

Paying Homage

"What kind of man did you go into the wilderness to see? ... I tell you the truth, of all who have ever lived, none is greater than John the Baptist" (Matt. 11:7, 11).

There are few people that Jesus paid greater tribute to than John the Baptist. Here Jesus starts off by asking what they expected to see in the wilderness. Surely not a weak person; someone blown this way and that by the wind. John was not spineless like a reed "moved by every breath of wind." And neither was he dressed up in extravagant clothes. John was a *heraut* (messenger) of God and not one of Herod's underlings. Did they expect to see a prophet of God? A prophet was trusted by God and announced the truth of God. Jesus declared that John was nothing less than a *heraut* who had been made holy, and who had to predict the coming of the Messiah.

> By the cross we know the gravity of sin and the greatness of God's love towards us.
> JOHN CHRYSOSTOM

This is how great the emphasis was on the homage paid to John the Baptist. Yet, in spite of this, the following sentence reads: "Yet even the least person in the Kingdom of Heaven is greater than he is!" (Matt. 11:11). What did John fall short of? What does the Christian have that John didn't? The answer is simple and fundamental: John never saw the cross! For this reason he was not able to know the love of God in all its dimensions. Those who saw the cross, saw the heart of God in a way that the people who lived before the cross could never experience. John was merely one of God's road indicators. God needed John: God needs people who direct others to the right road.

Crucified Lord Jesus, thank You that I can be a child of the cross, and for this reason, know God's love.

Violence and the Kingdom

"From the time John the Baptist began preaching until now, the Kingdom of Heaven has been forcefully advancing, and violent people are attacking it" (Matt. 11:12).

Ever since the time of John the Baptist, the kingdom of God has suffered violence; it becomes a reality through violence, persecution and suffering. Therefore, only those who approach the Kingdom in earnest and with dedication will inherit it. This Scripture could also have been a warning of the persecution and violence still to come, and a challenge to prove that dedication to the Kingdom is mightier than the violence against it.

It does seem quite strange that we read in verse thirteen that "all the prophets and the law prophesied up until John," but this was the law declaring that the voice of prophesy would never be silenced. Thus it is written in Deuteronomy 18:15: "The Lord your God will raise up for you a prophet like me from among your fellow Israelites. You must listen to him." And again in verse 18: "I will raise up a prophet like you from among their fellow Israelites." The reason why the orthodox Jews hated Jesus was because, according to them, Jesus broke the law; and yet both the law and the prophets referred to Jesus.

> It is always right that a man should be able to render a reason for the faith that is within him.
> SYDNEY SMITH

God can send His messenger and people can still refuse to acknowledge Him. God can send His truths and people can refuse to take notice of them. God's revelation is powerless without humankind's response. This is why Jesus ends this conversation with the words: "Anyone who is willing to hear should listen and understand!"

Holy Spirit of God, make me a trustworthy witness of the kingdom of God.

A Somber Reprimand

"To what can I compare this generation? It is like children playing a game in the public square. They complain to their friends, 'We played wedding songs, and you didn't dance, so we played funeral songs, and you didn't mourn'" (Matt. 11:16-17).

Jesus was deeply saddened by the perversity of human nature. In His view people acted like children in a public square, refusing and finding fault with everything they were offered. John came and lived in the wilderness, cut off from all human contact, but that was not good enough for the people. Jesus came, mingled with the people, shared their joy and sorrow, but still this was not good enough.

The simple truth is that when people don't want to listen to the truth, it is easy to find an excuse not to. Then Jesus concludes: "But wisdom is shown to be right by its results" (Matt. 11:19). The final judgment does not lie with the fickle critics, but in the deeds done. The Jews might have criticized John for his isolated life, but John moved people's hearts to God. The Jews might have criticized Jesus for keeping company with dubious characters, but those people were busy finding a new life: new kindness, new strength and new access to God the Father.

> If you have not the Spirit of God, Christian worker, remember that you stand in somebody else's way; you are a fruitless tree standing where a fruitful tree might grow.
> CHARLES H. SPURGEON

It would be good if we stop criticizing people and churches, and measuring them by the yardstick of our own prejudices and perversities. We should start thanking people from any church or community for bringing others closer to God, even if their methods are methods that don't really suit us.

Holy Spirit of God, remove all negative criticism from my life and make me a positive witness for God.

Judgment from a Broken Heart

Then Jesus began to denounce the towns where He had done so many of His miracles, because they hadn't repented of their sins and turned to God (Matt. 11:20).

We must pay close attention to pick up the emphasis in Jesus' voice when He speaks these words. The accent is one of sadness and not of hatred and revenge. The emphasis is on someone who offered people the most precious thing in the world and had to look on as they completely disregarded it. The words emphasize the heartache of someone watching a tragedy unfold, but who cannot stop people from charging towards their own destruction. It is holy anger caused by a broken heart. Why was the sin of Korazin, Bethsaida and Capernaum worse than that of Sodom and Gomorrah, Tyre and Sidon? This was the sin of people who had forgotten the responsibility of privileges. Korazin, Bethsaida and Capernaum had the opportunity that the other cities never had: they actually saw and heard Jesus. We must remember that the greater our spiritual privileges, the harsher our judgment if we neglect to meet the responsibilities that come with those privileges.

> To take up the cross of Christ is no great action done once for all; it consists in the continual practice of small duties which are distasteful to us.
>
> JOHN H. NEWMAN

This is the sin of indifference. These cities did not attack Jesus; they simply ignored Him. Omission destroys just as easily as deliberate murder. It is also the sin of doing nothing. There are deeds of sin, but also the sin of an absence of deeds; doing nothing. The latter was the sin of Korazin, Bethsaida and Capernaum. Our defense must never be: But I didn't do anything! This breaks Christ's heart.

Lord Jesus, give me the will to transform my faith into deeds.

Authority

At that time Jesus prayed this prayer: "O Father, Lord of heaven and earth, thank You for hiding these things [the truth] from those who think themselves wise and clever, and for revealing them to the childlike. Yes, Father, it pleased You to do it this way" (Matt. 11:25-26).

Here Jesus is speaking from personal experience: the Rabbis and wise men rejected Him, while the "childlike" accepted Him. Jesus in no way scorns intellectual ability, but He despises intellectual pride. The heart, not the brain, is the home of the gospel. You can be as wise as Solomon and yet have the simplicity, faith and innocence of a child's heart.

> The first and most important thing we know about God is that we know nothing about Him except what He Himself makes known.
>
> EMIL BRUNNER

This Scripture reading concludes with Jesus laying claim to something greater than He ever did, and which is the essence of the Christian faith. This is the fact that only Jesus can reveal the Father to the human being: "No one truly knows the Son except the Father, and no one truly knows the Father except the Son and those to whom the Son chooses to reveal Him" (Matt. 11:27). Others may be children of God, but He is the Son. John puts it like this: "If you had really known Me, you would know who My Father is. From now on, you do know Him and have seen Him!" (John 14:7).

What Jesus is in fact saying is: If you want to see what God is like; if you want to understand the way God thinks, the heart and nature of God – look at Me! It is the Christian's conviction that we see what God is truly like only in Jesus Christ, and Jesus can reveal this to anyone who is humble and trusting enough to receive it.

Thank You, Lord Jesus, for revealing the God of love to me.

Compassion

"Come to Me, all of you who are weary and carry heavy burdens, and I will give you rest. Take My yoke upon you. Let Me teach you, because I am humble and gentle at heart, and you will find rest for your souls" (Matt. 11:28-29).

Christ speaks to people who are desperate in their search for God, trying hard to live a good life. Jesus' invitation is meant for those who have become tired in their search for God and have been driven to despair. He invites those who have to shoulder heavy burdens in their search for the truth to come to Him. The Greeks believed it was hard to find God and when you did, it was difficult to tell anyone about Him. Zophar asks Job, "Can you solve the mysteries of God? Can you discover everything about the Almighty?" (Job 11:7).

Give me a stout heart to bear my own burdens. Give me a willing heart to bear the burdens of others. Give me a believing heart to cast all burdens upon Thee, O Lord.

JOHN BAILLIE

The only way to get to know God is to focus on Jesus. The religion of the orthodox Jews was a heavy burden to them (see Matt. 23:4). It was a matter of endless rules and regulations, which weighed heavily on them in all the spheres of life. The life Jesus gives us is not a burden that weighs us down, but a life that is specially made to suit each of us.

Christ's yoke is put on our shoulders with love, and love makes even the heaviest load light. When we think of the love of God, when we know that our "burden" is to love God, to love our fellow humans, then the burden becomes a song. The burden given with love is carried with love and therefore it is always light.

Loving Father God, thank You that Your burden never becomes too heavy for Your children.

How Jesus Taught

He taught them by telling many stories in the form of parables (Mark 4:2).

In this Scripture reading we see Jesus deviating in a refreshing way from orthodox methods: He didn't teach in the Synagogue anymore, but at the Sea of Galilee. First He followed the orthodox approach; now He used a new approach. We must take note that Jesus was always prepared to employ new methods. He was ready and willing to remove religious preaching and teaching from their orthodox picture in the Synagogue, and teach and preach to the crowds of ordinary people outdoors, in the open air.

There must have been many of the orthodox Jews who were shocked at Jesus' new style of preaching and regarded it as seeking sensation. Jesus, however, was sensible enough to know when it was time for new methods and adventurous enough to put them into practice. It would be good if the church were just as sensible and adventurous.

> I sometimes wonder what hours of prayer and thought lie behind the apparently simple and spontaneous parables of the gospel.
> J. B. Phillips

This new deviation required a new method. The new method that Jesus chose was to use parables when speaking to people. A parable is an earthly story with a heavenly meaning. Something on earth is compared to something in heaven so that the heavenly truth can be understood better in the light of the earthly illustration. Why did Jesus use this method? And why did He use it so often that it became synonymous with Him, so that He became known forever as the Master of the parable? We'll wait till tomorrow for the answer.

Lord Jesus, thank You that Your parables reveal many profound truths to me.

Why Jesus Used Parables

He taught them by telling many stories in the form of parables
(Mark 4:2).

Jesus chose the method of parables simply to get people to listen. He did not preach to a congregation in the Synagogue that was more or less obliged to stay put till the end of the service. He was speaking to people in the open air who were free to leave whenever they wanted to. So the first principle was to capture the crowds' interest. If this didn't happen, they would simply leave. The best way to keep the people interested was to tell stories, and Jesus knew that.

Furthermore, when Jesus started using the method of parables, he was using a method that was well known to the Jewish audiences and teachers. There are parables in the Old Testament, the most important being that of David and Bathsheba in 2 Samuel 11:1-7.

When Jesus used the method of parables He was making abstract ideas concrete. It is better to see a picture than to attempt to visualize it.

> The teaching of Christ is more excellent than all the advice of the saints, and he who has His Spirit will find in it a hidden manna.
> THOMAS À KEMPIS

Jesus was a clever Teacher who transformed abstract ideas into stories.

Lastly, the great advantage of the parable is that it forces people to think for themselves and to discover the truth in this way. The truth always has a much greater impact when you discover it for yourself. Jesus didn't want to do their thinking for them, but He wanted to guide them into using their own thoughts. In this way, they could discover the truth for themselves.

Thank You, Lord Jesus, for the meaningful parables You gave us.

Here and Now to There and Then

"Listen! A farmer went out to plant some seed. As he scattered it across his field, some of the seed fell on a footpath, and the birds came and ate it" (Mark 4:3-4).

Jesus was sitting in a boat close to the shore where a crowd had gathered. Then He drew their attention to a farmer who was busy sowing on the other side of the lake, and immediately adapted His parable to this everyday occurrence: "A farmer went out to plant some seed." This is the essence of the parable method: Jesus started with the here and now to get to the there and then. He used something happening on earth to guide the thoughts of people heavenwards. He started with visible things that led to the invisible. He started with the simple things that even a child could understand.

> I am nothing, I have nothing. I desire nothing but the love of Jesus in Jerusalem.
> WALTER HILTON

With this Jesus showed that He believed in a connection between heaven and earth. He believed that people could see God in everyday life. Jesus didn't see this earth as a sad and lost place; He believed if you looked around you, you would see God.

The essence of parables is that they were spontaneous and unprepared. They were created in the heat of the moment. Parables are not stories that came into being and were pondered in a study; they were born of the requirements of the moment. This brings us to the point that we must always remember in our efforts to interpret His parables. In the first instance they should be heard and not read. It is wrong to try and find a deeper meaning in every detail of a parable. We should ask: What main thought flashes through our minds when we hear this story the first time?

I kneel before Your heavenly wisdom in worship, Lord Jesus.

The Secret of the Kingdom

"You are permitted to understand the secret of the kingdom of God. But I use parables for everything I say to outsiders" (Mark 4:11).

This has always been the most difficult part of Scripture to understand. It doesn't mean something that is too complicated and mysterious in our sense of the word. It means something that is totally impossible to understand for someone who is not aware of its existence. In the pagan world they spoke about the mystical religions. This referred to communication with, and being united to some or other god by which the fears and terrors of life and death would be taken away.

Our Scripture verse refers to Isaiah 6:9-10 where God says that the people had become so slow-witted that they didn't understand His words anymore. This is why Jesus spoke in parables – He meant them to flash in people's minds and expose the truth. He claimed that so many people were blinded by prejudice, and doped by wishful thinking that they had become too lazy to think for themselves.

> The Bible is the Word of God in such a way that when the Bible speaks, God speaks.
>
> B. B. WARFIELD

What Jesus says here, He doesn't say in anger or irritation. He says it with the sincere desire of frustrated love, a completely different type of sorrow. It doesn't tell us about God who deliberately blinds people and hides His truth, but about people who find it so difficult to understand that even God thought it would be pointless to try to penetrate the curtain of their ignorance. May God keep us from hearing His Word in this way!

Holy God, You are the truth. Let Your truths become clear to me through Your Spirit.

The Harvest Is Secure!

"If you can't understand the meaning of this parable, how will you understand all the other parables?" (Mark 4:13).

E very detail of Jesus' parable is clear to His listeners because the story is taken from everyday life.

First there is the hard ground at the side of the road. The seed could fall on this type of ground in two ways. The fields of Palestine were in the form of long, narrow strips and these strips were separated by narrow paths. These paths were there to walk on with the result that they became as hard as a sidewalk because they were used so often. As the farmer scattered the seed, some of it fell on this hard ground where it didn't stand a chance of growing. But there was also another way to sow seed in Palestine. Sometimes a bag of seed was put on a donkey's back. There was an opening in the corner of the bag. The animal was then led up and down while the seed flowed from the bag. Inevitably, as some of the seed fell onto the hard footpath, the birds swooped down and ate it.

> Untilled soil, however fertile it may be, will bear thistles and thorns; but so it is with man's mind.
>
> TERESA OF AVILA

The Christian message can find no access to some people's hearts. The reason why it cannot enter into the listener's heart is because of the person's lack of interest; and that lack of interest is because of the inability to realize the importance of the Christian decision. Christianity will have no impact on people who are unconcerned about it. They think it is irrelevant and they can do without it. Many people discover their mistake too late!

Holy Master and Savior, grant that the seed that falls in my life will sprout and bear fruit.

Rocky Soil

"The seed on the rocky soil represents those who hear the message and immediately receive it with joy. But since they don't have deep roots, they don't last long" (Mark 4:16-17).

Then there was also rocky soil. It was a narrow footpath of hard ground, not strewn with loose stones, but a path of limestone. Many parts of Galilee were like this. In some parts of the country, limestone rocks showed above the ground. The seed that fell there did sprout, but because the soil was shallow and not fertile and it didn't hold much dampness, the heat of the sun soon made the young plants die. It is always easier to start with something than complete it.

An evangelist said on occasion, "We have learnt that it takes about 5% effort to win someone over to Christ, but to keep them in Christ and see them grow to maturity, takes 95%." Many people start off on the Christian road and some of them fall by the wayside. Two things cause this spiritual decline. One is our un-

> Some people's religion reminds me of a rocking horse, which has motion with no progress.
> ROWLAND HILL

willingness to reflect on the matter; to think it through, and our inability to realize what it costs and means before we start. The second is that thousands of people are drawn to Christianity, but they don't allow it to show above the surface of their lives. We are only safe if we give ourselves to Christ unconditionally and totally! But that is enough for today; tomorrow we will resume our discussion.

O Holy Spirit, I pray that the gospel won't fall on rocky soil in my life.

Among the Thorns

"The seed that fell among the thorns represents others who hear God's Word, but all too quickly the message is crowded out by the worries of this life, the lure of wealth, and the desire for other things, so no fruit is produced" (Mark 4:18-19).

The third kind of soil was overgrown with thorns. This Palestinian farmer was lazy. He cut down the thorn bushes so that the land looked clean and the thorns seemed to be destroyed, but the roots were still there. As time passed, the thorn bushes grew back to their former abundance. The weeds grew so quickly and zealously that they choked the life out of the seed. It is easy to cram life with so many interests that there is no time for Christ. The more complicated our life becomes, the more necessary it is to get our priorities right.

Finally, there is the seed that is sown in "good soil" so that it can thrive. If we really want to learn from this parable, there are a few things we must do. We must hear, and we can't hear unless we listen. We are often so busy talking and arguing that we forget to listen. It is necessary that we receive the message. It is not enough to only hear the message; it must be absorbed by our thoughts. Then we must put it into action. The harvest was thirty, sixty, even hundredfold. It was asking a lot, but the volcanic soil in Galilee was very fertile. Christian faith must always culminate in action. The Christian is challenged, not to speculate, but to act. Sow the seed and leave the rest to God. Then you are sure of the harvest.

> We must always change, renew, rejuvenate ourselves; otherwise we harden.
> JOHANN WOLFGANG VON GOETHE

Grant, Holy Spirit of God, that I will sow my deeds of faith only in fertile soil.

The Light Must Be Seen

Jesus asked them, "Would anyone light a lamp and then put it under a basket or under a bed? Of course not! A lamp is placed on a stand, where its light will shine" (Mark 4:21).

J esus had unique control of the language; He could say the most pointed things that stuck in the minds of His listeners. One of the memorable things Jesus said was that one would surely not light a lamp and then hide it; it is after all meant to give light. Here Jesus wanted to teach us two things ...

Firstly, the truth is meant to be seen, not hidden. There are times when the truth is the shortest way to persecution and trouble. However, the true Christian stands by the truth in the face of all circumstances and people. Martin Luther did it by nailing 95 statements to the church door in Wittenberg.

Secondly, our Christianity must be seen. In the early church it often meant death. There they worshiped the emperor as a "god." Once the citizens had acknowledged the emperor as god, they could worship the god of

> Ask yourself, if building God's church depended on me, would it ever get done?
> Anonymous

their choice. They were given a certificate to do this. All that Christians had to do in those times was to perform the formal act and then get their certificates; then they were safe. The early Christians could hide the fact of their Christianity, but they felt strongly about it that they had to testify to their Christianity in the presence of all people. We have to thank people like these for our Christianity today. It is often easier to keep quiet about our membership of the church of Christ, but our Christianity must always be like a lamp on a stand.

Holy Master, make me willing to be a faithful witness of Your grace and love.

The Truth Cannot Be Hidden

"For everything that is hidden will eventually be brought into the open, and every secret will be brought to light. Anyone with ears to hear should listen and understand" (Mark 4:22-23).

It was Jesus' conviction that the truth could not be suppressed or hidden. This is applicable to the truth itself. There is something about the truth that is indestructible. People may refuse to face up to the truth; they can disguise the truth; they may even try to ignore the truth or refuse to accept it, but the truth is big and will triumph in the end. We must watch out that we don't fight the truth.

It is also applicable to our own lives and behavior. Usually when someone does something wrong, their first instinct is to run away. This is what Adam and Eve did when they disobeyed God (Gen. 3:8). But the truth will out! It has an uncanny way of doing that. In the last instance you cannot hide the truth from yourself. A person with a secret is always an unhappy person. The web spun by deception is never a permanent hiding place. No person can have any secrets from God. Ultimately it is true that there is no secret that won't be revealed in God's presence. If we remember this we will feel the need and the urge for God to take a look at our deeds without us feeling any shame.

> Truth is not always popular, but it is always right.
> ANONYMOUS

Holy Spirit of God, may Your truth set me free.

Balance in Life

"Pay close attention to what you hear. The closer you listen, the more understanding you will be given – and you will receive even more" (Mark 4:24).

There is always balance in life: What we receive unfailingly depends on what we give. It is true of a study of the Bible. We often feel that there are certain parts of the Bible we cannot relate to. If, however, we study these parts, they are often the sections that yield the richest harvest. A superficial study of any topic doesn't really interest us, while intensive study always excites and fascinates.

It is especially true of worship. The more we bring to the house of the Lord in worship, the more we get out of it. There are wrong ways in which we go to the house of the Lord. We might go only to receive. It is then that we criticize the organist, the choir and the preacher. We see the whole service as a performance that is presented to entertain us. No,

> The perfect church service would be one we were almost unaware of: our attention would have been on God.
> C. S. Lewis

we must be willing to give. We must remember that worship is a corporative act. It is also wrong to go to church without any expectations at all. It might just be a custom in our lives. Then we go without expecting anything; the result of habit or routine. We should remember that we go to church to meet with God and when that happens, anything can happen.

We may also go without preparing our thoughts or our hearts. Often we are in such a rush simply to get there in time. We need to meet God in prayer before going to church and asking for His blessing on our gathering.

Thank You, Lord Jesus, for moments of worship where I am blessed by my meeting with God.

The Law of Increase

"To those who listen to My teaching, more understanding will be given. But for those who are not listening, even what little understanding they have will be taken away from them" (Mark 4:25).

This might sound like a harsh law at first, but it is proved to be fundamentally true in life. It is true of knowledge: The more you know, the more capable you are of knowing more. You cannot really get the best out of music before you have learnt something about the structure of a symphony. If you don't make a point of increasing your knowledge, the little you have, will also be taken from you.

This is also true of effort. The more physical strength you have, the more you are able to acquire. The opposite is also true: If you don't increase your physical strength and neglect your body, you will lose also the strength you have. Likewise, the more you develop the skills of the eye, hand and mind, the more these skills will develop. If you are happy to simply go with the flow, never try something new, learn no new techniques, you will get stuck just there where you are. If you neglect your God-given skills, you are sure to lose them.

> God's gifts now take the place of God, and the whole course of nature is upset by the monstrous substitution.
> MEISTER ECKHART

The same goes for your ability to take responsibility. The more responsibility you assume, the more you will be able to take on. But if you shirk your responsibilities, you will become spineless in the end and have no ability to make decisions. It is one of the basic laws of life and one that we forget, and this leads to our downfall.

Father God, You gave me certain virtues. Give me the grace to develop them.

Jesus Heals a Blind Man

When they arrived at Bethsaida, some people brought a blind man to Jesus, and they begged Him to touch the man and heal him (Mark 8:22).

Blindness has always been one of the great curses in the East. It is caused partly by the sharp sunlight and made worse by people's ignorance of hygiene. This interesting story is told only by Mark and it mentions a few unusual things.

Once again we notice how uniquely considerate Jesus was. "Jesus took the blind man by the hand and led him out of the village" (Mark 8:23). This man was probably born blind and Jesus knew that if his vision was suddenly restored, he would have been overwhelmed by what he saw. Jesus knew the heart and thoughts of his patients and this is why He was so great and remarkable.

> If I have ever made any valuable discoveries, it has been owing more to patient attention, than to any other talent.
> ISAAC NEWTON

In addition, Jesus used methods that this man would understand. The ancient world strongly believed in the healing power of saliva. Even today, a hurt finger automatically goes into the mouth to get spit on it. Normally Jesus' miracles took place instantly, but He knew that this man's sight had to be restored gradually. There is something symbolic in this: no one suddenly sees God's truth all at once. Contrary to what we believe, conversion is not a final point, but in fact a starting point. Even if we live a million years, we cannot discover the mysteries of God completely. With all God's undeserved goodness and glory before us, the human being can, however, gradually grow towards spiritual maturity.

Divine Father God, I beg You to gradually introduce Your mysteries to me day by day.

Jesus Is the Messiah

Then He asked them, "But who do you say I am?" Peter replied, "You are the Messiah" (Mark 8:29).

⌒ꚙ⌒

Philippi was outside the borders of Galilee. It was not in Herod's region, but in Phillip's. It was a pagan place of worship where the Roman emperor was god, and it was there that Peter recognized the homeless Galilean carpenter as the Son of God. There of all places and contrary to all reason, history and religion, Peter discovered that the wandering Teacher of Nazareth, who was headed for the cross, was the Son of God. This proves the sheer strength of Jesus Christ's personality.

This Scripture reading was written right in the middle of Mark's Gospel. In a certain sense this incident was a crisis in Jesus' life.

> Jesus Christ is not revelation if He is recognized by nobody as the Christ, any more than He is Redeemer if there is nobody whom He redeems.
>
> EMIL BRUNNER

Whatever His disciples might have thought, He knew He was headed for the cross. Things couldn't go on like this much longer. The opposition was ready to strike. Jesus' problem was that He wasn't sure if He had made an impact or not. Had He achieved anything? Had anyone discovered who He really was? If He had lived, worked and taught among people and no one saw God in Him, everything had been in vain.

He must have written His message on the heart of at least one person. That is why Jesus asked this question to test His disciples: "Who do you say I am?" Suddenly Peter realized what he had always known: that Jesus was the Messiah, the Anointed one, the Son of God. That answer told Jesus that He had not failed.

Thank You, Master, that we know You are the Messiah sent by God.

The Path of the Disciples

Then, calling the crowd to join His disciples, He said, "If any of you wants to be My follower, you must turn from your selfish ways, take up your cross, and follow Me" (Mark 8:34).

Here we get to the heart and essence of the Christian religion. First there is Jesus' amazing honesty. No one can say that they followed Jesus because of false promises He made. Jesus never tried to bribe people by offering them an easy path. He didn't promise people peace, but glory. Telling someone to take up a cross is the same as telling them to die like a criminal.

Secondly, we find that Jesus never demanded people to do what He wouldn't do Himself. This is the true character of a great leader of people. Thirdly, Jesus said, "If any of you wants to be My follower ... you must turn from your selfish ways, take up your cross, and follow Me." Simply and literally this means saying no to yourself and yes to Christ. You must say no to your own natural love of comfort. You must say no to every path of self-love and selfish ambition. You must say no to all the instincts and desires that lure you to touch and taste forbidden things. You must answer Jesus' voice and commands with an unmistakable yes. You must be able to say like Paul, "It is no longer I who live, but Christ lives in me" (Gal. 2:20). You don't live to follow your own will anymore, but to follow and obey Jesus' will. One finds perfect freedom in this service.

> The cross is laid on every Christian. It begins with the call to abandon the attachments of this world. It is that dying of the old man which is the result of his encounter with Christ.
>
> DIETRICH BONHOEFFER

Lord Jesus, once You have set me free from myself, I know I will be truly free.

Find Life by Losing It

"If you try to hang on to your life, you will lose it. But if you give up your life for My sake and for the sake of the Good News, you will save it" (Mark 8:35).

It is quite possible to make a success of your life and lose it in a certain sense. The true meaning of what Jesus says in this Scripture verse is: Where do you place your values in life? You might switch honesty with profit. You might crave material things to the extent that it doesn't matter how you get hold of them. The world is full of temptations to make a dishonest profit. The question is: What does your balance sheet look like to God? God is the auditor and all people must answer to Him one day.

You might sacrifice principles for popularity. Easy, tolerant people save themselves a lot of problems. The question is not, "What do people think of my actions?" but, "What does God know about them?" It is not the judgment of public opinion that determines your final destination, but God's judgment.

> The relationship between God and man is more private and intimate than any possible relation between two fellow creatures.
> C. S. Lewis

You might swop valuable things for cheap stuff. Cheap success is always easier to achieve. You might spend your life busying yourself with trivial things and letting important things pass you by. Cheap things never last long.

We can summarize by saying that a person can exchange eternity for the moment. It is always safe to see everything in the light of eternity. There are many things that are pleasant for the moment, but destructive in the long run. The best test is to see things the way God sees them: then you will never waste your life on things that cost you your soul.

Holy Spirit, teach me to see things like God Almighty sees them.

When the King Comes into His Own

"If anyone is ashamed of Me and My message in these adulterous and sinful days, the Son of Man will be ashamed of that person when He returns in the glory of His Father with the holy angels" (Mark 8:38).

One fact about Jesus stands out clearly in this part: His unequalled trust. He has just spoken about His death on the cross, but nonetheless He is convinced of triumph in the end. One thing that is as clear as daylight is that when the King comes into His kingdom, He will be true to those who were true to Him. Christianity is under pressure, and if anyone is ashamed to be known as a Christian under these circumstances, they cannot expect a place of honor in the kingdom of God.

In Jesus' time Christianity had practically no future and some people did not expect it to survive long. In fact these pessimists had every reason to think like this. But what happened? Within thirty years Christianity spread over virtually all of Asia Minor. Antioch became the great Christian gathering place. It penetrated Egypt. Rome became the basis of Christianity. Greece was also evangelized. Christianity was an unstoppable tide all over the world. So what Jesus had said was perfectly correct.

> Christianity has died many times and risen again; for it had a God who knew the way out of the grave.
>
> G. K. CHESTERTON

Something remarkable about Jesus was that He never knew despair. In the face of deadness in the thoughts of people, in the face of opposition, crucifixion and death, Jesus never doubted God's final victory. He was always sure that the things that looked impossible to human beings were possible for God.

Grant, Merciful Master, that I will be true to You, even in the darkest circumstances.

The Glory of the Mountaintop

Six days later Jesus took Peter, James, and John, and led them up a high mountain to be alone (Mark 9:2).

Here we are at one of the mystical moments in Christ's life. It is said that the transfiguration of Jesus took place on Mount Tabor. But Tabor is in the South of Galilee and Philippi far on the northern side. Tabor is only 1 000 feet high and in Jesus' time it had a fort on top. It is more likely that it happened on Mount Hermon, which is 9 200 feet high and much closer to Caesarea Philippi.

We will never be able to say for sure what really happened. We can only bow in worship while we try to understand. Mark says that Jesus' clothes became "dazzling white." At the end a cloud covered them. A cloud always featured when God spoke in the Old Testament: God spoke to Moses in a cloud; a cloud settled on the Tabernacle when God was inside; a cloud filled the Temple of Solomon when God occupied it.

> To be in Christ is redemption, but for Christ to be in you is sanctification. To be in Christ is to be fit for heaven, but for Christ to be in you is to be fit for earth.
>
> ANONYMOUS

Jesus' transfiguration was something very precious to Him. He now knew He had God's approval to continue on the road He had taken. But it was also a very special experience for the disciples. They were devastated by Jesus' announcement that He was going to Jerusalem to die. They were shocked and didn't understand. Jesus' transfiguration gave them something to hold on to. They had the story of His transfiguration in their hearts and could tell it to everybody.

Lord Jesus, grant that I will glorify You in my heart and life, like the Father glorified You.

Come Down from the Mountain!

When they returned to the other disciples, they saw a large crowd surrounding them, and some teachers of religious law were arguing with them (Mark 9:14).

This is exactly what Peter wished to prevent. He wanted to stay on the mountain in the presence of Christ's glory. Why leave there? But in our religion indefinite seclusion is not permitted. Seclusion is necessary for us humans to make contact with God, but it must not isolate us from others. Being in seclusion with God should just enable us to handle the demands of everyday life better.

The church, the body of Christ, was a supernatural institution to many people; it was called His unblemished bride, the oracle of God Himself, and was given many other romanticized titles. The transfiguration was over and kept secret, and Jesus appeared on the scene again. The crowds were arguing so much that they didn't see Him come down from the mountain. Jesus was ready to accept the cross and at the same time He was willing to handle any insignificant problem. This shows that we can accept any human crisis in His name. This was the wonder of Jesus. He could endure the cross and at the same time deal with the everyday things in life. He followed God on the daily paths of life.

> The church is her true self only when she exists for humanity.
> DIETRICH BONHOEFFER

Christ came to the world to save the world and yet He could give His undivided attention to a single person. It is easier to proclaim the gospel than to meet the need of one person; easier to be filled with sentimental love for the human race than to help an individual in trouble. Jesus possessed the Godly gift of giving Himself completely to anyone who needed His help.

Holy Master, thank You that You are always there for me!

The Call to Faith

Jesus said to them, "You faithless people! How long must I be with you?" (Mark 9:19).

This cry is wrung from Jesus' heart. He has just come back from the mountaintop where His task was outlined for Him. He has decided to give His life for the salvation of humankind. Now He finds His own people afraid and in low spirits. At that moment Jesus must have despaired of the possibility of saving humankind. How does He deal with this moment of despair? He says, "Bring the boy to Me" (v. 19). This is how He handles the problem He is confronted with at that moment. When we think of the condition of the world, we have every reason to despair. Then we should consider what to do in the particular place on earth where God has put us.

> The secret behind getting more faith, is to get to know God more.
> LESTER SUMRALL

The surest way to overcome despair is to take immediate action regarding the things we are experiencing. Jesus asks the boy's father the question which is the condition for all miracles: "What do you mean, 'If I can?' ... Anything is possible if a person believes." It is as if Jesus wants to tell the man the healing of his child lies with him. The father instantly replies, "I do believe, but help me overcome my unbelief!" Please take away all my doubts and fill me with true faith.

It sometimes happens that people are disappointed by some church or another or a certain preacher. The believer forges ahead, past the church and the preacher and reaches Christ Himself. The church does sometimes disappoint us, and His servants on earth might do so too. But if we wrestle until we are face to face with Jesus, we are never disappointed.

I believe, Lord Jesus. Take all my doubts away, please.

Jesus Announces His Death

"The Son of Man is going to be betrayed into the hands of His enemies. He will be killed, but three days later He will rise from the dead" (Mark 9:31).

This part of Scripture is a milepost in Jesus' history: He was now going to Jerusalem where the cross awaited Him. Jesus carried on teaching His disciples, because a teacher must leave students behind that will continue to proclaim His message. But there was a traitor among Jesus' disciples and Jesus knew this. He knew how Judas' mind worked – possibly better than Judas himself. Jesus was not only stating a fact here, but also gave the person planning to betray Him, a warning and a last chance.

Yet, the disciples still didn't understand Him when He told them He would rise from the dead. At that moment they were aware of the atmosphere of tragedy, but they didn't understand the wonder of His resurrection. It was a miracle that was just too big for them to grasp; they would only understand it when it had become an accomplished fact.

> As well could you expect a plant to grow without air and water as to expect your heart to grow without prayer and faith.
> CHARLES H. SPURGEON

Because they didn't understand, they were afraid to ask any more questions and to be given more bad news. We might be surprised that the disciples didn't grasp what they were so clearly being told. The human mind has the special ability to reject what it doesn't want to hear. Are we any different to the disciples? We hear the Christian message over and over again; we know what will happen if we reject it. And if we accept it? We still accept certain parts of the gospel that appeal to us and refuse to understand the rest.

Holy Spirit of God, give me clarity and insight into each word of Jesus.

Worthy Ambition

"Whoever wants to be first must take last place and be the servant of everyone else" (Mark 9:35).

This part is proof that the disciples didn't understand the concept of Jesus as Messiah. They still thought of Him in terms of an earthly King and of themselves as important officials in that Kingdom. When Jesus asked them what they were arguing about, they were ashamed and fell silent. Jesus treated this matter seriously. He told them that if they were in search of true greatness in His kingdom, they had to look for it in being last; not by being masters, but servants. Instead of getting others to do things for them, they should do things for others.

This is the point of view of common sense. The really great people who are remembered and who made the greatest contribution to life, are not people who asked, "How can I use the state and community to reach my own goals?" but, "How can I use my personal talents and gifts in the service of others?"

> For Christ is of those who are humble-minded, and not of those who exalt themselves over His flock.
>
> CLEMENT OF ROME

Sincere unselfishness is scarce and when it manifests, it is remembered. Every economic problem would be solved if people would live for what they could do for others instead of what they could take for themselves. Every political problem would be solved if people's ambition was to serve the state and not themselves. The division and disputes that cause the rift in the church would not happen if the church would see itself as a servant of others. Position doesn't count as long as service is rendered. In this respect, Jesus revealed one of the greatest practical truths to the world.

Lord Jesus, grant that I will faithfully follow Your example of humility.

Helping the Helpless Is Helping Christ

"Anyone who welcomes a little child like this on My behalf welcomes Me, and anyone who welcomes Me welcomes not only Me but also My Father who sent Me" (Mark 9:37).

Keep in mind that we are busy here with worthy and unworthy ambitions. A little child cannot influence a person's career; cannot teach us things; give us things. It is just the other way round. A child is typical of the person who needs things, and it is our duty to find and help those in the community who need things.

But this comes with a serious warning. It is easy to form a relationship with someone who can do things for us and whose influence can mean a lot to us. It is just as easy to avoid the company of someone who expects something from us. It is easy to nurture the kindness of important people and avoid the simple, humble person. It is easy to seek the company of people who are important in the community while neglecting your unimportant family member.

> Without humility of heart all the other virtues by which one runs toward God seems – and are – absolutely worthless.
> ANGELA OF FOLIGNO

Jesus is in fact saying to us not to find favor with those who can do things for us, but with those who we can do things for. In this way, we seek the fellowship of none other than Jesus. It is a different way of interpreting our Scripture verse for today and this is our duty as Christians from day to day.

Beloved Savior, keep me humble in my relations with my fellow humans.

Salt of the Earth

"For everyone will be tested with fire. Salt is good for seasoning. But if it loses its flavor, how do you make it salty again? You must have the qualities of salt among yourselves and live in peace with each other" (Mark 9:49-50).

Jesus discusses three diverse things: "Everyone will be tested with fire." According to Jewish law, each sacrifice offered to God had to be purified with salt (see Lev. 2:13). The salt for sacrifices was called a covenant of salt (see 2 Chron. 13:5). It was the addition of salt to a sacrifice that made it pleasing to God. According to the New Testament, fire does two things: it purifies and destroys. It purifies all a person's desires, and destroys all fear of persecution. Salt is good, but once it loses its saltiness, it loses its good qualities. Salt has two good qualities in particular: It adds flavor to things and it preserves something from decay. So salt preserves from corruption and the lowering of standards.

> We can influence others as much as God has influenced us.
>
> BOBBIE-JEAN MERCK

It is the Christian's duty to add flavor to life. Jesus is busy challenging the Christians: The corrupt world needs the flavor that only Christianity can supply. If Christians have lost that flavor, where will the world get it? "You must have the qualities of salt among yourselves and live in peace with each other." Here salt means the purity of life. The ancient world regarded salt as the purest of all things because it is created by two of the purest things: the sun and the sea. Jesus says that Christians must have the purifying quality of salt in themselves. Only the life that is emptied of self and filled with Christ can really live in peace with their fellow humans.

Thank You, Lord Jesus, that I may have the quality of salt.

July

Transformed by His Love

"This is My commandment: Love each
other in the same way I have loved you."
~ John 15:12

Love is a force more formidable than any other.
It is invisible – it cannot be seen or measured, yet it is
powerful enough to transform you in a moment, and
offer you more joy than any material possession could.
~ BARBARA DE ANGELIS

Lord and Savior, You are the Source of all true love.
Teach me to love truly and sincerely.
Make my love steady and sincere:
teach me that there is no problem that love cannot remedy;
no estrangement that love cannot bridge;
no misunderstanding that cannot be resolved;
no wall of silence that love cannot break down;
no transgression that love cannot forgive.
Holy Master, by Your grace, we now know
that no matter how hopeless a situation might be,
how deep the breach,
how terrible the offense –
sincere godly love can solve it!
Teach me, Lord of love, to love like You love –
unconditionally and to the very end.
Purify my love; refine it, even if it must go through fire.
Let my love burn brighter so that I may be
a reflection of Your love in Your world.
In the name of Jesus, who loved and will
love His own until the very end.

Amen.

Guard Your Destination

"All this I have told you so that you will not fall away" (John 16:1 NIV).

✧❖✧

The Christian way of life is to experience the presence of Christ every moment. He gives meaning and understanding to every day of your life. You can know His love every day and rejoice in the knowledge of His presence. When Christ is present in your life, you know that your faith is meaningful every day. It is never pointless. Every day you build on the foundation of faith that you established in the past. Thus your spiritual life is not static.

Faith is to develop an ever-deepening understanding of God and your eternal destination. This continuous development makes it necessary for you to erect a storehouse of faith that will support you and strengthen you in dark days that might await you. Just like a farmer prepares for a possible poor harvest by building up reserves in his storehouse, so those who are serious about their spiritual life, store up spiritual reserves.

> I don't know what tomorrow holds, but I know who holds tomorrow.
> ANONYMOUS

No Christian is guaranteed against times of depression. We all experience times that God feels far away. It is in times such as these that we need reserves that provide us with security and confidence. So, now is the time to start creating your spiritual reserves by a meaningful prayer life and by always being aware of Christ's presence in your life.

Don't put a time limit on God. He is with you *now* and He is already waiting in the future to enfold you in His loving arms. What you need is faith and trust in God when you take on the new adventures and experiences of the future.

Holy Spirit of God, help me to build my spiritual reserves so that I will be strong in dark days.

God's Message Is Announced

From then on Jesus began to preach, "Turn from your sins and turn to God, because the Kingdom of Heaven is near" (Matt. 4:17).

In a single sentence, Matthew gives us the gist of the message Jesus brought. Proclaiming the Word, or preaching, is from the Greek word *kerussein*. This is the word for a *heraut* (messenger) who brought the word directly from the king. Jesus' words in today's Scripture verse tell us about certain qualities that must be present in all preaching.

The *heraut* was a person who brought important news. His tone of voice was one of absolute certainty. Goethe said, "Tell me of your certainties: I have doubts enough of my own." Preaching is the proclamation of certainties – and no one can convince others if they are not convinced themselves.

> Preaching should break a hard heart, and heal a broken one.
> JOHN NEWTON

The *heraut's* voice is one of authority. He does, after all, speak on behalf of the king. Preaching is applying the kingly authority of God to the present situation.

The *heraut's* message comes from an outside source: from the king. The messenger is not expressing his personal opinion; it is the voice of God speaking to the people through a certain person.

Jesus' message consisted of instructions that would create a new situation. "Repent of your sins," Jesus said. Turn from your own path and turn to God! Look up to heaven. Stop turning your back on God and start walking towards Him. This command became essential because the kingship was starting. God came to earth in the form of Jesus Christ; therefore it was very important that people make the right choice by choosing God!

Father God, make my heart Your home, forever!

Jesus Chooses His First Disciples

One day as Jesus was walking along the shore of the Sea of Galilee, He saw two brothers – Simon, also called Peter, and Andrew – throwing a net into the water, for they fished for a living. Jesus called out to them, "Come, follow Me, and I will show you how to fish for people!" (Matt. 4:18-20).

Jesus did not choose educated men, influential people, or those with a high-class background as His disciples. They were poor, simple people without a beckoning future. Jesus needed ordinary people who would dedicate themselves to Him. Furthermore, they were good fishermen with qualities that would make them good fishers of people.

Fishermen have to be patient; able to wait for the fish to take the bait. We seldom see quick results in preaching and that is why we must learn to wait patiently.

A good fisherman needs to have staying power. They must learn never to become discouraged. This goes for the good disciple as well. They have to be daring people, willing to weather the violence of the ocean. A good preacher should know that there is always danger when you proclaim the truth. People who do so often take their reputation and their lives into their own hands.

> You must be willing to follow if you want God to lead.
>
> ANONYMOUS

True fishermen must know when the moment is right. And so the disciple should know when to speak and when to be silent. Good fishermen know what bait to use for the different types of fish. All people are unique and must be approached differently. True fishermen stay in the background, because even his shadow can chase the fish away. Likewise, true disciples stay in the background to ensure that the Lord is placed in the forefront.

Leader of life, thank You that I could become Your humble disciple.

The Homing Instinct

To illustrate the point further, Jesus told them this story: "A man had two sons" (Luke 15:11).

We humans experience an attachment to our surroundings, a longing for home, or a homing instinct which is clearly perceptible and also indelible. The implications of these words, as spoken by Jesus, affects each person deeply: "A man had two sons." Or, "Two sons had a father and mother and they lived on a farm." An entire world of relationships, places and experiences is conjured up in our minds.

Do you ever feel the nostalgic longing for home? Songs or poems about the place where we grew up often make us yearn for the things of the past.

What a complexity of emotions anchor you to a fatherland, a father's home. Just think of the feelings that go through your mind when you visit your "roots" again after a long absence; the place where you were born and raised. You first have to pull off and stop at the side of the road because your eyes suddenly grow misty and your throat is dry. A person's origins do this to you. You can never be cut loose from these ties, not in your entire lifetime, no matter how long you have been away.

> This is the true nature of home – it is the place of Peace; the shelter – not only from injury, but from all terror, doubt and division.
>
> JOHN RUSKIN

God created humankind like this: to have a home, an anchor; a place where you come from and return to as often as life allows. Somewhere behind you is the place where you started, where you found a foothold in life; an acre where you were planted and put down your first tender roots before being transplanted elsewhere.

Thank You, Lord Jesus, that You are the only one who can satisfy our homing instinct.

My People, My Home

"A man had two sons" (Luke 15:11).

It makes no difference if you suffered in your hometown. In fact, it is often the suffering which strengthens the ties with your place of birth. It doesn't matter where it was: In the North West with its huge quiver trees; the Boland with its breathtaking beauty; the flat Karoo plains; the foot of the towering Drakensberg mountains. It doesn't matter where it is – as long as you know: this is my world; my people ... home.

And don't think that this instinct is based purely on sentiment. It is not merely an affinity for an environment, a longing for the place where you played as a child. It is the conclusive symbol of our attachment to an eternal Fatherland; an eternal Father's house; a loving Father. We belong with God and we cannot separate ourselves from Him.

> The goal of every married couple, indeed, every Christian home, should be to make Christ the Head, the Counselor and the Guide.
> PAUL SADLER

We ask ourselves about the strife and confusion in the world today. The answer is: humankind has lost its homing instinct! We have become citizens of the world; we are without an anchor, without a home. Consequently, we are also without direction and purpose. We come from nowhere and we are on our way nowhere. We have become separated from God, our Father's house and our Fatherland.

These connections in our lives are not merely coincidental. There is a reason why this "man had two sons." It is an image of our bond with God. God placed eternity in our hearts. This is the reason for our homesickness, our longing for God and Christ. God's devoted children sometimes long for heaven with the same deep longing we have for our place of birth.

Lord Jesus, I pray that the Father's house will be my home forever.

The Parental Home

"A man had two sons" (Luke 15:11).

Parental home; birthplace; children's paradise. The relationship between a parent and child is something very special. It is this relationship that makes us part of God's creation plan. It is a reflection of our heavenly origin. No wonder the first commandment about human relationships reads: "Honor your father and mother." This helps us to respect and honor God. The parent/child relationship is not just a coincidence: It is an order from God, and those who understand the joy of parenthood also understand the wonder of God's Fatherhood. Those who know a father's house are able to form a vague image of the eternal Father's house. The love between a parent and child helps us to understand the love of God.

> Salvation is a work of God for man, rather than a work of man for God.
> LEWIS SPERRY CHAFER

The Lord Jesus teaches us to pray, "Our Father ... " What an incredible privilege: we have a loving Father and an eternal home. "For His Spirit joins with our spirit to affirm that we are God's children" (Rom. 8:16). And the wonder of God's grace is that if we are His children, we are also heirs.

This Father's house is not just a fair-weather stronghold. In peace and in war, in prosperity and adversity, in happiness and sadness, in success and failure – the child is always welcome in their parents' home. The boy in our story came back in his failure and shame, and his father welcomed him back home. Perdition is a condition without God, without anchors, without any ties; a condition of being totally unattached. But in Jesus Christ, God comes to meet you. Won't you come home?

Lord Jesus, I heard Your voice calling me to come home. Thank You that I obeyed.

The Extent of God's Love

Don't you see how wonderfully kind, tolerant, and patient God is with you? Does this mean nothing to you? Can't you see that his kindness is intended to turn you from your sin? (Rom. 2:4).

It is only when you take note of all the evil in the world and take into consideration the changing disposition of man, that you become aware of the full extent of God's love. People ignore Him, they forget His manifestations of grace, they are disobedient to Him, they rebel against Him, and they blame Him when things go wrong in their lives. Nevertheless, in His love, God sent Christ to live amongst people and to die for them so that they could rest assured of salvation and eternal life.

> Peace does not dwell in outward things, but within the soul.
> FRANÇOIS FÉNELON

It is highly improbable that any human being would have tolerated the attitude that mankind displays towards God, and still persevere in infinite love as God does towards His people. That is what one starts to appreciate as the true meaning of the Christian faith. Christianity is the only religion rooted in the great love of God that transcends our understanding.

Acknowledge His gracious acceptance of you as His child. Surrender yourself unconditionally to His Son. Follow Him and live life to the full as He offers it to you (see John 10:10). Praise the Lord, because He is good. His love is infinite.

God of love, thank You that Your love and grace enables me to find You.

Godly Grace

Jesus went into the synagogue again and noticed a man with a deformed hand (Mark 3:1).

Estate agents believe that for every house, there is a buyer for whom that house will be absolutely perfect. Their job is to find that buyer, show the house to him or her and then negotiate the buying price. One person is involved in meeting the exact needs of someone else.

This is what happened in the meeting place that Jesus went to. Jesus brought with Him grace, healing power and love. A man went to the synagogue with a crippled hand. He needed healing. He met Jesus, but not just by chance. They came together to worship God and to hear His Word. But a higher power brought them together. Jesus could offer precisely what the crippled man needed.

> In God alone there is faithfulness and faith in the trust that we may hold to Him, to His promise and to His guidance. To hold to God is to rely on the fact that God is there for me, and to live in this certainty.
>
> KARL BARTH

God has an abundant provision of grace, power and blessing for the deepest needs of every person. Whatever your need might be, He has the power, love and compassion that you need in your unique situation. If you are overwhelmed with sorrow, He offers to embrace you in the darkness until the light shines through. If you are threatening to snap under pressure, He promises to renew your strength like that of an eagle.

If the future looks uncertain to you, He promises to walk the road with you. If changes are unsettling you, he offers you the courage to work through them. No matter what situation you find yourself in, he comes to meet you to show you grace and to offer you His help.

Meet me anew today with Your inexpressible grace, O Lord.

Love and Growth

This means that anyone who belongs to Christ has become a new person. The old life is gone; a new life has begun! And all of this is a gift from God, who brought us back to himself through Christ (2 Cor. 5:17-18).

This verse is firmly linked to two important spiritual concepts: new life and growth, and love for God and other people.

May God in this time open your heart to His love; your thinking to His wonders; your ears to His voice; and your entire life to His loving presence. May you receive from His hand peace for your unrest, forgiveness for your guilt, His presence in your loneliness, His guidance on your pilgrimage, and His love.

Many people fervently wish they could start their lives anew. There are many ignoble things they would like to make undone. The living Christ offers you just such an opportunity! Despite what you have done, He asks you to allow Him to come into your life and take control. He waits for you to open the door and make Him a dynamic part of your life (see Rev. 3:20).

> He who counts the stars and calls them by their names, is in no danger of forgetting His own children. He knows your case as thoroughly as if you were the only creature He ever made, or the only saint He ever loved.
> CHARLES H. SPURGEON

While you are reading, ask Him to take control of your life and to fill it with His Holy Spirit. Confess to Him everything that causes you sorrow. Do it without shame, because you know that He will understand.

Then accept in faith the "new life." He erases the past completely. Follow Him wherever He guides you. He waits for you at the point of departure to a new, meaningful and joyful life.

Holy Lord Jesus, I open my life to Your Holy Spirit.

The Gifts of the Spirit

There are different kinds of spiritual gifts, but the same Spirit is the source of them all. There are different kinds of service, but we serve the same Lord (1 Cor. 12:4-5).

The Christian faith finds expression in many ways. It changes people's lives radically; it alters attitudes; it brings healing for the sick; in more ways than one it makes God a reality and it proves that the teachings of Jesus Christ are more than a neat philosophy – in short, it is a practical way of life.

Because you as a Christian love and serve the risen Lord, you may perhaps continually be looking for signs to confirm your faith. Perhaps you desire one of God's extraordinary gifts to be able to do mighty things in His name. The gift of tongues, healing, teaching, performing miracles, and discernment are but a few of God's fantastic gifts. You probably think that if you had only one of these gifts, you could probably reach the pinnacle of all spiritual experiences.

> Use what talent you possess: the world would be very silent if no birds sang there except those that sang best.
> HENRY VAN DYKE

However, Paul calls upon us to strive for the most excellent gift when he says, "You should earnestly desire the most helpful gifts" (1 Cor. 12:31). Then he reveals to us that love is the greatest of all God's gifts. Therefore, we can say that the climax of all spiritual experiences is to love God above all else and to love our neighbor as ourselves.

Love changes ordinary things into something divine, and causes the most humble gift of the Spirit to reveal the living Lord. That is our calling in this world.

Grant me, Lord Jesus, a greater awareness of Your love, so that my life may reflect Your glory every day.

Victory Is Yours

You belong to God, my dear children. You have already won a victory over those people, because the Spirit who lives in you is greater than the spirit who lives in the world (1 John 4:4).

⌒◯⌒

The true Christian life is often described as a battle, and this becomes true when a disciple is struggling against the forces of darkness.

It is true that Christians find themselves in continuous conflict with demonic powers, temptations that threaten to overwhelm them, and subtle forces that carry out their destructive purposes before their presence has been perceived.

Unfortunately, it is also true that many disciples rely on their own strength and resources when they come face to face with forces over which they have no control. They do their best, but it is just a matter of time before they break down.

However, followers of the living Christ have spiritual reserves that they can call on when they are confronted by the Evil One in his many disguises. Deep within them lives a Spirit that is sensitive to the intervention of Jesus Christ and empowers them to fight confidently against any evil force. Never trust in your own resources, but rely on the indwelling Christ, particularly during moments when you feel weak and helpless.

> Little by little, with patience and fortitude, and with the help of God, you will sooner overcome temptations than with your own strength and persistence.
> THOMAS À KEMPIS

In the power of Christ and through His wisdom you can overcome dark forces if you realize that your help and strength come from the Holy Spirit who lives in you.

Holy Master, through Your indwelling Holy Spirit I am able to live victoriously.

More Than Conquerors

No, despite all these things, overwhelming victory is ours through Christ, who loved us (Rom. 8:37).

Paul maintains that one of the ways to experience peace with God is by realizing that, together with Christ, you are a conqueror. He declares God's pardon. His words forcefully declare: God is for you! This turns the faithful into more than conquerors. Paul reveals our debt before God, Christ's payment of that debt and our pardon through faith in Jesus Christ.

The children of the Lord desire to live a life of victory in which sin and weakness are conquered. But all too often we have to confess with Paul, "When I want to do what is right, I inevitably do what is wrong" (Rom. 7:21). Then we humbly confess to the Master that we are not conquerors, but that our circumstances have conquered us.

> Christ alone can bring lasting peace – peace with God – peace among men and nations – and peace within our hearts.
> BILLY GRAHAM

That is not what the Master wants for His followers. He desires that we live a life of victory and triumph in everything. Thank God that we do not have to triumph in our own strength. His Word declares that it is through Him who loves us that we not only become conquerors, but more than conquerors!

To experience this wondrous promise fully, we must meet with Him every day to receive new strength. We will never be denied that. Whatever happens, whatever afflictions and problems may surface, you must remember that "in all things" He grants us victory. Then we will be conquerors through the power of Somebody who loves us and who always fulfills His promises.

I praise and thank You, Lord Jesus, that in Your strength I may be the conqueror.

Joy-Filled Grace

You will show me the way of life, granting me the joy of Your presence and the pleasures of living with You forever (Ps. 16:11).

Our lives here on earth change constantly; we are engaged in new experiences and circumstances every day. We learn and grow and move on. Sometimes there is a lot of sweat and hard labor, but little beauty and rest. Although we enjoy a measure of success we also often taste failure, disappointment and pain. We mostly find human joy in relationships with friends. But even those are simply a mixture of highs and lows; they come and go. When we are happy and all smiles, when love is strong and warm, we wish that things could go on like that forever. But all earthly joy fades.

There is, however, one joy that is steady and eternal, and that is the presence of God. Many people shy away from God because they fear that He will make their joy disappear. They have the feeling that He will not approve of their lifestyles or that He will be shocked by their faults and the horrors of their sins. He does not, however, do that. But in striving after those temporary earthly pleasures they walk past the single greatest joy there is in life – to know God and to live close to Him.

> We may think God wants actions of a certain kind, but God wants people of a certain kind.
> C. S. Lewis

If you believe in Jesus Christ and follow Him faithfully, you will know that He does not in any way destroy earthly pleasures; He makes them richer and deeper. He adds a joy that does not fade with the passing years – a personal, tender and life-enriching friendship with Him! What is more, this joy is only the beginning of an even greater joy when this life comes to an end.

Father God, let me remain in Your presence for all eternity so that I may taste real joy.

Do Something with Your Life

Focus on this one thing: Forgetting the past and looking forward to what lies ahead, press on to reach the end of the race and receive the heavenly prize for which God, through Christ Jesus, is calling us (Phil. 3:13-14).

Within the human personality there are many forces at work, which all strive for recognition and fulfillment. The complexity of human nature is emphasized by the fact that every personality contains a parent, a financier, a politician, a religious person, a student, as well as many other characters.

During different phases of your life you move from one category to another without being aware of it. You are forever moving between forces that strengthen or weaken your character. People who achieve success know the importance of specialization. They set themselves goals and strive to achieve them. Make sure that your goal is worthy of your very best.

> Faith is not knowing
> what the future holds,
> but knowing who
> holds the future.
>
> ANONYMOUS

Some people strive for success in the academic world, while others want it in commerce of the arts. Whichever field you choose, you will want to live fully. If you are a disciple of the Master you will want to make the world a better place for having lived there.

The highest goal in your life is to conform to Christ. Perhaps it sounds too idealistic to be practical, but such a goal is just practical common sense. Christ calls you to the most noble way of life that you can ever achieve. He does not only call you, but equips you to achieve heights that you would not have been able to achieve alone. Let your life be meaningful and achieve its utmost potential through the power of the indwelling Christ.

Guide and Lord, help me to achieve the goal that You have for my life, through the work of Your Holy Spirit.

Called by God

*I, a prisoner for serving the Lord, beg you to lead a life worthy of
your calling, for you have been called by God (Eph. 4:1).*

It is amazing how many Christians have a poor opinion of
themselves and their calling. They live under the false impression that excessive modesty is acceptable and pleasing to God.
Even though these people may have special gifts and qualities,
they never achieve what God intends them to.

If, in your quiet moments of prayer and meditation, you
conclude that you will never be able to achieve anything
worthwhile, you might ask yourself why you have come to that
conclusion. Be absolutely honest with yourself and with God.
If you claim that you know your
shortcomings and are living within
those limits, it is possible that you
are looking at your natural potential
without considering what God can
do through you. If you combine your
resources with those God has put
at your disposal, you could achieve
great things!

> All things are possible to
> him who believes, yet more
> to him who hopes, more
> still to him who loves, and
> most of all to him who
> practices and perseveres in
> these three virtues.
> BROTHER LAWRENCE

Don't waste your time and spiritual resources lamenting the things that you cannot do. Hold on
to the glorious truth that if you dedicate yourself to the Master
to the best of your ability, He will use you beyond your wildest
imagination. Place yourself in His hands and let your prayers
always be: "Use me, Lord." Such a commitment to the will of
God will reveal hidden talents that you never realized you
possessed. You will experience the deep satisfaction that is the
reward of those who strive to do the will of the Lord.

*I lay my weakness in Your hands, Lord, so that I can be strong in
Your strength.*

Life to the Full

You are the fountain of life, the light by which we see (Ps. 36:9).

Never allow life to become an unbearable burden to you, because it is God's greatest gift to you. He only gives to you what is good and you should be exceedingly grateful for that. Unfortunately it is possible to make your life an unbearable burden through degenerating and negative thoughts, and by the total neglect of your spiritual life and principles.

If you want to lead a full and blessed life, there are certain principles that must be accepted. One of the most important principles is that you must be grateful for your life, because it is the best thing God has given you. Of course this doesn't mean that everything must always be plain sailing, but when you accept the goodness of life with gratitude towards God, you will stop fighting it. When you start co-operating with life, you become a collaborator with the almighty God.

> Gratitude is a course from which we never graduate fully.
> FRED BECK

When you accept that life is good, you become aware that it has a clear goal and plan. This acceptance removes all impatience and frustration, and life becomes an exciting and satisfying experience. But, in order for you to understand the great plan of life, you need to know the Planner. You need to accept the fact that God exists and allow your life to be controlled by godly principles, until eventually you become an expression of those plans.

When you have this experience and make it your own, you possess a unity with the Creator and your life is filled with the fullness of God. How can you possibly thank and praise Him enough for this in one lifetime?

Creator God, I thank You that in Jesus Christ I can overcome any obstacle, and be a shining light for You.

Comfort for the Future

"Look, God's home is now among His people! He will live with them, and they will be His people. God Himself will be with them" (Rev. 21:3).

In our day fear has cast a very dark shadow over the future. On the international scene there is ever-increasing tension; clashes between races and the seeming inability of leaders to handle even the most basic issues cause people to wonder what kind of world is awaiting their children and grandchildren. It is impossible not to personalize national and international affairs, because of necessity you are part of humanity.

To be sheltered in the living Christ elevates your view above the temporal, giving you an exceptional appreciation of life. You realize that the times you live in, regardless of how tense and ominous they might appear, are still under God's control. The Lord God Almighty still reigns and has not rejected His creation.

If you do believe in the omnipotence of God and if your faith is built on a steadfast foundation, it will

> The only light on the future is faith.
> THEODOR HAECKER

have practical results in creating a positive attitude in your life. You will not fear the extinction of mankind, but rather believe in God's redemptive work that will come to fulfillment in mankind.

To believe that God is working out His divine plan with us, in spite of our sin, enables us to maintain a well-balanced and calm attitude. The choice is yours: you can look to the future without God and experience depression and fear, or you can believe in God's plan of redemption and approach the future comforted, and with trust.

Eternal and all-powerful God, I believe with conviction that I can trust the future to You.

Eternal Comfort

All praise to God, the Father of our Lord Jesus Christ. God is our merciful Father and the source of all comfort. He comforts us in all our troubles so that we can comfort others. When they are troubled, we will be able to give them the same comfort God has given us (2 Cor. 1:3-4).

Often, shortly after you have been through a harrowing situation in your life, and have found comfort, you meet someone who has to handle a similar situation. It is God who leads us to these people because the comfort that we offer is sincere and they know that we have wrestled with a similar experience ourselves.

In this letter, Paul praises God for using the church of Corinth to "give them the same comfort God has given us." What would it take for you to proclaim God as your Help and Deliverer? What would it take for you to look to God alone for the solution to your problems? When you find yourself or an acquaintance in a difficult situation, approach His

> In Christ the heart of the Father is revealed, and higher comfort there cannot be than to rest in the Father's heart.
> ANDREW MURRAY

throne of grace in prayer. Declare boldly to God that you trust in Him alone to deliver you.

In prayer and with gratitude, consider all the ways in which God has comforted you in times of affliction and tell God that you are willing to let Him use you to bring comfort to others.

Gracious God, thank You for the comfort You granted me so undeservedly. Use me to comfort others in turn.

Flee or Trust?

Oh, that I had wings like a dove; then I would fly away and rest! (Ps. 55:6).

The way in which one deals with problems will reveal much about one's Christian character. The psalmist here point to two methods people use to deal with their problems. There is "flight" in which you try to escape or evade your problems. Then there is the "stand steadfast and trust the Lord" method in which we deal with our problems and overcome them in the name of the Lord.

Jonah started by running away. God sent him to Nineveh. At Joppa, he then bought his ticket for a voyage by boat to Tarshish – situated far away from his responsibilities. But Jonah never reached Tarshish. There is no place on earth where we can escape our problems completely. Instead of solving his problems, Jonah only multi-plied them. One cannot escape from yourself, your responsibilities or your problems. When Jonah eventually chose the path of obedience and went to Nineveh to carry out his task, the Lord supported him with strength and he worked miracles in the name of the Lord.

> Jesus whom I know as my Redeemer cannot be less than God.
> St. Athanasius

At one time or another we all face the temptation of trying to flee from our problems or to sidestep our responsibilities. Even Jesus was confronted by temptation in the desert. However, He accepted God's will for His life and did what He had to do. If we are obedient and faithful, if we trust God completely, He will support and help us.

Holy Trinity, I trust You with my life and my problems. Make me obedient and faithful through Your Holy Spirit and through the power of my Redeemer, Jesus Christ.

Strength for Every Day

Be strong in the Lord and in His mighty power (Eph. 6:10).

When we are faced with problems that seem irresolvable, we often cry out in despair, "What can I do? I cannot go on like this!" This might be the result of a personal setback, a business failure or a disappointing national or international situation. Whatever it is, the consequent feelings of hopelessness leave you alone and vulnerable.

There is one thing that you can be absolutely certain about and that is the fact that God will never leave you to wrestle with life and all its problems on your own. He who has promised never to leave you in the lurch and never to forsake you (see Heb. 13:5) is with you in every area of your life. He is simply waiting for you to call out to Him. You can be sure of His all-powerful help.

> God can give only according to His might; therefore He always gives more than what we ask for.
> MARTIN LUTHER

Instead of continuously laboring under the heavy burden of life, put your trust in your heavenly Father. Let Him be completely in control of your life and affairs, and let Him unconditionally lead you on His path. As you walk in obedience with the Lord, you will experience the trust, assurance and peace that are born from the presence of His Holy Spirit in your life.

Lord Jesus, strengthen my faith so that I may live my life in the power and might of God.

God in You

All who confess that Jesus is the Son of God have God living in them, and they live in God (1 John 5:12).

The simple doctrines of Jesus Christ have enormous power. People from all walks of life experience their impact. Theologians may debate the various guidelines of Christ's doctrines and, in doing so, cause confusion in the mind and spirit of ordinary people.

However, if you acknowledge and embrace the deity of Christ, you will have a force in your life like you have never experienced before. Such an acknowledgement, which is found on the Scriptures, gives you energy, strength and inner life. Just by stating, "Christ is the Lord" causes that force to sparkle in your life.

> We can be tired, weary and emotionally distraught, but after spending time alone with God, we find that He injects into our bodies energy, power and strength.
>
> CHARLES STANLEY

The miraculous truth is that you will not live alone with God, but that He will live in you. This is the most significant and amazing experience that you will every witness, because it will mark a complete revolution in your existence. Your disposition towards people and circumstances changes, you notice the beauty of life instead of staring yourself against dreariness. Your objectives are creative and your work positively towards them. Your entire life becomes a pilgrimage to an ever-growing relationship with God.

Acknowledging the deity and sovereignty of Christ results in such far-reaching consequences that you will stand amazed each day about that which God has achieved in your life.

Lord God, I wish to celebrate Your power. Make me victorious in battle through Your Spirit.

God Is Always Near

We thank You, O God! We give thanks because You are near. People everywhere tell of Your wonderful deeds (Ps. 75:1).

Don't ever forget that God is near to you! At times He performs mighty miracles to remind us just how close He is. But there are many times when we are not so consciously aware of His might and righteousness. This prayer addresses this problem directly. If we feel tempted to question whether God is even aware of our problems, we should begin to praise Him for His might. We should also remind ourselves that God is close to us and we should think of all the times that we have seen His power at work in the world. God promised to bring justice to this world, but in His own time. While we wait for God to act, we should keep praising Him.

> Jesus Christ is God's everything for man's total need.
>
> RICHARD HALVERSON

When we experience problems in life, it is often extremely difficult to wait on the Lord. The Israelites who were under the yoke of the Roman Empire felt exactly like that. They couldn't wait for the Messiah to come. After centuries of waiting, their hope was fulfilled in the Baby who was born in Bethlehem. All that they had to do was wait for His perfect timing.

Whatever situation you might find yourself in today, think of one thing God has done for you recently, and sincerely thank Him for it. Praise Him because He is always near to you and rest assured that you will receive an answer to your prayers.

Holy and loving God, it comforts me to know that You are always close to me. Thank You for this reassurance.

Anchored in the Peace of God

Trust in the LORD always, for the LORD GOD is the eternal Rock (Isa. 26:4).

When idols are mentioned we usually see in our mind's eye many of the gods that form an integral part of the life, culture and tradition of heathen gods. There were rain gods, fertility gods, war gods – the list is endless. People lived in fear and trepidation because it was possible that they could anger these gods and then the gods would seek revenge.

However, idols don't have a religious connotation only. In our day people have elevated money into an idol and they are trying their very best to hoard riches. Yet others seek security in their earthly possessions; while others make liquor and drugs their idol in an effort to escape the pressures of modern life.

Covetousness, jealousy and lust are just as real to some people as their idols are to pagans. Just like the pagan idols they create fear and anxiety in the hearts of those who worship them. They fear the loss of their earthly possessions, or they cannot cope without the crutch of drugs and alcohol.

> You can either win your peace, or you can buy it. You can win it by resisting evil; you can buy it through compromising with the Evil One.
> JOHN RUSKIN

Most people, if not all, intensely yearn for tranquility and peace of mind. And this is to be found only with the one true God. It happens when you surrender your life to the living Christ and when you love Him above all else. Live your life in Christ, open up your heart to Him. Spend time in His presence and draw your strength from Him. In this way, His love will expel all fear and tension from your life and you will have a safe haven where you can live in peace.

Lord Jesus, I thank You for being my Safe Haven.

The Love of the Lord

This hope will not lead to disappointment. For we know how dearly God loves us, because He has given us the Holy Spirit to fill our hearts with His love (Rom. 5:5).

People all around the world can testify of their love for Jesus Christ. These people are of different nationalities, traditions and cultures. Nevertheless, they bear witness to their love and faith in Jesus Christ, who died on a cross two thousand years ago. They are convinced that He is alive today. How is this possible? They never even saw Him. His earthly ministry lasted about three years and even the reports on that are rather fragmentary.

The secret of His unique attraction does not live in one or other theological formula or religious organization – regardless of how important these things may be in the right context. But He promised to grant His Spirit to everyone who accepts Him and confesses His rule. Through the ages He has kept His promises. He said that His Spirit would live in every person who loves Him and who serves Him. Countless followers of this century believe that this experience with the living Christ is valid and true for our time.

> Though our feelings come and go, God's love for us does not.
> C. S. LEWIS

If you want to sit on the sideline, remember that Christ can convert your life. A new, unparalleled strength will take possession of your spirit. It will enable you to do those things that are pleasing to God. This change in your life and this new strength will assure you of Christ's presence in your life. If you have the Spirit of Christ you will know the reality of His holy presence. Love for Him will radiate from your heart and your life.

I praise You, Lord, that I can experience the power of Your living presence through the work of the Holy Spirit.

God Is Faithful

True, some of them were unfaithful; but just because they were unfaithful, does that mean God will be unfaithful? (Rom. 3:3).

The wonderful and comforting truth is that God *is* faithful. When you trust someone and they disappoint you, you feel deeply hurt. You probably declared publicly that you would never trust anybody again. At the time you meant every word, but you can seldom persist, because our whole life is based on trust. Without trust society would fall apart.

Because man's nature is so fragile and unreliable, people are easily disappointed. Disappointing someone is not always intentional and sometimes it is unavoidable, but because of our imperfect and sinful nature, it is something we have to accept. The only Unchangeable One in a changing world is God! He is forever the same. His promises in the Bible are certain and unfailing. People have been confirming His faithfulness from time immemorial. Even though He did not always act according to their plans and desires, He did prove in His own, unique way that He is faithful and true. He brings His plans to pass in the lives of those who trust Him unconditionally.

> In God alone there is faithfulness and faith in the trust that we may hold to Him, to His promise and to His guidance. To hold to God is to rely on the fact that God is there for me, and to live in this certainty.
> KARL BARTH

God expects your unqualified trust. When clouds of doubt and sorrow threaten and when it seems as if everybody has disappointed you, hold on tightly to God's trustworthiness. The clouds will disappear and you will be able to rejoice in God's faithfulness once more.

Lord, I may not always understand everything, but I trust You unconditionally.

Jesus Taken Captive

"Who are you looking for?" He [Jesus] asked, "Jesus the Nazarene," they replied. "I AM He," Jesus said (John 18:4-5).

There are few scenes in Scripture that reveal Jesus' character as clearly as this one. His heroism is revealed. During Easter, it was full moon in Jerusalem; the moonlight was almost as bright as daylight. Yet Jesus' enemies came with lanterns and blazing torches – things they certainly wouldn't have needed. But they thought they would have to search for Jesus in dense bushes and caves in the hills. Yet instead of hiding, Jesus came forward at their arrival and asked, "Who are you looking for?" "Jesus the Nazarene," they replied. And Jesus' answer was, "I AM He." Instead of hiding, Jesus revealed the courage of someone who would see things through till the very end.

> Every virtue is a form of obedience to God. Every evil in word or act is a form of rebellion against Him.
> STEPHEN NEILL

This Scripture verse also reveals Jesus' authority. There He stood: alone and unarmed, and yet, when they saw Him they "all drew back and fell to the ground." Authority flowed from Jesus and even in His isolation it made Him stronger than His enemies.

We also see here that Jesus chose to die. He could have walked away from the scene and disappeared. But He didn't – He even helped His enemies to capture Him and only asked them to let His disciples go. We see Jesus' total obedience: "Shall I not drink from the cup of suffering the Father has given Me?" (John 18:11). What was taking place was God's will and this was enough for Jesus.

Thank You, Lord Jesus, for Your example of complete obedience to the Father.

Why Have Christian Love?

"But you are to be perfect, even as your Father in heaven is perfect" (Matt. 5:48).

⌒✦⌒

We have now seen what Jesus meant when He ordered us to show Christian love. Why must we have this love of unconquerable goodwill? The answer is in fact quite simple: because it makes humankind become like God.

God's actions in this world equal unparalleled goodwill. He lets the sun shine on good and bad; He lets His rain fall on the righteous and the unrighteous. God's love is of such a nature that He doesn't take pleasure in the destruction of the creatures His hand made. "The eyes of all look to You in hope; You give them their food as they need it" (Ps. 145:15). God demonstrates this universal kindness even toward people that violate His commands and break His heart. Jesus says we must have this same kind of love so that we can become God's children.

> Love is the fulfillment of all our works. There is the goal; that is why we run: we run toward it, and once we reach it, in it we shall find rest.
>
> St. Augustine

To be perfect in love means to be perfect. On the face of it, this looks like an instruction we cannot carry out because none of us see ourselves as perfect. But it is a goal we must strive for, that we were created for, and sent out into this world for. Human beings will only be perfect if they reach this goal: "Then God said, 'Let us make human beings in our image, to be like us'" (Gen. 1:26).

This is the teaching of the entire Bible; that we realize our human nature only when we conform to God. One thing that makes us like God is our love that never stops caring for people: to care like God cares, and to love like God loves.

God of love and undeserved goodness, strengthen Your love in my heart every day.

Prepare for Your Eternal Destination

"Don't be so concerned about perishable things like food. Spend your energy seeking the eternal life that the Son of Man can give you. For God the Father has given Me the seal of His approval" (John 6:27).

There are depths to God's nature that no human could ever estimate, but few people have taken the time and gone to the trouble of getting to know God to the best of their ability. They believe in Him and yet refuse to totally and unconditionally entrust their lives to Him. They say they trust Him and yet worry themselves sick about trivialities. They are surrounded by the glory of the living God, and yet they become involved in petty religious issues that dishonor His name.

One of the most glorious facts about Christ's teachings is their simplicity. Jesus invites the human being to a new and blessed relationship with the living God and Father. One of the basic requirements for this relationship is sincere spiritual hunger and willingness to accept Jesus as Redeemer and Savior.

> For a small reward, a man will hurry away on a long journey; while for eternal life, many will hardly take a single step.
>
> THOMAS À KEMPIS

This acceptance is not the result of an emotional experience or following a specific religious formula, but total and unconditional surrender to the Father. You should get into the habit of speaking to God as you go about your daily tasks, like you would speak to a friend, which is exactly what He is. As you start having more intimate fellowship with Him, He will become more of a reality to you, until every aspect of your life is made holy by His presence and you are ready for your eternal destination.

I praise and thank You, Father God, that You share my daily life with me.

What If Christ Hadn't Come?

"They would not be guilty if I had not come and spoken to them. But now they have no excuse for their sin" (John 15:22).

If Jesus had not come to earth, our world would have been without love. Because this is the good news of Christmas: God is love! It was for this reason that He sent His Son. God loves us and that's why we love Him and one another. If Christ hadn't come to us, our world would have been without a gospel and a church. Christ is the very essence of the gospel and the cornerstone of the church. Picture a world without prayer, without baptism and Holy Communion, without church services and songs of praise. Imagine a world without a cross where we can go and lay down our burdens and walk away as redeemed people.

> It is good to be children sometimes, and never better than at Christmas, when its mighty Founder was a child Himself.
> CHARLES DICKENS

If Jesus had not come to the earth, we would have had no expectations for the future. Then death would have been final for all of us. Everything would have ended in darkness without God and without hope in the world.

But Jesus came: Hallelujah! He completed His salvation work; His tomb is empty; He interceded for us with the Father; and He promised that He would come again to fetch us so that we can also be where He is. Then Christ will be celebrated forever in the house of the Father!

Thank You, Lord Jesus, that You were prepared to come to this world to save us.

The Disciples' Assignment

That Sunday evening the disciples were meeting behind locked doors because they were afraid of the Jewish leaders. Suddenly, Jesus was standing there among them! "Peace be with you," He said. As He spoke, He showed them the wounds in His hands and His side. They were filled with joy when they saw the Lord! Again He said, "Peace be with you. As the Father has sent Me, so I am sending you" (John 20:19-21).

The disciples were under a lot of pressure and feared that the bitterness of the Jews who planned Jesus' death would put them next on the list. They locked the doors and feared every footstep, every knock at the door. While they were sitting there, Jesus appeared among them.

Jesus greeted them: "Peace be with you!" This meant far more than being spared from trouble. The literal meaning was: May God provide you with every good gift! Then Jesus gave the disciples their assignment. Jesus said that just as God sent Him, so He also sends them. This is the covenant of the church. This is exactly what Paul meant when he later said, "And the church is His [Christ's] body" (Eph. 1:23) and "The human body has many parts, but the many parts make up one whole body. So it is with the body of Christ" (1 Cor. 12:12).

> We are all missionaries. Wherever we go, we either bring people nearer to Christ, or we repel them.
> ERIC LIDDELL

Jesus came with a message for all people and now He was going back to His Father. He would not be able to bring that message to everybody, unless the church took over. The church is Christ's messenger. Jesus could never become the Savior and Redeemer of the world unless the church proclaims His message.

Lord Jesus, help Your church to faithfully carry out Your assignment so that all people may find You.

The Church as God's Messenger

Suddenly, Jesus was standing there among them! "Peace be with you," He said. As He spoke, He showed them the wounds in His hands and His side. They were filled with joy when they saw the Lord! Again He said, "Peace be with you. As the Father has sent Me, so I am sending you" (John 20:19-21).

Jesus trusts His church absolutely, but at the same time this means that the church urgently needs Jesus. People who are sent out need someone to send them out; they need a message to deliver; they need the authority to confirm this message, someone they can turn to should any trouble or doubts arise. The church urgently needs Jesus. Without Him there is no message and the church has no authority. This means that the church is dependent on Jesus.

The mission that Jesus gave to His disciples is the same mission for which God sent Jesus to earth. The relationship between Jesus and God depended entirely on Jesus' obedience to and love for God. So it follows that the church can only be God's messenger if it loves God absolutely, and fully obeys Him. The church dare not propagate its own message; it must propagate Jesus' message. The church dare not follow man-inspired doctrines; it must follow God's will. The church fails if it tries to solve problems in its own strength and wisdom. The church must constantly seek Christ's will and guidance.

> Obedience is the only virtue that implants the other virtues in the heart and preserves them after they have been so implanted.
>
> GREGORY THE GREAT

Holy Father, give Your church wise and loving leaders who want to obey You.

August

And the Word Became Flesh ...

In the beginning the Word already existed. The Word was
with God, and the Word was God ... So the Word became
human and made His home here among us.
~ John 1:1, 14

Jesus Christ is God in the form of man; as completely God as if He
were not man; as completely man as if He were not God.
~ A. J. F. BEHRENDS

Holy Master, when the days are short, gray and cold,
when the nights are long and dark and full of worry;
let this song of praise rise up from my heart:
The Word became human!
When not even loved ones, friends or colleagues
know my pain, fear and torment,
then open my ears to hear this song of praise:
The Word became human!
When my faith is low and I think in
my heart You are far away from me,
let Your Spirit of Truth touch my heart and jubilantly say,
The Word became human!
Your Word and the flesh and the life became one
to prove Your love.
So, let me always look up so that I can clearly see:
The Word became human!
O Holy Child of Bethlehem, descend on me in love;
cleanse me from my sin;
come and live in my heart.
Be born in me again.
Our Lord! Our Immanuel!

Amen.

Love of Another Kind

"Just as I have loved you, you should love each other" (John 13:34).

L ove is probably the most misused word in the English language. All too often the discussion about love becomes a substitute for the practical act of loving.

When Jesus told His disciples that they "should love each other," He wanted to make clear to them exactly what He meant. He told His disciples to love each other in the same way He loved them. He drew close to them, teaching them and encouraging them to strive for things which were good and honorable. He showed them what it meant to put others first; to give love freely, without trying to profit from it. In terms of spiritual welfare, He wanted the best for those He loved. In short, He would show His disciples how far true love would go: till death. For this love He gave His life on the cross. Later many of them would also come face to face with death for the sake of their faith and love for Jesus and each other.

> For love to be possible we need the courage to create space between us and to trust that this space allows us to dance together.
>
> HENRI NOUWEN

Christ's kind of love is far more than simply feeling sorry for someone or a once-off act of kindness. It is ongoing and constant love for another. It is to persist in love with purposeful single-mindedness. It is bold and contagious caring for others. It is giving others nothing but the best. This love does not ask for thankfulness, for payment or reward. You know this kind of love only when Christ lives in you, because it is ultimately a superhuman kind of love. You cannot just decide on your own to love like this. It is the beautiful awakening of Christ's presence in your heart and life.

Loving Lord Jesus, let Your love live in and through me.

Your Actions

"Your love for one another will prove to the world that you are My disciples" (John 13:35).

〜⟳〜

Christianity is all about God speaking to us: in the Bible, in His creation, and through others who tell us about God. He also speaks through Christ, the Word that became flesh for our sakes. All of this implies a "speaking" God. Sometimes people think that's all Christians ever do: talk and talk and talk!

Jesus knew that much more would be necessary than talking. There needed to be practical action to confirm the sincerity of His followers' faith, demonstrating that their faith really did make a difference. Their love for one another would have to do the talking. It would be proof to everybody to whom they belonged, and that His love was alive in them. This would emphasize the fact that God loved the world in the same way in which Christ loved them. And just like Christ spoke to them about an eternal life, and offered it to people, the disciples' love for others would reinforce this idea. Their special love for each other would have a supernatural quality. It would be an indication of God's presence as well as evidence of their mutual brotherhood.

> It does not take a perfect church to introduce a man to the perfect Christ.
>
> RICHARD WOODSOME

We must be a witness for Christ by our love for our fellow Christians, which does not mean love only for our close friends. It means love for people of other denominations and races, levels of education, and economic circumstances. It is never easy to witness for Christ. It is in fact often difficult and demanding. Witnessing with love is even more taxing. Are you willing to pay the price?

Holy Lord Jesus, help us to show Jesus' love to the world by our love for one another.

Stumbling Loyalty

Jesus answered, "Die for Me? ... Before the rooster crows tomorrow morning, you will deny three times that you even know Me" (John 13:38).

～ つ⌒ ～

What was the difference between Peter and Judas? Judas betrayed Jesus and Peter denied Him. While Judas is tainted with the dirtiest shame, there is something appealing about Peter. The difference is that Judas' betrayal was a planned action whereas in Peter's denial there was no sign of premeditation. His heart was always in the right place. There is a difference between deliberate sin and the sin of a situation you find yourself in; between the sinner who knows exactly what he's doing and the sinner who commits a sin in a moment of weakness. May God keep us from deliberately hurting anyone.

> The love of Christ is like the blue sky, into which you may see clearly, but the real vastness of which you cannot measure.
> ROBERT MURRAY MCCHEYNE

There was something special about the relationship between Jesus and Peter. No one ever knew Peter as well as Jesus did. He knew that Peter was impulsive. He knew that Peter spoke first with his heart, before thinking about what he was saying. Jesus was well aware of Peter's loyalty, but also that he didn't always stand by his intentions.

Jesus also knew that Peter had a lot of love to give. He knew that no matter what Peter did, he always loved Jesus. If only we could make allowances for this when people disappoint or hurt us. It would save us a lot of heartache if we would remember that the person who sometimes hurts us, loves us. Jesus knew who Peter was and what he would become in the future. He would walk the road of martyrdom, and emerge a hero. Jesus sees who we are, and can make us what He sees in us.

Lord Jesus, thank You that You know I love You.

"Don't Be Troubled"

"Don't let your hearts be troubled. Trust in God, and trust also in Me" (John 14:1).

↶ ♋ ↷

In spite of being told often not to allow our troubles to get to us, many of us still do. We worry about our financial affairs, family relationships, health and security. People are troubled about their jobs, the country's political climate and the economy. Unless you live in a dream world, there is much to worry about.

One can understand that Jesus' disciples were troubled by Jesus' announcement of His imminent departure. Aware that they were starting to panic, Jesus tried to calm them down. Being troubled served no purpose. Jesus' death was near and it would be better for them to be calm. They would survive it. It would be a horrific judgment, but they would reach a new dimension of faith and trust in dealing with the tension and shock. The best way to confront it was head-on, with the calm assurance that God was busy working through it. They would emerge from the experience with a stronger faith.

> Nothing is really lost by a life of sacrifice; everything is lost by failure to obey God's call.
>
> HENRY P. LIDDON

Whatever it is you worry about, just listen to Jesus' words in today's Scripture. It is more than good advice; it is a command you must obey. Whatever problem you have to handle, place your complete trust in the Lord God Almighty. Say with a believing heart, "Lord, I really don't know how everything will turn out. But I know Your omnipotence. Hold me tight, Lord, and never let me go." God has the whole wide world in His all-powerful hands – He will also hold tightly onto you.

Lord Jesus, strengthen my faith in You and in the Father of love and grace.

Big Enough for All

"There is more than enough room in My Father's home" (John 14:2).

People live in a great variety of places that are "home" to them. For some it is a cardboard box. To others, "home" is a castle or a mansion. There are those that are quite content with mud huts, while a suburban three-bedroom house is "home" to millions of people. A typical short advertisement describes a home as "a house with parking. Sleeps eight."

Jesus grew up in the town of Nazareth, as a carpenter's son. But He used the town Capernaum as His base when He started His earthly ministry. As a carpenter He probably helped build both big and small houses. But He didn't yearn for His father's house in Nazareth or for the carpenter's house in Capernaum. He knew He was on His way to the house of His "other" Father; a house with many rooms.

> Entrance into heaven is not at the hour of death, but at the moment of conversion.
>
> BENJAMIN WHICHCOTE

This is a home where you will be warmly welcomed, no matter how you journeyed to get there. Its most important element is the loving Father's presence, and that of the gracious and faithful Son. The Father's home is spacious and has many rooms. Songs of praise and love resound through the house. The godly people are there – and many sinners, who also found their way there.

There is also room for you! You will meet familiar faces and there will be much joy – pure, sincere joy. Then the things of this world will fade away in the light of the glory and grace of God Himself who is always present.

Heavenly Father, thank You for the glorious prospect of living in Your house.

Jesus Goes Ahead of Us

"I am going there to prepare a place for you" (John 14:2 NIV).

When we relocate from one place to another, it helps a lot to know someone familiar. It makes us feel less like strangers.

Jesus told His disciples that He was going ahead of them to His Father's house. He was going to "prepare a place" for them there. There is a specific picture behind these words. In the Middle East there were many structures along the road known as "resting places." Travelers journeying by camel, donkey or on foot would stay over at these places. There were no servants – only shade and basic amenities. Some travelers sent servants ahead to prepare the resting place for their master's overnight stay. When describing His Father's house, Jesus included these temporary resting places promising to go ahead to get everything ready for their arrival. This meant that He would be there Himself to welcome them and everything would be ready for their stay.

> There will be little else we will want in heaven besides Jesus Christ. He will be our bread, our food, our beauty, and our glorious garment. The atmosphere of heaven will be Christ; everything in heaven will be Christ-like; yes, Christ is the heaven of His people.
> CHARLES H. SPURGEON

Never fear death. Look forward to it, knowing that whatever it might hold, and whoever might be there, Jesus will also be present. He goes ahead of us and when we arrive, everything will be in place. He will know our names, be familiar with our strong and weak points, our background and our personality. In the great unknown, you can entrust yourself to Him as Your Savior, Friend and Guide. He will never let you down here on earth, and He won't let you down in the world to come!

Lord Jesus, I eagerly look forward to being in Your presence forever.

All about Jesus

"When everything is ready, I will come and get you, so that you will always be with Me where I am" (John 14:3).

～✺～

Through the ages, many diverse doctrines and thoughts on heaven have been put forward. Some were taken from the Bible and some not. Hymns and songs in particular focused on the particulars and beauty of heaven. These images helped the Christian disciples to get an idea of what heaven would be like one day. These hymns are lovely and it is fine for us to use and enjoy them.

However, when Jesus spoke to His disciples about heaven, He rarely mentioned any of these details. He did emphasize that He, Jesus Christ, would be part of it. He said He was going ahead to prepare a place for us and then He would come again to escort us on our journey to our final and eternal place of rest. He promised that we would be where He is. The essence of the argument is that Jesus Himself is the main concept of heaven.

> My home is in heaven. I'm just traveling through this world.
> BILLY GRAHAM

Jesus Christ is present there in His glory and majesty; in His infinite love. His knowledge of His children and God the Father is complete. He is present *in* and *with* His followers. He is present in *His* perfection and He will bring everything *to* perfection. He is the risen, transfigured Jesus, the Lamb who sits on the throne. All people and all things will praise Him, honor Him and worship Him. We have the opportunity to prepare ourselves to become part of the songs of praise to Him, of honoring and worshiping Jesus, our Lord.

Transfigured Lord Jesus, I'm looking forward to be in Your glorious presence for all eternity.

Pathfinders

"You know the way to the place where I am going" (John 14:4 NIV).

The road you travel always depends on your destination and your guide. A stranger lost his way and stopped to ask someone for directions. The answer he got was: "Well, if I was on my way there, I wouldn't have started here."

To Jesus, however, the road traveled was more important than the destination. The expression "the way" was commonly used in the Jewish faith in which Jesus and His disciples grew up. Years later Christianity became known as "the Way." To the Jewish believer, following "the way" was obedience to the law and glorifying God. To Christ, however, it was not obedience to laws. He Himself was "the Way." And because the disciples traveled with Him for three years, they must have known about the concept that faith was about a personal relationship with God and with Christ, and not obedience to rules and regulations.

> The young Christian must realize that the test of his religious life is what he is and what he does when he is not on his knees in prayer, not reading his Bible, not listening to great preachers and not participating in religious meetings.
> DR JOHN MEIGS

Make sure that you also find the true "Way." If you lose your way, you won't reach the destination Jesus meant for you: an ongoing deepening unity with God the Father and with Himself. There are many short-cuts, highways and byways, detours and dead-ends. Follow them and you will get lost and stray from "the Way." Put your hand in the hand of the Man who calmed the storm and He will keep you on the right track to the glorious end: the Father's house with its many rooms.

Help me, Lord Jesus, to find the Way and walk it with You up until the very end.

"I Am the Way"

Jesus told him, "I am the way" (John 14:6).

A couple was touring Switzerland and arrived in the beautiful city of Berne. They were on their way to a caravan park on one of the highways leading out of the city. In the strange city, unsure of which road to take, they stopped to find their bearings. The wife crossed the road to ask for directions. Fingers were pointed in different directions. At last she went back to the car and told her husband, "That man will take us there. Just follow the blue car." The voluntary guide was as good as his word. He took them right up to the entrance to the caravan park, going more than two miles out of his way. For a short time the man was their pathfinder – he was their way.

In a much more meaningful way, Jesus was, and still is, "the Way." He didn't give people lists of laws and instructions. He lived the life of God before them and among them. To this day He doesn't tell you where to go and what to say. His every word and deed is "the Way" that is demonstrated for you to follow. And what is more: He leads you every step of the way, through a maze of byways and shortcuts, of deviations and wrong roads that could very easily make you lose your way.

> Jesus does not give recipes that show the way to God, as other teachers of religion do. He is himself the Way.
>
> KARL BARTH

In the end, the life of a Christian is more about how you travel and the adventures on the road, than your final destination. Make sure you always follow Jesus as "the Way" in your life, live in line with His will, and do what pleases Him.

Lord Jesus, I acknowledge You as the Road to life and I ask You to lead me every step of the way.

He Who Is the Truth

Jesus told him, "I am the way, the truth, and the life" (John 14:6).

In the quest for justice in a court case, it is often necessary for a judge to work through masses of conflicting ideas, lies, claims and counterclaims. Before they can prove someone's guilt or innocence, the judge must get as close to the truth as possible. Some cases are judged on a "balance of probabilities." Sometimes truth shows the correct version of what happened. It could also be the knowledge of one single fact, or many facts. We often think of the truth as "something far away."

To Jesus the truth was something totally different. The truth was not so much about getting the facts right as getting the person right. It was not something in the distance, but rather knowing God, understanding His love and undeserved goodness, and building a relationship with Him. To Christ the truth is God who presents and reveals Himself to us, and our response in loving and obeying Him. The truth is something you do – not facts you learn. And seeing that Christ is the perfect revelation of God the Father, He is the perfect embodiment of God's truth in everything He says and does.

> Knowing God is more than knowing about Him.
>
> J. I. PACKER

It does help to know as much as possible about the Bible. But it is so much more important to know Jesus as Friend, Savior, Redeemer and Guide. In this way, you achieve spiritual truth instead of just spiritual knowledge. They are not the same thing! Don't go chasing after some theory or clever formula. Just get to know Jesus better and obey Him.

Lord and Master, lead me in all Your truth until the end of the road.

A Life Worth Living

Jesus told him, "I am the way, the truth, and the life" (John 14:6).

People are in search of something that will give their life meaning. A character in one of William Barclay's books says, "I never knew what life meant until I saw it in your eyes." Love brought life (*The Gospel of John*, vol. 2). Love brought people to life. Some people find joy and life in the beauty of creation around them. Others find it in works of art, in music or in their flower garden. Then there are many who find the deepest meaning of life in the birth of their children and in raising them.

To those who worked and walked with Jesus, He was the one who made their lives worthwhile. He was the beauty and joy of life to them; He was the beginning and end in their lives. He was the way and the motivation to live; the light and perfection of life. Real life began for James and John, for Peter and Andrew when Jesus came to them where they were fishing and called them to follow Him.

> Life's like a play: it's not the length, but the excellence of the acting that matters.
> SENECA

Life starts for many people the minute they say yes to Jesus. Suddenly there is joy where there used to be sorrow. All of a sudden there is hope where there used to be despair. A new future beckons, where feelings of guilt reigned before. Discover your life in Christ and you will discover that life really is worth living. Make Jesus the center, the power, the pivot around which your entire existence revolves, and spiritually, you will suddenly start moving. Allow Him to be your captain and commander, and you will start to live life like never before.

Thank You, Lord and Master, that You called me to real life. It is truly a life worth living.

The Road to the Father

"No one can come to the Father except through Me" (John 14:6).

If you know what it feels like to lose your ticket for an important event or journey, you will know how embarrassing it is to explain what happened; and to ask to be allowed access because you did in fact pay for it. You will also know how frustrating it can be if the person in control will not under any circumstances give you permission without your ticket. But if someone you know arrives on the scene, and has the authority to tell the person to help you, you will probably think, "This is my lucky day!"

Christ is your "ticket" to the eternal and holy presence of the Father. Do you know Him as your "in"? There is, however, much more to what Jesus says in this verse. Jesus was emphasizing how He and the Father are one. They know and enjoy complete fellowship and unity with each other. For this reason, those who know Jesus and are given right of admission by Him, also have access to God the Father.

> The Son of God, in the form of Jesus Christ, hung on that cross at Calvary in all that shame and agony just for the joy of greeting you in heaven.
> BOB WELLS

Jesus' pronouncement raised many questions. But in fact everything is straightforward and easy to understand. It simply means, "Get to know Jesus. Stay with Jesus and always be "in" Jesus, as Paul puts it. As long as you have fellowship with Him, you will also have fellowship with the Father. Don't look for inferior ways to find God. You find Him in Jesus and in Jesus only. So make Jesus your road to follow, acknowledge Him as the highest truth of the world and of life. Look for nothing bigger and more glorious than the life you find in Him, and He will lead you to the Father.

I come to You, Lord Jesus, and to the Father, now and always.

Like Father, Like Son

"If you had really known Me, then you would know who My Father is. From now on, you do know Him and have seen Him!" (John 14:7).

Sometimes, as a child grows, they will be the spitting image of one of their parents, so much so that people will comment on it. The child will have the same color eyes and hair, the same build, voice and possibly also the same hairstyle. A boy who looks just like his father might even grow a moustache that looks just like his dad's.

One of the objectives of Christ coming to the earth was to reveal to people what the mystical and unknown God actually looked like and how He acted. Prophets learnt from God and passed His messages on to the people. The commandments gave people an idea of how God expected them to live. But His own Son was necessary to reveal what and who He really was. In addition, by living and working with Jesus, His disciples entered into a relationship, not only with the Son, but also the Father. Before Jesus came, they didn't really know God as their Father. Jesus brought this truth home to the people in a whole new way.

> Remember, Christ was not a deified man, neither was He a humanized God. He was perfectly God and at the same time perfectly human.
> CHARLES H. SPURGEON

Don't speculate about God's nature in a lighthearted way. Don't accept what every Tom, Dick and Harry tells you about Him. Think only of Jesus. Get to know Him intimately. Hear God's words in Jesus' teachings. Note the way in which God loves through Jesus' deeds and actions. Accept His love in your heart and you will draw as close to God as you possibly can.

Thank You, Lord Jesus, for the picture of God You revealed to me.

It Really Happened

"From now on, you do know Him and have seen Him!" (John 14:7).

It is amazing to actually experience history and remember it as such. How we all held our breath to catch every word when the first man landed on the moon forty years ago. Up until then, this was something most people regarded as impossible, or at the least, highly unlikely. Afterwards we knew that we were living in a new era.

In Christ's time people had already for a long time been talking about the vague possibility that God would send a Messiah to this world. And then, out of the blue, it happened. He was *there*, flesh of their flesh and bone of their bone, walking among them. They were so used to thinking that it was going to happen somewhere in the future, that when it happened it was difficult to convince them that He had actually materialized. God had really come and Jesus Himself was the great event. Ordinary fishermen and the working class saw Him face to face, spoke to Him, ate, walked and prayed with Him.

> He became what we are so that He might make us what He is.
> ST. ATHANASIUS

This changed the entire concept of life, of themselves, of God, of love, of faith and of history. And it took place right in front of their eyes. Just as God drew nearer to those first disciples through Jesus Christ, He draws close to you today. It was not only a one-time occurrence, limited to the people who lived during that period in time. It is an ongoing occurrence. And you and I have the privilege of seeing to it that others also experience it.

Holy Jesus, help me never to stop seeing and knowing You.

Show Us the Father!

Philip said, "Lord, show us the Father, and we will be satisfied" (John 14:8).

⟨ つ◠ ⟩

The Christian faith, to some people, is something that shows you how to live. To others it is a way of understanding the universe. Faith can be regarded as part of a person's culture and heritage, to be preserved at all costs. There are also those that believe it lays down the laws to maintain civilization and ensure its survival.

Philip, one of Jesus' disciples, asked the simple yet astonishing question, "Lord, show us the Father, and we will be satisfied." This request touches the heart and essence of all true religion. The religious life, that is to say, faith, is about God. It gives expression to the deep-felt need of humans to have fellowship with God. To Christians this does not refer to just any idol, but to the one Paul names as "the God and Father of our Lord Jesus Christ." Philip spoke on behalf of all believers in Jesus Christ and everybody who seeks to be believers.

> The love of God is like the Amazon River flowing down to water one daisy.
> ANONYMOUS

Every time you open your Bible to read it, ask the same question that Philip did: "Lord, show me the Father!" When you take part in communal worship with other believers, use this verse as a prayer before the service. Pray for those leading the worship; that they will be reminded of the main purpose of worship: to reveal the Father. To meet God is the core of any activity concerning the Christian faith. Christianity is far more than merely a friendly gathering. It is much more than healthy teaching or prescribing good behavior. It is a group of people who knows the Father and shows Him to the world.

Father God, enable Your children to show the Father to the world.

Quick on the Uptake?

Jesus replied, "Have I been with you all this time, Philip, and yet you still don't know who I am?" (John 14:9).

Do you remember how some kids at school were always the first to put up their hands when the teacher asked a question? It was like they knew the lesson before the teacher had even discussed it. Others just never caught on. Many situations in life are the same.

When the disciples began to follow Jesus, they started attending a completely new school – to learn about Christ and spiritual things. There was so much to learn. They had to learn who Christ was and the purpose of His mission. Thus their experiences in life became a learning curve. Sometimes they understood what Jesus taught them, but often they misunderstood Him or didn't understand at all.

> Grow in the grace and knowledge of our Lord and Savior Jesus Christ.
>
> 2 PETER 3:18

In this verse we see that Philip was slow to understand. Jesus showed them the Father in His doctrines, teachings, healings and caring for no less than three years. The Father could be evidenced in everything Jesus said and did. Philip saw all this, but didn't immediately understand.

Don't be too hard on Philip. You and I might also be slow to understand, and even slower to react to the things God did for us through Jesus Christ. We might understand some things, but not others. There are also mysteries we have not yet encountered that await us; things the Master wants us to know. We should always be aware of our need to learn more, to grow and mature in spiritual matters. So, always be ready when Jesus is trying to get through to you, when He is trying to tell you something in some other way.

Lord Jesus, make me sensitive to spiritual truths.

The God We Can See

"Anyone who has seen Me has seen the Father" (John 14:9).

༼༦༽

There are many kinds of gods in the world. The ancient people worshiped idols made of wood or metal. They could see their idols. The Hebrews knew that Moses saw God from behind, but that no one had actually seen His face. To this day people worship false gods – health, science, money, pleasure and power are the most common.

The invisible God became visible in Jesus Christ. Christ was the human face of God that millions of people yearned to see. He was not a ghost or a spirit. He was not an animal or some or other part of a physical creation that was worshiped by some nations. He was a human being, *the* human being. He was just like any other human: born into a human family; had a human occupation; struggled to make a living; learnt the lessons of life; experienced human pressure and stress; had to provide for Himself; suffered; and in the end, died as a human being.

> Anything that one imagines of God apart from Jesus Christ is only useless thinking and vain idolatry.
> MARTIN LUTHER

Not all gods are the same. Different religions may have similar characteristics, but those who don't define God by acknowledging that He revealed Himself to us in Jesus Christ, are not true Christians. It is easy to accept a substitute for God or to worship an entity claiming to be the true God. Political leaders like to think of themselves as gods. But don't be deceived. Stay with Christ and the true God He reveals to us. Then you can never be misdirected!

Holy Father, help me to always focus on Jesus, so that I may get to know You.

Revealed through the Son

"Don't you believe that I am in the Father and the Father is in Me?" (John 14:10).

When two people work together for a long time, they get to know each other very well. One knows how the other acts, and responds perfectly. One knows how the other thinks, and acts accordingly. Marriage partners, siblings, and sometimes twins, build a special relationship in this way.

Did Jesus learn the art of carpentry so well in His father's carpenter shop that He drew a parallel between this and His relationship with His heavenly Father? We certainly see in Jesus the glory of the Father coming to earth in human form. Put differently: God's glory became "domesticated." But we also clearly see the love of God the Father for the human race at work in Jesus Christ. We can believe that God loves us just like Jesus loved people, and the other way round. We see the love of God demonstrated in the love of Jesus.

> God is best known in Jesus Christ; the sun is not seen but by the light of the sun.
>
> WILLIAM BRIDGE

The way that Jesus loved people was much purer than any human form of love. It was love that asked no reward – only mutual love! This is because Christ's love comes from the Father's heart, flowing abundantly to you and me. The strong bond between the Father and the Son meant that they were of one mind.

Jesus sincerely desires a similar spiritual oneness between Him and us. He wants us to know about His glory and His desire is for us to share in it. He longs for us to share in His love and to go and spread that love in the world that needs it so badly.

Holy Master, live Your life also in me.

Words and Works

"The words I speak are not My own, but My Father who lives in Me does His work through Me" (John 14:10).

Sometimes an actor in a play, or a movie star, will portray a character so precisely and realistically that the viewers begin to feel it is the real person. But the words were written by the playwright or scriptwriter, so we should in fact say, for example, "The voice is that of Lawrence Olivier, but the words and the work are those of Shakespeare."

In Jesus' early ministry, He was the personification of the Word or message of God. He wasn't merely playing a role He was given. He was God Himself, speaking in the flesh. What He said and did was God speaking and acting in and through Him. And when He spoke through Jesus, God was busy doing His work: bringing light, truth, hope, salvation and eternal life to the people of this world. Jesus was so totally one with the Father that He knew exactly what to say, how to say it and to whom.

> Although Christ was God, He took flesh; and having been made man, He remained what He was, God.
>
> ORIGEN ADAMANTIUS

Jesus' words have been preserved for us in the Bible. By reading and believing them, we are entrusting ourselves to God's spoken word, so that eternal life is made possible like in Jesus' time. Just as God lived in Jesus, He lives in each of us today if we are "in" Christ and Christ is "in" us. God does this work in us while He shapes Christ in us, whether we are aware of it or not. For this reason, keeping ourselves occupied with the Bible and with Jesus' words is of the utmost importance in everyone's lives.

Eternal God, speak through me and work in me and through me today and every day.

Two Kinds of Faith

"Just believe that I am in the Father and the Father is in Me. Or at least believe because of the work you have seen Me do" (John 14:11).

People travel different roads to find faith in God. Some have a dramatic experience with Him and never doubt Him again. Others struggle with conflicting and perplexing ideas that they finally resolve. There are those that live a promiscuous and ungodly life, and only when they are on the verge of despair, do they seek a better road and find it in Christ.

Jesus here speaks of two ways in which we can come to faith in Him: to see Him as He is or to get to know Him in all His fullness. In the first way, the person takes Jesus at His word, acknowledges Him as God in human form, and responds in love and surrenders. It can be called "intuitive faith," where people meet Christ in a deeply religious experience that fills their whole life with meaning, purpose and direction.

> Christ is the only way to God, but there are as many ways to Christ as there are people who come to Him.
>
> Os Guinness

In the second way, the person reasons things out. On this road to faith, the person says, "I see the world and it looks wonderful. It must have a Creator. I read about this remarkable man who healed the sick and died a brutal death on a cross. He must have loved us very much. I see the impact He has on many lives where He reveals miraculous grace. I will now walk this road myself."

Whichever route you choose to faith, just make very sure that you know Jesus Christ as your Friend; that you worship Him and serve Him as your Lord and Savior.

Holy Spirit of God, help me to know Jesus personally in His fullness, omnipotence and glory.

Do What Jesus Did

"I tell you the truth, anyone who believes in Me will do the same works I have done" (John 14:12).

Most of us have a hobby, something we enjoy a lot. We wish we had the time and talent to become an expert in it. When we have the opportunity of seeing a true expert in action we really wish we could do it just as easily. They either inspire us to do better, or drive us to despair.

Jesus displayed the works of God to His disciples both by what He said and what He did. The whole time He was busy preparing them for the day when He would leave them and they would have to continue the mission He started. He knew they would have to take the gospel He gave them out into the world and proclaim it to all people. He also knew that they would be inclined to ask, "Who? Me? Never!" So He began building up their faith in Him, making them an astonishing promise: He told them that they would also do mighty things.

> God does not begin by asking us about our ability, but only about our availability, and if we then prove our dependability, He will increase our capability!
>
> Neil A. Maxwell

There is no doubt that God can do great deeds through anyone who really trusts in Him and who believes God is waiting to use them. John Wesley, William Booth, Gladys Aylward and John White of Mashonaland, Angus Buchan from KwaZulu-Natal, were all born perfectly ordinary people, but they knew God intimately. They knew that He not only called them, but also equipped them to do extraordinary things through Him.

Christ also wants to do great things through you and me, plain and ordinary as we are. Are you ready to make yourself available to Him?

Use me, Lord, as and where You choose to do so.

Even Greater Works

"Anyone who believes in Me will do the same works I have done, and even greater works, because I am going to be with the Father" (*John 14:12*).

Some people like getting involved in conversations where they can tell a story to top all the others. Someone complains that the price of butter has gone up considerably, say by 11%. Then the following person says, "That's nothing. I bought a bottle of lemonade and the price had gone up by 15%." And so the percentage goes up with every contribution to the conversation. To do better things, to be bigger, to own something bigger is the crux of the type of competition most of us yearn for.

> To give real service, you must add something which cannot be bought or measured with money, and that is sincerity and integrity.
> DONALD A. ADAMS

At first the idea that Christ's disciples would do even greater things than their Master was seen as ridiculous. But Jesus performed only a few healings in a limited area among a small group of people. In His lifetime, His words were only heard by a few people who were in the vicinity at the time. The disciples were to go to the ends of the earth. They were to pass on Jesus' words to millions and millions of people. They were to provide the inspiration for extensive works of healing and grace by establishing hospitals all over the world. All this would happen because He was "going to be with the Father."

You are part of a Christian community whose task it is to do today the same things Jesus did, only bigger. However, you don't do these things in your own strength or know-how: Jesus does it in and through you. Are you willing to make yourself available?

Holy Master, enlarge my capacity to do Your mighty deeds.

Ask in Jesus' Name

"You can ask for anything in My name, and I will do it, so that the Son can bring glory to the Father" (John 14:13).

You are perfectly normal if you find prayer difficult. If you also feel that God doesn't often give you what you ask for, and that because of this your prayers have failed, then you are in good company. Maybe you also hear other believers talking about the wonderful answers to their prayers, and that just adds to your feeling of failure.

When Jesus spoke about prayer in the Upper Room, He didn't think about this the way we often do. We think: *How can I twist God's arm to get what I want from Him?* When Jesus told His disciples that they would do even greater things than He, He was thinking of the powerful and rapid spread of the gospel that would be achieved through their work. This kind of missionary effort often includes miracles of healing and conversion. The continuation of His work by His followers brought honor and glory to the Father by proclaiming His Son as the Savior and Redeemer of this world. They were to pray in His name for these mighty acts to take place so that God could be glorified.

> Live your beliefs and you can turn the world around.
> HENRY DAVID THOREAU

Try to extend your prayer requests beyond what makes you or your family happy or comfortable. Broaden your prayers to include the entire Christian mission all over the world. Pray that the church will strive to glorify God and not only to enlarge its own authority and influence. Pray for missionaries in the most dangerous parts of evangelical outreach. Try to formulate your prayers around matters that truly bring the Father honor and glory.

Lord Jesus, let my prayers and life honor and glorify God through Your good Spirit.

A Matter of Love

"Yes, ask Me for anything in My name, and I will do it!" (John 14:14).

Billy Graham said on occasion, "The only time my prayers are never answered is on the golf course." Older translations of our Scripture for today led to the misconception that we could ask for absolutely anything we wanted (for example, a million dollars), on condition that we include in our prayer, "I ask this in Christ's name." Then our request would be granted.

On the face of it, it seemed that Jesus made prayer a blank check. What He said, however, was in the context of the crucifixion and resurrection, bringing honor and glory to God the Father and Son. He also said it was a follow-up to everything He said about our oneness with God. As a result of His complete unity with God the Father, Jesus prayed with an attitude of obedience and perfect love – like in Gethsemane.

> The first rule of right prayer is that we be disposed in mind and heart as befits those who enter conversation with God.
> JOHN CALVIN

Thus we should interpret what Jesus is saying here as: "If you live in perfect unity and love with Me and God the Father – in the same kind of oneness that I live with Him – you will ask only what is in perfect harmony with the Father's will. Then I will work in and through you in a way that glorifies God in His positive answer to prayer."

Persevere in prayer, no matter how inferior you might feel about them. Try to draw near to God in your prayer time, so that your love for Him may grow. Make an effort to discover His will for your life and bring your prayers in line with God's will. This is what real prayer is made of.

Lord Jesus, help me to pray with love and an increasing knowledge of You and the Father.

Proof of Love

"If you love Me, obey My commandments" (John 14:15).

～ ⬡ ～

Often one person in an ordinary relationship will take advantage of another's love to his or her own benefit: "If you love me, you will give me what I want." This is the ploy many people use to make the other person satisfy their selfish demands.

This is not what Jesus said when He made love the focal point of His disciples' relationship with Him. He said that love, and not obedience to laws and rules, should be their motivation to obey Him gladly and joyfully.

Julian of Norwich wrote: "The great honor we can give to Almighty God, greater than all our sacrifices and mortifications, is to live gladly, joyfully, because of the knowledge of His love." Wouldn't it be glorious if we could do that? Jesus would like us to.

> Love is an act of faith, and whoever is of little faith is also of little love.
>
> ERICH FROMM

Walk close to Jesus in your daily tasks and duties. Even if you are under severe pressure, set aside at least a few minutes for fellowship with Him. Find ways to show your love for Him, both in what you say and in what you do. Reflect on His love and let your love for Him thrive and grow in obedience that follows readily and joyfully.

Thank You, Holy Jesus, that I obey You because I love You.

The Promise of Help

"I will ask the Father, and He will give you another Advocate, who will never leave you. He is the Holy Spirit, who leads into all truth" (John 14:16-17).

Most of us need outside help at some stage in our lives. When pain pills won't bring relief from pain, we call in the doctor. We do this on a daily basis: we call in the help of electricians, plumbers, motor mechanics and many others.

We also need help from outside in our spiritual life. We try to love God, but don't always find it easy. We want to walk with God, but there are others who also want to walk with us, who is forcing Jesus into a less important position. We know we must live loving and caring lives, but we are often influenced by prejudice and cowardice. Our love for God cools and our faith in Him wilts easily. Is there anything we can do about it? Yes, we can try to stay in God's presence and consciously remember His promise that He will be with us always.

> The Holy Spirit is the secret of the power in my life. All I have to do is surrender my life to Him.
> KATHRYN KUHLMAN

Jesus knows our weakness and He sees our struggles. He loves us despite all our failures. He knows about both the reality and inadequacy of our love. And because of His love for us, He asked the Father to send us the Holy Spirit. The Spirit's role is to become the power of God inside us: our inner spiritual helper.

You are not alone. Christ promised to always be with you. He offers you the Holy Spirit who will be at work in you. He will strengthen your love for Christ and stimulate your spiritual development in such a way that Christ takes shape in you.

Father God, thank You for the Great Helper, the Holy Spirit, who is at work in me.

The Spirit of Truth

"I will ask the Father, and He will give you another Advocate, who will never leave you. He is the Holy Spirit, who leads into all truth" (John 14:16-17).

We would all like to be strong, because strength is life. Other people admire us if we are strong. There are, of course, different forms of strength. Some people are physically strong, but intellectually weak. Others, who are physically weak, have great emotional strength. Jesus, who spoke these words to His disciples in the Upper Room, knew that they would need strength – more than they could ever draw from their own resources. For this reason He promised them another Advocate that would be with them when He left.

The word that is translated as "advocate" conveys the idea of power. Your advocate would argue a case in court more forcefully than you could ever hope. Jesus didn't promise them a shoulder to cry on, but Someone who would boost their strength, make them more powerful and bolder, and more effective in taking His message across the entire world.

> There is no human power that can replace the power of the Spirit.
> LEWI PETHRUS

He offers you the same Holy Spirit to make us braver and to empower us. In this dark world we mustn't take on the struggle alone. The Holy Spirit, sent by the Father and prayed for by Jesus, is right beside us, encouraging and strengthening us. We needn't be crushed by the negative forces posted against us. Accept and live in the power God supplies you with.

Lord Jesus, live in me and make me strong from the inside.

Be Joyful

"I have told you these things so that you will be filled with My joy. Yes, your joy will overflow!" (John 15:11).

The central idea of this portion from Scripture is that Jesus tells His disciples that they are not the ones who chose Him, but that He is the one who chose them. We didn't choose God either, but God, in His infinite grace, chose us by making us an offer borne out of His love.

The importance of this verse lies in the fact that we can use it to make a list of things we have been chosen and called for. In the first instance, we are chosen to be joyful. No matter how steep and difficult Christ's road might be, both in its journey and purpose, it will always be a joyful road. There is always joy in knowing that you are doing the right thing. If we have sidestepped some duty or another, and then go back and do what had to be done, we experience special joy.

> To be simply ensconced in God is true joy.
> C. C. COLTON

Christians are cheerful people who live by the words in Philippians 4:4: "Always be full of joy in the Lord. I say it again – rejoice!" A heavy-hearted Christian is a contradiction and nothing in the entire history of Christianity has done more harm than the negative connotations of black clothes and long faces. It is true that Christians are sinners, but they are saved sinners – it is in this that the secret of their joy lies. How is it possible to be unhappy if you walk the road of life with Christ?

I praise and thank You, Lord Jesus, that You brought joy into my life.

Love Each Other

"My command is this: Love each other as I have loved you. Greater love has no one than this, that he lay down his life for his friends" (John 15:12-13 NIV).

We have been chosen by Jesus to love each other. We are sent into the world to show love to others. Sometimes it looks more like we have been sent into this world to compete with one another, to argue; yes, even to pick a fight with others.

But in truth Christians are sent into the world to live in such a way that they will demonstrate what is meant by love for each other. That's why John says, "Dear friends, let us continue to love one another, for love comes from God. Anyone who loves is a child of God and knows God" (1 John 4:7).

Jesus expects something significant from us with this command. One of the things we always instinctively ask when someone makes a serious demand is: What right do they have to ask it? If we were to ask Jesus, "What right do You have to demand that we love each other?" then His answer would be, "Greater love has no one than this, that he lay down his life for his friends." And this is precisely what Jesus did.

> The love of God and the God of love constrain you to love one another that it may at last be said of Christians as it was at first, "Behold how they love one another."
>
> RALPH VENNING

There are many people who proclaim from pulpits that we must love one another, while their own lives demonstrate nothing of the sort. But Jesus gave us a command that He first applied in His own life. Always measure your love against the love of Christ and ask the Holy Spirit to help you grow in love.

Holy Spirit of God, keep me from showing a lack of love towards my fellow humans.

Friends of Jesus

"You are My friends if you do what I command" (John 15:14).

⸎

Jesus calls us to be His friends. He says to His disciples, "I no longer call you slaves, because a master doesn't confide in His slaves. Now you are my friends, since I have told you everything the Father told Me" (John 15:15). They are no longer slaves *(doulos),* but friends. The title *doulos,* or slave of God, was not a mark of disgrace or shame; it was a title of the highest honor.

Moses was the *doulos:* the servant; the slave of God (see Deut. 34:5). And so were Joshua (see Josh. 24:29) and David (see Ps. 89:20). Paul regarded it as an honorary title (see Titus 1:1), and so did James (see James 1:1). The greatest men of the past were proud to be called *doulos* of God. Now Jesus says to them: "I have something more precious for you; you are no longer slaves, you are friends." This offer of Jesus is a blessing that not even the greatest men of Scripture knew before Jesus came to the world. With this, He offers an intimacy with God that was impossible before He came.

> True friendship is seen through the heart, not through the eyes.
> ANONYMOUS

Being a friend of God has an important history. Abraham was a friend of God (see Isa. 41:8). Christ calls us His friends and God's friends, an immense offer. This means that we don't have to yearn for God from a distance; we are not slaves who have no right to appear before their owners. Jesus did an amazing thing: He made intimacy with God possible for us, so that God is no longer a distant stranger, but a Friend. All of this came about because Jesus is our Friend.

Thank You, Jesus, that I could become a friend of God because of You.

Find Your Peace in Christ

He was despised and rejected – a Man of Sorrows, acquainted with deepest grief. We turned our backs on Him and looked the other way. He was despised, and we did not care (Isa. 53:3).

The story of Judas' betrayal, Jesus being captured, His suffering and the rejection of His own people, is undoubtedly one of the saddest events of all time. In spite of the fact that people rejected Him, Christ's love was so strong that He accepted death of His own free will to being about salvation for you and me.

Jesus rose triumphantly from the grave so that we could have the promise of eternal life. To convince us of the depth of His love, Christ forgave Simon Peter who denied Him, and entrusted God's flock to him. God made sure that we would be equipped with His power by giving us His Holy Spirit.

> If God be our God, He will give us peace in trouble. When there is a storm without, He will make peace within. The world can create trouble in peace, but God can create peace in trouble.
>
> Thomas Watson

There are occasions in the life of every Christian, that you turn your back on Jesus. Every time you fail to do a good deed; when you show signs of anger and a lack of love; when you are worried you will become unpopular and then keep quiet instead of standing up for what is right, you turn your face away from Jesus. Just like the people of Jerusalem when Jesus needed them most. It is not too late to turn back to Jesus. Do it right now and you will find perfect peace again.

Forgive me, dear Savior, for every time I turned away from You. Thank You that You always take me back again – just like I am.

September

The True Vine

"Remain in Me, and I will remain in you. For a
branch cannot produce fruit if it is severed from the vine,
and you cannot be fruitful unless you remain in Me."
~ John 15:4

There is not an inch of any sphere of life over
which Jesus Christ does not say, "Mine."
~ ABRAHAM KUYPER

Lord Jesus, we worship You as our Honorable King.
To many it would seem absolutely impossible to think that
You were born in a stable to poor and simple parents;
You taught the uneducated, using parables and stories;
You walked to work and slept under the stars;
You lived among the despised and the outcasts,
and mingled with them;
You used saliva to make the blind see;
and a soft word from You made the deaf hear.
You brought the dead back to life by words
You spoke with authority!
Your life was filled with people that kings did not approve of.
You blessed the poor and chastised the rich.
You tolerated no compromise – You refused kingdoms,
crowns and scepters!
Yet You are the Eternal King, and the heavenly beings call out
as they worship You, "Holy! Holy! Holy!"
Lord, Jesus of Golgotha, teach us in Your spiritual school:
that we must be servants here to reign with You one day;
that we must be humiliated before
we can rise to greater heights.
God Himself gave You the name above all names – and in Your
name every knee will bow and every tongue will confess:
Christ is the King! All this to the glory of God the Father.
We bow down before You, King Jesus, we pay homage to You,
worship You and sing songs of praise.
All the honor and glory are due to You,
Savior, Redeemer, King! Now and forever!

Amen.

The True Vine

"I am the true grapevine, and My Father is the gardener" (John 15:1).

In the Old Testament the image of Israel is repeated as a vineyard or vine. Isaiah describes the big picture of Israel as God's vineyard: "The nation of Israel is the vineyard of the LORD of Heaven's Armies. They are the vineyard of the LORD. The people of Judah are His pleasant garden" (Isa. 5:7). God's message comes through Jeremiah with the words: "I was the One who planted you, choosing a vine of the purest stock – the very best" (Jer. 2:21). Ezekiel compares Israel to a useless vine, and we find another comparison in Ezekiel 19:10: "Your mother was like a vine planted by the water's edge."

Hosea described Israel as being prosperous, like a lush vineyard laden with fruit. The psalmist sings in Psalm 80:8: "You brought us from Egypt like a grapevine; You drove away the pagan nations and transplanted us into Your land." Hosea was thinking of how God delivered the Jews from Egypt. It was often said that the vine became the symbol of the nation of Israel.

> Christ is not valued at all unless He is valued above all.
> ST. AUGUSTINE

Jesus calls Himself the "true vine." It is strange to note that the symbol of the vine is never used in the Old Testament except to warn of Israel's iniquity. Israel thought that because they were Jews, God's chosen people, they were part of the true vine. But it is not the nation that is the true vine; it is Christ. You are not saved because you are a Jew, but only if you have an intimate relationship with Christ. Only Jesus can put our relationship with God right.

Grant, Lord Jesus, that I will be joined inseparably to You, the true vine.

Always with Us

"He will give you another Advocate, who will never leave you. He is the Holy Spirit, who leads into all truth" (John 14:16-17).

The movie *Far from the Madding Crowd* ends with a touching scene. After we have seen the heroine go through a number of disappointments, she suggests that she and the hero should get together again. He replies, "That's fine with me. As long as you're there every time I look up, I'll be there every time you look up." We all need someone who will always be there every time we look up!

God is always there! He was with Abraham, Jacob and Moses during the bad times of their spiritual struggle, and at other times as well. Aware of the fact that His personal presence would be withdrawn, Jesus promised His followers that the Holy Spirit would always be with them.

> When led of the Spirit, the child of God must be as ready to wait as to go, as prepared to be silent as to speak.
>
> LEWIS SPERRY CHAFER

Up to this day that promise holds good for you and me. Whether we are new Christians or have been disciples for years, He is always with us. Whether we are in Africa, the Pacific Islands, Europe or the ice fields of Canada, God's Holy Spirit is with us. Whether we are young and enthusiastic and life is exciting; or old and tired; clever or not so clever; strong or weak – the Holy Spirit is always there for us!

Holy God, thank You that You are always there for me through Your Spirit.

The Truth about God

"He is the Holy Spirit, who leads into all truth" (John 14:17).

There are two important aspects of the truth. We can call the first one "objective facts," for example an event that really took place. The other one is the way a person sees, understands and interprets what is going on, or what took place. This second aspect of the truth not only includes physical perception, but insight, wisdom and understanding.

Jesus' disciples saw how He lived and died. These were the objective facts, but what did they make of these facts? How did they understand them? And what effect did they have on their faith and testimony? The Holy Spirit that Jesus promised would switch on their inner understanding and give them insight into what God was doing in and through Jesus, and therefore also what He wanted to do in and through them. These insights would

> The Holy Ghost has called me by the gospel, and illuminated me with His gifts, and sanctified and preserved me in the true faith.
> **Martin Luther**

enable them to know exactly who God was, how He acted and worked. The Holy Spirit would also activate the virtues of love, joy, peace, goodness and self-control in them.

We will never know the truth about God if we rely on our own limited efforts. Every time we understand something more about God, it is the Holy Spirit working in us, making us aware of Jesus, while leading us into deeper fellowship with Him. Pray that God reveals more and more of Himself to you through the Holy Spirit so that your walk with Christ will be more fruitful.

Holy Father God, fill me with the insight and wisdom of the Holy Spirit.

Those Who Refuse to See

"The world cannot receive Him, because it isn't looking for Him and doesn't recognize Him"(John 14:17).

～◯⌒～

During the Communist domination of Russia, it was said of the president that he knew the Bible from Genesis through Revelation. But he wasn't a Christian believer. Under him the persecution of Christian churches carried on. In spite of his intellectual capacity and "head-knowledge," this wisdom never penetrated his heart and he never got to know Jesus.

This is why many people are good, friendly and peace-loving, and yet they don't believe in Jesus Christ and they don't feel the need for His power and presence in their lives. Their spiritual eyes have never opened to the truth of Jesus Christ; their hearts have never been warmed by His love, and Jesus' presence is entirely absent in their way of life.

> The Holy Spirit's great task is to carry on the work for which Jesus sacrificed His throne and His life – the redemption of fallen humanity.
> ALAN REDPATH

If they would only acknowledge Him as the Son of God, accept Him as their Lord and Savior, and seek to love and serve Him, their faith would grow considerably.

We need to know that it is the presence or absence of the Holy Spirit that determines whether people become disciples. His presence awakens faith and leads to Christian maturity. Make very sure that the Spirit is at work in you and that He continues providing you with the fullness of Christ.

Savior and Redeemer, let Your Spirit build Your image in me.

Knowing the Spirit

"But you know Him, for He lives with you and will be in you"
(John 14:17 NIV).

⌒ ᴐᗕ ⌒

When a new invention or discovery appears on the scene, some people welcome it and sing its praises. Others wait a while to see if it isn't just a passing gimmick. Yet others refuse to have anything to do with it.

When Jesus called His disciples to follow Him, He was starting a process in which He would expose them to something new that God had brought into the world – Himself! As He gradually began occupying a larger part of their lives, the Holy Spirit who was alive and working through them, also started touching their lives. While some of them responded to Him quickly, and others more slowly, they felt the influence of the Holy Spirit more and more. Jesus' impact on them meant that the Spirit had taken possession of them in a special, creative and dynamic way. He would still make His presence

> A church in the land without the Spirit is rather a curse than a blessing.
> CHARLES H. SPURGEON

known in a powerful and dramatic way, bursting forth in all His glory at Pentecost. But the Spirit was not born at Pentecost. He was already busy in and through them at the time of Jesus' ministry on earth.

Allow the Holy Spirit to be with you. He usually works in and through the community life of Christian believers; so allow Him to build your relationships with His other disciples in your community. Make sure that He also works in you by helping you to live in Christ. Always remember, where the Spirit is present, there is true Christian fellowship.

Help me, Lord Jesus, to promote true Christian fellowship to Your honor.

The Promise of Hope

"No, I will not abandon you as orphans – I will come to you"
(John 14:18).

There is something terribly painful about losing a parent, even if the person was elderly and forgetful. When a second parent dies, the child's small world of comfort and security that they grew up in is something of the past. Often students who finish their course and leave college feel the same when they say goodbye to lecturers they got to know well.

Jesus knew that this was precisely what His disciples would experience at His death. Without Him they would feel lost, like orphaned children. He knew they would be heartbroken. But He would come back again; back from the dead to comfort them and inspire them to accomplish their mission. Tragedy would change to triumph. They would not despair any longer. Their night would be changed into a bright day. The miracle of His resurrection would change their whole world. And Jesus would be with them again.

> Nature is too thin a screen; the glory of the omnipresent God bursts through everywhere.
> RALPH WALDO EMERSON

If you feel lonely, or if despair makes you feel that life is pointless, or if painful experiences have made you a broken person, think about this promise the Master made. It comes from Jesus Himself. It is as true for you as it ever was for those first disciples. It often seems that the world is without God and one can easily feel rejected. Don't give in to these feelings. There is a greater Presence, whether you sense it or not. He is with you today, tomorrow and every day of your life. He will hold you tight through all tragedy and trauma that might still await you.

Stay with me, Lord Jesus, as I approach the future.

To See and Believe

"Soon the world will no longer see Me, but you will see Me. Since I live, you also will live" (John 14:19).

～◯◯～

We often say, "Seeing is believing!" When someone makes a promise we don't think will be kept, we say, "I'll believe it when I see it!" But then it also sometimes happens that the sincerity of the person making the promise is enough to convince us. Then we say, "Frank saw it happen and he doesn't talk just for the sake of talking." We believe the facts on the grounds of Frank's credibility.

In this conversation in the Upper Room before His crucifixion, the Lord turned everything upside down. He was saying, "Seeing is believing." Within a few hours He would be taken from them by death – everyone would see it happen in public. Then He would be raised from the dead, but the soldiers wouldn't see Him; Pontius Pilate wouldn't see Him; the priests and the crowds of Jerusalem wouldn't see Him. But those with the faith to know Him and recognize Him would see Him. Mary would see Him and Peter would see Him. And even Thomas would see him, temporary doubts and all.

> Destiny is not a matter of chance, it is a matter of choice. It is not a thing to be waited for, it is a thing to be achieved.
> WILLIAM J. BRYAN

The truth of God – and Jesus is God's truth – is revealed to those who believe in Him. Those who don't believe are not given the opportunity and this just reconfirms their unbelief. Place your complete trust in Jesus and you will see more and more of God. You will be filled with more and more of His love. You will be increasingly strengthened by His presence and empowered by His Spirit.

I believe, Lord Jesus. Help me to see and understand.

Life before Death

*"You will see Me. Because I live, you also will live" (John 14:19
NIV).*

A group of young people were on a flight from Europe to
South Africa. They were chatting about the country they
had just visited. One young man gave his opinion at the top of
his voice: "Good grief! They haven't got a life. They merely exist!" Everyone who heard him laughed loudly and confirmed
his opinion. We have different opinions about what exactly having a "life" is. Is it a life of pleasure, to get rich or to make your
influence felt? For millions it is simply having enough food every day to keep them alive.

The Jewish religion was interwoven with the law: the Torah.
According to Deuteronomy, the law
would give life. It succeeded in co-
ordinating the relationships in the
nation's community and this led to a
better life. But it was not enough for
the fullness of life Jesus had come to
give – He called it eternal life. When
He came, He knew that life would be
experienced in a relationship with Him. But there was more: By
dying and rising again, Jesus came to extend the meaning and
duration of life. Then and now, living in a relationship with Him
meant understanding His resurrection. Many people at the time
asked what many still ask to this day: "Is there life after death?"
The answer is, "In Christ there is life before and after death!"

> Life is not a holiday,
> but an education. And
> the one eternal lesson
> for us all is how better
> we can love.
> HENRY DRUMMOND

If you live *in* and *with* Christ it won't be necessary to ask if
there is life after death. It is just a continuation and fulfillment of
the life before death.

*Lord Jesus, give me the assurance in my heart that I will live
with You forever.*

Then We Will Understand

"When I am raised to life again, you will know that I am in My Father, and you are in Me, and I am in you" (John 14:20).

～ ⌒ ～

Sometimes we simply cannot see our way through some difficult issue. After thinking about it a lot and considering the options, we decide to drop the matter and leave it unsolved. Then the moment comes when the light breaks through, and we can sigh with relief: "Now I understand."

Jesus knew that few of His disciples really understood the perfect oneness between Him and the Father. He also knew that He would die within the coming hours and then be brought back to life again. The day of His resurrection would be the opportunity that would open their eyes. They would see God's almightiness in a dramatic way, and the things that Jesus had said that were so vague to them at the time that they seemed to be spoken in darkness, would now shine like a bright light. They would see the truth of His claim

> The empty tomb of Christ has been the cradle of the church.
> PRESSENSE

that He was the Son of God and that They worked together in perfect harmony. The disciples would get to know God, and also Jesus, in a new way.

Let the truth of Christ's resurrection penetrate your understanding. Allow it to dominate your faith and determine your actions. Let it inspire your hope and awaken your imagination; let it give you nerves of steel and stir your love; let it broaden your horizons, motivate your plans and direct your footsteps. Let it be of paramount importance in your life and the final goal at your death.

Lord Jesus, fill me with a deep awareness of Your resurrection power.

At One with Jesus

"You will know that I am in My Father, and you are in Me, and I am in you" (John 14:20).

If you have ever watched a world class sports team train, you would have seen to what extent the players are in harmony with one another. They anticipate what their teammates are going to do, for example how a player is going to pass the ball, and then make sure they are in the right position to take it and run with it. They work together like the parts of a well-lubricated machine.

Jesus and the Father were in perfect harmony with each other and the resurrection would clearly reveal it. It would also strengthen the relationship between Jesus and His disciples. The Spirit was already at work among them and the resurrection would merely strengthen their faith and calling. Then Pentecost would bring the Holy Spirit in all His fullness and they would go out to do the work Jesus had done up to then. The Father, the Son, the Holy Spirit and the disciples would work together like a well-oiled machine!

> Be careful how you live: you might be the only Bible some person ever reads.
> WILLIAM J. TOMS

The main aim of the Christian disciple is always to become completely one with Jesus. He lives in us and we live in Him. We are filled with Jesus' thoughts and He controls and directs our every thought, movement and action. Don't think for one moment that this means we will never have problems, be under pressure or experience tension; but it does mean that we will be able to meet those problems in the power of Jesus. And because we overcome our problems, we will be spiritually stronger. Strive every day to become one with Jesus.

Holy Jesus, make me more and more like You.

Love and Obedience

"Those who accept My commandments and obey them are the ones who love Me" (John 14:21).

⟨∘⟩

There are different kinds of love. Sexual attraction is one of them. Mutual caring, responsibility and working hard to be part of a family is another. There is the love friends have for one another. Then there is also God's sacrificial, selfless and outgoing love.

Jesus expects this last kind of love from us. When He spoke the words of our Scripture verse today, He was moments away from the cross where He would sacrifice Himself for human beings. He knew that many of them would eventually sacrifice themselves for Him in exactly the same way – on condition that they were obedient to Him. When He calls us to live for Him, He also calls us to die for Him. This means to let go of our old selves and obey Him, even if that obedience means dying for Him. The obedience He demands is absolute obedience.

> God loved us; not because we are loveable but because He is love.
> C. S. LEWIS

Not all the types of love include obedience. Two people can have a relationship in which both are equals and the issue of obedience is never even mentioned. But being Jesus' friend means we accept Him as our Lord as well as our Friend. He gives the orders and we obey and fulfill them. We do it because we love Him deeply, and we love Him out of thankfulness for what He did for us. Never lose sight of His great love for you, because this is the foundation of your entire relationship with Him.

Loving Master, I want to love You more and more.

Receiving God's Love

"Those who accept My commandments and obey them are the ones who love Me. And because they love Me, My Father will love them. And I will love them and reveal Myself to each one of them" (John 14:21).

When a couple is planning to get married, you get people who raise the question of whether the man is marrying the bride only, or the bride's family as well. In some marriages, deep and advantageous relationships develop between the couple and the in-laws. Often, however, this ends in broken relationships in both families.

Jesus was speaking to His disciples in the Upper Room the night before the crucifixion, and He knew that their relationship with Him was not only crumbling, but that His Father was also involved in this. Jesus knew that while He loved them, the Father also loved them. Jesus knew that they also had to love the Father in order to love Him. He knew something they didn't: The Father would love them with a special kind of love because they loved Him.

> Nothing binds me to my Lord like a strong belief in His unchanging love.
> CHARLES H. SPURGEON

While God loves all of humankind in general, He also has His special love for those who love His Son. However, you can't earn this special love by doing good deeds and behaving yourself. This special love is given because of God's undeserved goodness. Those who love the Son are particularly open to receiving that special love.

Let your love for Christ deepen as the years go by. He will enlarge the capacity of your love for both God and other people. In the process He will reveal more and more of Himself to you.

God of Love, enlarge my capacity for loving and for being loved.

The Academic Question

Judas [not Judas Iscariot, but the other disciple with that name] said to Him, "Lord, why are You going to reveal Yourself only to us and not to the world at large?" (John 14:22).

⌒◌⌒

W hen it comes to issues about faith, we are overwhelmed by many questions: Why does God allow natural disasters like earthquakes and floods? Do all religions worship the same God? Is any religion better than the others? Many of the most difficult questions don't seem to be answered in the Bible.

The disciples were often confused by the things Jesus said and taught. Here, during the Last Supper in the Upper Room, Judas asked Jesus the question in our Scripture verse. It wouldn't make any sense for Jesus to reveal Himself to them only, the inner circle of His followers.

It would make much more sense to reveal Himself to the world. It would convince the world and make many people believe. But Jesus was not pre-pared to give a superficial answer to this particular problem.

> Believers who have most knowledge, are not therefore necessarily the most spiritual.
>
> JOHN NEWTON

The Bible does not give academic answers to academic questions that don't intensify people's faith, but in fact only salve their academic vanity. The answer was: Don't worry about those intellectual and speculative issues. Put your trust in God and walk with Jesus. He will give you enough truth to understand, and enough light to walk in. Leave the rest to Him and the theologians.

Do this in faith and don't worry about those perplexing questions that can never be solved this side of eternity. Follow Jesus faithfully, and simply obey His instructions.

Lord Jesus, help me through Your Spirit to concentrate on the important things in my spiritual life.

Who Lives with You?

"All who love Me will do what I say. My Father will love them, and We will come and make our home with each of them" (John 14:23).

Sometimes people who make their home with you can be a help or a hindrance. Loud people can be particularly trying. Capable people can be of great help – especially in an emergency.

Jesus evaded Judas' question and continued with the spiritual truths He was sharing with His disciples. After all, the issue under discussion was about loving Him and obeying Him – not pointless speculation about what God did or didn't do. Both He and the Father would make their home with anyone who loved Him and did what He taught them and gave them to do.

> Do your utmost to guard your heart, for out of it comes life.
>
> WALTER HILTON

Practical Christianity has a practical result: the continuous presence of a good family of friends.

God is always on His way – to Adam in paradise, to Moses in the burning bush, to the manger in Bethlehem. Now He is on His way to you. He wants to come and stay with you. He and Christ will not be occupants only. The Scripture verse puts it more strongly: It says they will come to you and *live* with you! They will not be neighbors, but residents who have found a home.

Make sure your "house" – your deepest inner soul – is a suitable home for the Father and the Son. Make sure you care for Them and make Their stay a happy one. And They might just come disguised as people you don't know.

Father and Son, make Your home with me forever.

He Has Come to Stay

"My Father will love them, and We will come and make our home with each of them" (John 14:23).

~∽◦∾~

A man once joked with a visitor who was leaving and said, "Come again ... when you can't stay so long!" There are indeed some people that you wish wouldn't stay long, and others that you wish would never come and visit. But then there are those who would make you very happy if they could stay longer; they are helpful, interesting and stimulating.

When Jesus said that He and the Father would come to live in the hearts of those who loved and obeyed Them, He meant it would be permanently. They wouldn't just pop in for a short visit; They would come forever and in more ways than one.

When the Son and the Father live in your heart it means that They will communicate with you. They will empower and boost and reassure you; They will encourage you to strengthen your faith. You will know more about God and Jesus Christ; grow in the grace of God and be

> Don't think so much about who is for or against you, rather give all your care that God be with you in everything you do.
> THOMAS À KEMPIS

more and more dedicated to spiritual things. Furthermore, They will be of comfort to you when you are under pressure. They will heal you when you experience pain and suffering. They will bring renewal when you feel despondent and deserted.

Reflect for a moment on what a great miracle this is – the powerful and mighty God, and the Savior of the world, make Their home with you in your tiny, anxious, guilt-ridden soul. They come to transform you, to change you and to be your permanent guests. This is the extreme miracle of undeserved grace of the Triune God.

Father and Son, make me a worthy host for You.

The Final Authority

"Remember, My words are not My own. What I am telling you is from the Father who sent Me" (John 14:24).

The best students are thoroughly schooled in the writings of others in their field of study. They often quote freely from their works and are always meticulous about acknowledging their sources. In fact, some students do very little else than quote bits and pieces from the works of others.

In Christ's time, the Scribes and the Pharisees quoted from the Old Testament and from Commentaries. Jesus spoke on His own authority and He came across more clearly because He spoke and taught with so much authority. He was in fact proclaiming the message that He received directly from God the Father. He was well-informed about the truth of God, and He and the Father were one to the extent that He became the Father's mouthpiece. And there is no higher authority than God. These words of Jesus enabled people to receive the final truth that came from the final Authority. It was so deep, so convincing and so devoid of speculation that it was in fact God speaking through Jesus to the people who were listening to Him.

> Authority without wisdom is like a heavy axe without an edge, fitter to bruise than polish.
>
> ANNE BRADSTREET

Listen to Jesus' words. Read His words again and again. Become familiar with them. Don't choose only the encouraging and comforting parts; read them all – even those parts that are very difficult to reconcile with a "Gentle Jesus, meek and mild!" Know that when you open your inner ear to Him, you receive the message directly from the final Authority.

Father God, thank You for the eternal truths that You spoke through Jesus Christ.

Jesus' Gifts of Grace

"I am telling you these things now while I am still with you"
(John 14:25).

～✺～

W e are often reminded to draw up a last will and testament before it's too late. But sometimes, before someone dies, they realize that they don't have enough room to store all their possessions, and then they start handing out many of their treasures to loved ones and friends. These people often cherish these gifts because they remind them of someone very special. Jesus had no treasures to give people in the community. But every word He spoke was a precious gift from God, seeing that He was the original Sender of the message.

Jesus' words are gifts from God. In one way or another, most of them have our names written on them. Contrary to the gifts we might receive from others, these gifts that God gives through Jesus, are something each of us can receive. They last forever and grow in meaning and importance.

> Christ has transformed all our sunsets into dawn.
> CLEMENT OF ALEXANDRIA

Jesus' words were of great importance to the first disciples. They would remember the occasion on which He spoke the words for the first time. They might have remembered the sound of His voice, the look in His eyes and the effect His words had on people. And like someone looking at a precious photo of a loved one who is no longer with them, they would have thought of Jesus time and time again, and found new meaning in His words.

Reflect deeply on the things Jesus said, not just as something you should learn and remember. Think of them as His great gift of grace to you personally.

I praise Your holy name, Lord Jesus, for everything You said and did for my sake.

The Spirit Teaches Us

"When the Father sends the Advocate as My representative –
that is, the Holy Spirit – He will teach you everything and will
remind you of everything I have told you" (John 14:26).

You are probably familiar with the saying "We live and learn!" We usually say it when we are somewhat embarrassed because of a mistake we made. What we are in fact saying is, "I won't make the same mistake again." Sometimes we learn our lesson, but often not.

Jesus knew there was so much He said and did that the disciples didn't understand. At that point in their growth and understanding it was beyond their ability to comprehend everything that was happening. Without help they would never live and learn. This is where the Holy Spirit would be of so much importance. He was another of the gifts that Jesus had prepared for them. But first He had to go through the suffering of the cross and then raised from the dead.

> If we hold on to God's truth, we won't be trapped by Satan's lies.
> ANONYMOUS

Many things the disciples would only understand later. And it was the Holy Spirit that would unlock their thoughts and minds so that they would fully understand who Jesus was and what God was doing in and through Him.

To this day the Holy Spirit still teaches Jesus' disciples. Every time you are given new insight into Jesus, the Holy Spirit is quietly and unnoticeably ushering you into the truth of Christ. Whether you are reading, listening, speaking, observing, or battling with some problem, and you succeed in understanding, it is the Holy Spirit teaching you – and all along, Christ is growing in you.

Lord Jesus, thank You for Your Spirit that is continually teaching me what truth is.

A Farewell Gift

"I am leaving you a gift – peace of mind and heart" (John 14:27).

⤳ ᴏᏮ ↫

When we die, we leave everything we own behind. But we also leave behind memories, traditions, experiences and relationships. Sometimes there are small gifts, treasures and photos.

Jesus had no possessions to leave behind. But He had other things that would never spoil and were more precious than anything else. One of them was peace. When conflict was rife outside the Upper Room; while violence was being planned; when death was knocking at the door, Jesus gave them peace.

This was the peace created by complete trust in the presence of God. It was absolute faith in His omnipotence and the acceptance of His holy will. It was also Christ's own peace. By this gift of peace, He gave them something of Himself. He knew they would be confronted with danger, opposition, suffering and even death. They would need peace more than anything else.

> No God, no peace –
> know God, know peace.
> Aesop

Open up your heart now to receive Jesus' gifts. Like the disciples, you probably need them more than anything else. If you are grappling with problems, confusion, opposition, resistance, ridicule, temptation, loneliness, pain or suffering, cling with all your might to this farewell gift Jesus gave us. Allow His peace to calm your anger. Allow His peace to take over your prejudices, your doubts and your grievances. Let it take over your entire attitude, your speech and your relationships. And whenever possible, give this peace away to someone else. The more of it you give away, the more it grows inside you.

Lord Jesus, Source of all my peace, please give me more and more of Your peace.

Going and Coming

"Remember what I told you: I am going away, but I will come back to you again" (John 14:28).

Sometimes when a loved one has died after a long and painful illness, a family member might remark, "We will miss them terribly, but we wouldn't want to wish them back. They have been set free from pain and are in a much better place."

If a parallel is drawn between this example and Jesus' death on the cross, His resurrection and ascension to heaven, they are not exactly the same. On the night of His betrayal and the Last Supper in the Upper Room, Jesus clearly had deep feelings for His disciples that He would leave behind. But He also knew and understood what was happening, while they didn't. He knew that His final destination was complete oneness with His Father in their collective glory.

> For however more devoted you are to God, you may be sure that He is immeasurably more devoted to you.
> MEISTER ECKHART

When this was reached, His earthly mission, with its inevitable humiliation, suffering and pain, would be perfect and complete. Anyone who loved Him would wish Him greater peace and glory, in the same way that love compels us to believe that death brings final healing, and is preferable for someone who suffers constantly and intensely.

The kind of love that God tells us about through Jesus makes us think of the spiritual advantage of death for very sick people; rather than wanting to have them with us longer and having them suffer. So if God loves us like this, our love for others must make their interests top priority. Is this the case in your life?

Holy Master, give me the grace to put other people first at all times.

The World Must Know

"I will do what the Father requires of Me, so that the world will know that I love the Father" (John 14:31).

～∽～

It is an astounding fact that the death of a carpenter two thousand years ago, in an insignificant small town, led to a movement that has something like two billion followers today. Jesus was, however, not speaking here of "the world" in the sense of "all people." In the New Testament, "the world" refers to the organized forces of evil that stand united in total opposition to God with a spirit of antagonism against His will and purpose for humankind.

Even while Jesus was still busy speaking, "the ruler of this world" was ready to strike. Jesus knew that He was acting out of love for and in obedience to God. The salvation of the people in the world that God loved was fundamental to His entire mission. With time, His words acquired deeper meaning and became applicable on a much wider scale. After Pentecost, the disciples started with their mission of telling people about Jesus, of His love for them and His love for the Father.

> One loving spirit sets another on fire.
> St. Augustine

The world, that is to say the forces that are hostile towards God, still need to hear about the love and the omnipotence of God and where exactly the final power of the universe is concentrated. Millions that don't follow or believe in Him know it. Christian believers of all denominations should focus less on the interests of their own group and rather look wider, with worry in their hearts about the great many people that still need Jesus.

Leader and Master, teach me to show people Your love.

The Vine Gives Life

"I am the true grapevine, and My Father is the Gardener" (John 15:1).

One Christian author said, "God wraps His omnipotence in the friendly, everyday, close-at-hand things" (H. Thielicke, *I Believe*). God meets with us and speaks to us, not in high-flown theological doctrines, but using familiar pictures, things, places and people.

Vines grew luxuriantly in Israel and grapes were plentiful. Wine is and was one of the most important products of the country. Centuries before Christ, the Hebrew prophets used the image of the vine to illustrate the relationship between the people of Israel and God. It is possible that the cup of wine that Jesus drank during the Last Supper, indicates the relationship that should have existed between Him and Israel. The old vine of God failed and was not fruitful anymore. Jesus was the new and true vine.

> All the resources of the Godhead are at our disposal!
> JONATHAN GOFORTH

Vines bear fruit and soon Jesus' lifeblood would be shed to bring life to the world in the way the vine gives life with the juice from the grapes. In the way Jesus unfolded the truth by means of the familiar image of the vine, God, as the vine that gave itself and renewed lives, was doing the same. Those at the table with Jesus weren't doing much more than quenching their thirst by drinking the wine; they claimed His sacrificial love for themselves, and in this they found a new depth of God's work in and through them.

Let God's work be a flood of life-giving spiritual power in you that empowers those around you and gives them a deeper dimension. And let Christ bear fruit through you.

Living Lord Jesus, let Your life-giving power also work through me.

God Is the Gardener

"I am the true grapevine, and My Father is the Gardener" (John 15:1).

⌒つℭ⌒

There are people who say that gardening brings you into close contact with nature. It also enhances your property, provides flowers for the house and food for the table. In spite of being hard work, it gives great joy to those who do it.

People in Israel were familiar with the gardener who looked after the vineyard and harvested the grapes. The role of the gardener and of the shepherd, the farmer and the judge was a reference to God. The gardener was in control of the vineyard and the vines were his pride and joy. Christ was God's vine and thus the "Father" was the Owner of the vineyard and the primary Agent in taking care of the vineyard and yielding a crop. The small and insignificant Christian community who followed Jesus' teachings, soon realized that God, the Owner of the vineyard, had planted a new vine and that these branches were now given preference over the old vine, Israel. In reaching His goal, God was in control of His "garden" and, like any hardworking gardener or farmer, He did everything possible to ensure a good and abundant harvest.

> It is the laden bough that hangs low, and the most fruitful Christian who is the most humble.
> ANONYMOUS

Take note that, above the buzz and din of the world's business, God is still there and at work, looking for ways to motivate His missionaries so that He may be sure of a good and fertile crop. Sometimes He plants more vines and patiently carries on working until the first fruit is seen and He can gather the harvest He has been waiting for. Always be aware of His handiwork.

Father God, may Your vineyard become fruitful again.

The Problem of Barrenness

"He cuts off every branch of Mine that doesn't produce fruit, and He prunes the branches that do bear fruit so they will produce even more" (John 15:2).

A strange feature of many plants and trees is that the more you cut them back, the better they grow. If you want the plum tree in your garden to produce better and bigger plums, prune it back heavily and you will get better fruit.

The same goes for the vine. Jesus saw gardeners doing this all His life. The disciples also saw it. Sometimes branches are bare and bear no fruit. It is necessary that these branches be pruned back.

According to Jesus, there was a lot to get rid of in the people of Israel – spiritually speaking. In Jesus' words, God was doing precisely that by planting a new vineyard. But there in the Upper Room, among the leaves, was Judas. And as a result of his spiritual death he would shortly be pruned back by God, the Gardener.

> It is no use to anybody for a tree to bud and blossom if the blossom does not develop into fruit. Many are the fold who perish in blossom.
> MARTIN LUTHER

God cut off all the barren branches in His mission for the human race. Individual branches had to go. Sometimes a good many branches felt the effect of the pruning shears. So, guard against barrenness. Watch the group activities of your Christian community so that they don't become like those of a social club – enjoyed by the members but without any spiritual power that attracts new members. And take care that you produce fruit only in honor of the Gardener.

Lord Jesus, let me live to bear fruit for You.

The Purifying Word

"You have already been pruned and purified by the message I have given you" (John 15:3).

⌘

At times we feel inspired and motivated in some people's company. But then there are others whose presence weighs us down with pessimism, boredom and negativity, and we try to avoid them.

By the time the Master had finished speaking to His disciples during the Last Supper, they had shared many hours of conversation and teaching with Him. Being in His presence was a unique experience. They bombarded Him with questions, looked at old scripts in a new way, in light of His ideas on the kingdom of God. They gained insight into the "mighty works of God." They began looking at the world in a totally new light. In addition, they were beginning to understand the future – everything under the Master's leadership.

> Most people are in favor of progress, it's the changes they don't like.
> ANONYMOUS

To be with Him was to be inspired, to be challenged and purified. Something of His faith, His love, His hope and His joy rubbed off on people. They became completely different beings, filled with hope, joy and love. And some of the impurity of this world that had also rubbed off on them was purified.

To know Jesus was to experience the transforming influence of His friendship. To hear His voice was to submit yourself to the future and eternal life that He came to offer. Each one of us can also experience that transforming influence. Open up to Jesus and you are instantly introduced to wholeness, holiness, pure love and deep joy.

Lord Jesus, thank You for being a life-changing Friend to me.

United with Christ

"Remain in Me, and I will remain in you. For a branch cannot produce fruit if it is severed from the vine, and you cannot be fruitful unless you remain in Me" (John 15:4).

Have you noticed how easy it is to lose contact with people you knew earlier and whose friendship really means a lot to you? The years fly by and you don't know each other's addresses anymore. Relationships must be treasured and kept.

Jesus encouraged His disciples to do more than just stay in touch. He knew they would become ineffective if they weren't in contact with Him at all times. The image of the branches that stay attached to the vine was a good representation of what would be expected of them. As far as Jesus was concerned, it was a promise. Jesus was saying, "You make the effort to stay connected to Me, and I will stay connected to you." Only in this permanent unity would they find the spiritual ability to bear fruit for Him in their work as His witnesses.

> Develop a passion for learning. If you do, you will never cease to grow.
> ANTHONY J. D'ANGELO

You and I also need to remain united with God. We must make up our minds to stay in Jesus as long as He can provide us with the sources that strengthen our spiritual abilities, and at the same time make us effective in our creative relationships with others. We cannot do it on our own. We must get our spiritual life from Jesus Himself.

Lord Jesus, let me live in unison with You; You are the true vine.

Achieving Success

"Yes, I am the vine; you are the branches. Those who remain in Me, and I in them, will produce much fruit. For apart from Me you can do nothing" (John 15:5).

All farmers dream of having rich, beautiful and abundant harvests. Whatever they grow, be it grain, potatoes or sugar cane, success is always determined by their know-how. The right weather is necessary, pest control, well-cultivated lands and very hard work. There is no shortcut to success.

Jesus knew His disciples would understand what it meant to dream of a rich harvest in a country where farming was the most important concern. An abundant harvest could mean the difference between ruin and survival. The major feast of the Jewish faith was the Harvest Feast; the feast of the gathering of the harvest. It included the grape harvest. The only way in which they could bring in a successful spiritual harvest was for them and Jesus to consolidate completely and to stay that way. Like all farmers, He wished for a good harvest and He wanted them to yield a good crop.

> We plough the fields and scatter the good seed on the land, but it is fed and watered by God's Almighty hand.
>
> JANE MONTGOMERY CAMPBELL

You will achieve success in spiritual development and in serving others only if you allow the power, love and joy of Christ to work in and through you. You will be an overflowing blessing to others if Christ lives in you. When He is at work in you, He will reach others that you come into contact with and influence them positively to learn more about faith, hope and peace. Someone who might be a doubter at present could become a disciple of Jesus. This is indeed a rich harvest.

O Holy Spirit of God, stand by me so that I can gather a rich harvest for Christ.

The Christ We Cannot Do Without

"Apart from Me you can do nothing" (John 15:5).

W e all have an inherent wish to "prove ourselves," to "make our mark" or to "make a name" for ourselves. In a highly competitive world, it is a praiseworthy achievement when someone is a success. It requires much dedication and competence to become this successful.

Because we all wish to achieve great success, we find it difficult to accept the idea that we can never achieve success in spiritual matters through our own abilities or skills. When we are motivated by the desire to shine, to reach the top, or to become known as a great spiritual person, we have already failed. One of the first lessons we must learn is that we must stand back, hand the matter over to God and allow Him to control everything.

> If God can work through me, He can work through anyone.
> St. Francis of Assisi

To be fruitful, we must be a branch and we can only bear fruit if we are anchored to the stem of the plant. Cut yourself off from Jesus and you are a useless branch, separated from the mother plant. Even if we know all this, many of us still try to achieve success on our own. This is a recipe for failure and frustration.

The truth is right in front of you: Face up to it and find out how to achieve success in the spiritual world. No matter how talented you might be, how gifted you are or how hard you work, if Jesus isn't at the center of everything, you will fail to bear fruit in matters that are important to Him.

Holy Savior, work in and through me to Your glory.

In Whose Service Are You?

"When you produce much fruit, you are My true disciples. This brings great glory to My Father" (John 15:8).

In our day and age many people become famous because of the publicity they get via the mass media. The media glorify heroes. Ordinary people become famous because they are often seen on television. And some live to be seen and praised.

Jesus knew that the disciples' wish for fame would be one of their greatest temptations. They might seem to be serving Him, but deep inside they would nurse the secret wish for their names to become well-known, that their successes would be remembered and their achievements noticed. The greatest hurdle in the life of the Lord's servant is the desire to be in the limelight, and to seek their own glory. Jesus saw it coming and solved the problem by warning His disciples and telling them that they should seek the glory of God and not their own. They would do this by bearing fruit, by becoming purpose-driven missionaries and doing everything to God's glory only.

> A man can no more diminish God's glory by refusing to worship Him than a lunatic can put out the sun by scribbling the word "darkness" on the walls of his cell.
>
> C. S. LEWIS

When you do something for Christ, always ask who will get the most out of it: you or God? Accept that you will need to argue points in this field, but make sure you aren't doing it for your own publicity; not so that people would remember your name, but that Christ would become known and glorified, and that the honor would be God's. Do this as well as you can and be as successful as you can – and give God all the glory!

Father God, may You be glorified in all I say and do.

The Four Dimensions of Love

"I have loved you even as the Father has loved Me. Remain in My love" (John 15:9).

We often say that marriage consists of much more than simply falling in love and organizing a wedding. It is taking on responsibilities, learning to understand someone else, starting a family and caring for someone in sickness and in health.

Receiving and gaining knowledge of the love of God is much more than the bliss of a mountaintop experience. It means accepting God's love and being receptive to the infinite love that the human mind can barely grasp. It means allowing that love in our lives, so that it can overcome our feelings of guilt and fear about our own shortcomings. It is to accept ourselves as children of God. It means to get to know Jesus, to acknowledge His claim on our lives and to allow His wonderful love to flow through us to others. It means that our whole life, our attitude and deeds, are filled with the love of Christ.

> Jesus did not come to make God's love possible, but to make it visible.
> MARTYN LLOYD-JONES

This extraordinary love has four dimensions. God loves Jesus, the Son. Jesus loves you, even if you aren't worthy of His love. He loves you unconditionally. Your duty is to love Christ and to remain in that love. Eventually you will be sent out to love other people. Loving God is far more than experiencing a warm feeling. It is much more than being religious. It is a lifelong giving of yourself to God, to Jesus and other people without reward, popularity or praise. It is hard work, but it gives you joy; and is eternally fulfilling.

Lord my God, fill me with Your love so that it will flow out to others.

October

Love That Touches the Heart

"I will ask the Father, and He will give you
another Advocate, who will never leave you.
He is the Holy Spirit, who leads into all truth."
~ John 14:16-17

The Holy Spirit is not a blessing from God, He is God.
~ COLIN URQUHART

Holy Spirit of God who lives in us,
Who leads us back to God's forgiveness
through remorse and confession of guilt, and
Who gives us a new life through Jesus Christ;
we worship You as the Spirit of life and growth.
We thank You that You are at work in our lives
and that You live in us, and that through You,
Christ lives in us and we in Him.
We worship You as the Source of renewed life because
You lead us back to the heart of God.
Thank You that You are the Teacher who makes us understand
the difference between right and wrong.
You make us part of one another as Christians,
because we all possess the same Spirit.
You brighten up our minds with Your gifts.
You equip us and send us out to go and proclaim
the gospel. You open up the Holy Word for
us so that we can get to know God's will.
Through You, O Spirit, God is present in
our hearts – therefore we live!
Touch my spirit generously with the fruit
of Your love, joy and patience,
friendliness, kind-heartedness, trustworthiness,
humility, and self-control.
Thank You, O Holy Spirit, that You help me to put my
imperfect prayers into words,
and that You enable me to speak to the Father.
I praise You for the wisdom You give me
and for enriching my life beyond measure!
In the name of Jesus, the Risen Savior.

Amen.

The Greatest Love

"Greater love has no one than this: to lay down one's life for one's friends" (John 15:13).

Harry Munn was the son of a farmer, and had very little schooling. He was an officer in the early days of the Salvation Army and was sent as lieutenant to the Midlands to work there. His handwriting was unreadable, his spelling poor and his knowledge of numbers pathetic. He admitted himself that he found reading difficult. But he was successful in persuading people and making them aware of the necessity of living a good life. He loved people sincerely and became a true soul winner for Christ.

Munn died of small-pox when he was stationed in Belfast. He caught the disease because he gave himself unconditionally to the sick. He went in and out of their houses, without minding the danger. After falling ill,

> Love is the greatest thing God can give us; because He Himself is love; and it is the greatest gift we can give to God.
>
> JEREMY TAYLOR

he insisted on persevering with his ministry of grace. He had learnt profound lessons in Jesus Christ's school.

But there were also many people who loved with the love of Christ and didn't die in His service. Others, like Henry Munn, followed where the Lord led them. Jesus says in this Bible verse that His disciples should be ready to give themselves until death, out of love for their fellow disciples. Many of those who listened to Him did just that. He gave the command and they obeyed. If you are not expected to go this far, how far will you go in your love for God and your fellow disciples?

Loving Father, show me how far my love should go.

Friends of Christ

"You are My friends if you do what I command" (John 15:14).

A few years ago a woman from Cape Town celebrated her eightieth birthday. She had never married and only one of her sisters was still alive. She planned a breakfast for this occasion and invited all her friends. There were friends from her childhood, professional colleagues, people she had worked with, neighbors dating back years, and dozens of her friends from church. A cousin and her husband came all the way from England for the occasion. Other friends flew in from Durban.

> Life has no pleasure higher or nobler than that of friendship.
>
> SAMUEL JOHNSON

The big hall she had hired for the party was packed. She had hundreds of friends because she was a friend to hundreds of people. She was also a friend of God, and because of that, she had become a friendly person.

Jesus also gathered His disciples around Him. He needed human friends, in spite of His godliness. He treasured His circle of friends. His main purpose with His choice of friends was to prepare and train them for His mission, and evangelization. He needed their friendship as well as their support, faith and love. His heart reached out to them and He did not journey through this world alone. Abraham was also called a friend of God because he was faithful and loyal, and obeyed God.

Be a friend of God, like Abraham; you also have Jesus Christ as a role model. Be a friend to others. This command that Jesus gave us has a wonderful reward.

Lord, it gives me indescribable joy to be called a friend of Yours.

Slaves No More

"I no longer call you slaves, because a master doesn't confide in his slaves. Now you are My friends, since I have told you everything the Father told Me" (John 15:15).

⌒◯◯⌒

One of the most important tasks for any person is handling human relationships. Being able to do this requires understanding, wisdom and maturity.

Jesus called His intimate followers to be His disciples. When He called them and they responded, He became their Master and Teacher. He raised them to a higher level by calling them His friends, and their relationship took on new stature.

A master didn't share his secrets with his slaves, but Jesus did with His friends. He was now revealing God's great plan to His disciples – God's plan for the salvation of humankind, and they would be entrusted with this task.

> The crowning wonder of His scheme is that He entrusted it to men. It is the supreme glory of humanity that the machinery for its redemption should have been placed within itself.
> HENRY DRUMMOND

Jesus confided in His disciples so that they could start thinking about salvation the way He thought about it. Jesus shared His secrets with His friends, and by doing this, He included them in His plans. Soon putting those plans into action would become their life work.

And now it has become our responsibility. In a certain sense it is a privilege to be God's slave. But being a friend of God is much better. It means that we are in close contact with God and He entrusts us with His plans and dreams.

Holy Master, help me to conscientiously carry out the plans You give me.

The Holy Selector

"You didn't choose Me. I chose you. I appointed you to go and produce lasting fruit" (John 15:16).

✦◦○◦✦

When a national sports team is selected, there is normally a panel of selectors who choose the team. Sometimes a player is so good that he is an automatic choice. When explaining this selection, commentators say, "He selected himself."

Jesus knew that some of the disciples He chose were fairly strong, forceful people who could act with authority. They would want to take control of the group when Jesus had left them. They would compete with each other for the role of leader.

Jesus affectionately reprimanded all of them and reminded them that they hadn't chosen themselves, and neither did they choose Him. He, and only He, chose them. They were His choice, His people, appointed by Him. They responded to His authority and carried out their tasks on His command. They were not their own people, but belonged to Jesus.

> It is a good thing God chose me before I was born, because He surely would not have afterwards.
>
> CHARLES H. SPURGEON

Some people are in a dominating position in Christian churches and communities, to such an extent that they seem to think the church is their own group; under their authority. Some leaders are so self-centered that they create the impression that God is there to meet their needs and to give them the glory they think is due to them. You, a disciple of Christ, must remember that this is precisely what you are – a learner called by the Teacher. You are there to serve Him, not yourself. From all the available people He chose you and it is an honor and a privilege to be chosen. Therefore, always be God's man or woman.

I thank You, Leader and Master, that You chose me, in spite of ... (name the things that hold you back from serving the Lord).

Will the Fruit Last?

"I appointed you to go and produce lasting fruit" (John 15:16).

In days gone by, traveling evangelists held large rallies that drew big crowds. Sports stadiums were used, there was massive publicity, and prayer chains were established to support the mission. Altar calls were made and those who responded were trained, led, helped and supported. However, this always brought into question whether those who responded to the altar calls became members of the local church, and whether their Christian convictions lasted. The answer was usually: some did, but others didn't.

Jesus was worried that the evangelization work He sent His disciples to do would not last long. He wanted them to do more than just arrive at a place, deliver a few sermons and then continue their journey to win more victories along the road. At a later stage, Paul worked out a more effective strategy. He stayed in some places for a long time where he taught and trained people in the spiritual life.

> Evangelization is like a swimming pool; it is at its noisiest at the shallow end.
> ANONYMOUS

Sometimes he returned later to support new believers in their discipleship. Later, he sent his helpers to lead and guide believers. Sometimes he even appointed local leaders to carry on with the work so that the gospel would stay alive permanently in the community.

To produce fruit for Christ is not a once-off occurrence. It constantly requires work, patience, prayer and the encouragement of spiritual growth. Will your work for Christ last?

Lord of the harvest, grant that my work for You will be long-lived.

The Command to Love

"This is My command: Love each other" (John 15:17).

Dietrich Bonhoeffer was one of the great Christian thinkers of the twentieth century. He gave up his safe job as a teacher in America at the outbreak of the Second World War to return to Germany.

He was deeply aware of the sacrifices it would mean for him because of his opposition to the Nazi rule. He found great comfort in the compassion of his friends whose reputations and lives were at stake because they visited him in prison.

Love is made up of little things. Although romantic love is an important matter – for some the most important thing in the whole world – God's love that worked in the thoughts and hearts of His disciples, also manifested in little things and in deeds. Words and deeds mean the world to those who receive them.

> You learn to love by loving.
> FRANCIS DE SALES

Are you having doubts; are you in the depths of despair because of finances, relationships or confusion? Nevertheless, look for even the slightest ways in which you can show God's love to another. It will benefit them and you, if you remain in Christ and His love.

Holy Spirit of God, show me where and when I can give Christ's love to others.

Prepare to Be Hated

"If the world hates you, remember that it hated Me first" (*John 15:18*).

It is difficult in many respects to be a Christian. A South African girl, Manche Masemola, was murdered by her own parents because she accepted the Christian faith – and this happened not even a hundred years ago. Her statue is above the western entrance of Westminster Abbey in London. Many others are scorned, tortured and rejected because they follow Christ.

Jesus knew that when the disciples took up their crosses after His departure, they would also experience the fury and rejection of the "world." By the time John wrote his Gospel, about sixty years after Jesus' ascension, many of His followers had already died. In the following two centuries many more would die. Jesus was the example and model to all these martyrs. He knew that only those completely fill-

> Hate for others and hate within will eventually destroy the hater.
> HARRY E. FOSDICK

ed with the love of God would manage to withstand the bitterness, opposition and hate that awaited the witnesses of the newborn Christian faith.

You and I should take what Jesus said to heart. Christian believers try to become popular in the eyes of the world by watering down their faith, compromising their way of life and accepting the standards of the world. Jesus didn't do this and neither did the great believers. You and I must not do it either.

Know from the very beginning that Jesus experienced resistance. It is a normal part of discipleship. Take note that the world will not just "dislike" you. The world will hate you. However, you have a trustworthy ally in Jesus Christ.

Master and Savior, keep me on my feet, standing up to the world's opposition.

You Must Be Different

*"The world would love you as one of its own if you belonged to it,
but you are no longer part of the world. I chose you to come out
of the world, so it hates you" (John 15:19).*

If you live in a community that is saturated with the Christian faith it's not easy to imagine a condition where there is a marked difference between the regular community and Christianity. But it does happen in many countries.

The Christian community was a small minority when John recalled Jesus' prophetic words in this Scripture verse. There was a marked difference between the small minority of Christians and the world that loathed them.

> You never will be the person you can be if pressure, tension and discipline are taken out of your life.
> JAMES G. BILKEY

William Temple wrote in *Readings in St. John's Gospel*: "Are we not of the world? Is it not so that our origin or character is in agreement?" Yes, only too often. But this is not the distinguishing and functional factor that makes us different when we become Christ's followers. "You are no longer part of the world. I chose you to come out of the world, so it hates you" (John 15:19). The phrase "the world" is repeated, but with a difference. Linked to the verb "chose," it no longer represents origin and growth, but a place of separation, and consequently segregation. This is in part where the hate of the world is felt. The world dislikes Christians. It begrudges them their new character; it is tortured by their new character and furious about their joy in Christ. Can the world notice that difference in your life because you are a Christian?

Lord Jesus, You who were so different, help me to be different from the world as well.

Why Christians Are Hated

"Do you remember what I told you? 'A slave is not greater than the master.' Since they persecuted Me, naturally they will persecute you. And if they had listened to Me, they would listen to you!" (John 15:20).

It often happens that religion is put in a bad light. Secular news is always ready to emphasize the failures of religion. The widespread good things done by religion go unnoticed.

This has always been the case. In the first century after Christ, allegations were made that Christians were troublemakers. It was said that they wanted to disrupt the Roman Empire and were disloyal because they refused to worship the Emperor as god. They were also accused of cannibalism: They gathered to enjoy the "blood and body" of Christ and this cast suspicion on them. It was claimed that they were immoral because they greeted one another with a kiss at gatherings. Once a tremendous fire raged through Rome, and because Christians sometimes preached about the fire that would one day engulf the world, they were blamed for this also. They were blamed for creating division in families, because a wife or husband sometimes became a believer and the other one did not. There was sometimes some truth to this rumor.

> God didn't call us to be successful, but faithful.
> MOTHER TERESA

Today Christians are called fanatics. The world sees us as "superstitious and old-fashioned." They label us as spoilsports because we call for purer ethics than the world has. In spite of all these charges against us, we follow Christ and expect the same rejection He got from the world.

Gracious God, help me to stand firm in the face of rejection.

In the Master's Service

"They will treat you this way because of My name, for they do not know the One who sent Me" (John 15:21 NIV).

A student was hitch-hiking through an isolated part of South Africa when the car that gave him a lift had a flat tire. The driver had a spare wheel, but unfortunately no tools with which to change it. The student hitch-hiked to a village nearby, hoping to borrow a jack from the petrol station. The owner of the petrol station had lost too many "borrowed" articles and refused to help him at first. After looking the student up and down he asked, "Aren't you a Stellenbosch student; a 'Matie'? Well, one can always trust a 'Matie'." The student never found out why the man had been so accommodating because he was a *Matie*, but boy, was he thankful.

> To suffer like Jesus appears to be the same as to rule like Jesus.
> ANONYMOUS

It works just the other way round for Christians. We are rejected not for what we do or believe, but because we represent Christ. If the disciple represents Christ, Christ represents the Father. The world refuses to understand what Christ's mission was all about, because they are deaf to the voice of God and blind to everything God is busy doing. The first step of faith is to realize the connection between Christ and the Father. Only then will people open up their lives to God so that He may complete His salvation plan in their heart and soul.

Enduring rejection because you are a disciple of Jesus Christ is a noble lot in life. To be linked to Jesus, for better or for worse, is the deepest meaning of true faith.

Holy Master, strengthen those who have to endure persecution for Your sake.

The Consequences of Unbelief

"They would not be guilty if I had not come and spoken to them.
But now they have no excuse for their sin. Anyone who hates Me
also hates My Father" (John 15:22-23).

M any people think that believing is a purely intellectual exercise, something like a long, drawn-out joke that some catch and others don't. Many people find it extremely difficult to correlate the scientific description of the world with the religious viewpoint.

Jesus knew that it involved much more than only that. He knew that a huge element of surrender accompanied everything about religion, and that the will to believe was more important than intellectual conviction. He also knew that refusing to believe was an act that challenged God, and therefore a sin.

> Only he who believes is obedient, and only he who is obedient, believes.
> DIETRICH BONHOEFFER

When Jesus came, His presence on earth created a bigger opportunity than ever for humankind to see God for who He really was and to respond to that belief. But the magnitude of their hate would soon be revealed: Jesus was still speaking only a few hours before He was crucified by those very same people. They hated Him, and therefore also hated the Father.

If you experience problems understanding certain difficult parts of the faith – the Holy Trinity or the Virgin Birth – and because of this, lack the will to believe, know that you are robbing yourself of true knowledge of God and eternal life. It would truly be very sad, don't you agree?

Holy Spirit of God, strengthen my faith in the Almighty Father
and the Son each and every day.

Knowledge and Responsibility

"If I hadn't done such miraculous signs among them that no one else could do, they would not be guilty. But as it is, they have seen everything I did, yet they still hate Me and My Father" (John 15:24).

When we grow up we soon find out that adulthood includes responsibilities as well as privileges. The privilege of love and marriage brings the responsibility of parenthood. The ability to make a decent living brings the responsibility to pay tax. The right to vote carries the responsibility of serving your country.

By coming to the people of Israel as the Son of the Father, Christ emphasized the dual dimension of the privilege of having knowledge of God and the responsibility of knowing Him, believing in Him and serving Him. Most importantly, before the crucifixion and resurrection, the miracles that Jesus performed served as signs of the presence of God who worked in and through Jesus.

> See in the meantime that your faith brings forth obedience, and God in due time will cause it to bring forth peace.
>
> JOHN OWEN

To see Jesus at work was to see God at work. To meet Jesus was to meet God. To hear Jesus and believe Him was to hear and believe God. It was also to know eternal life as something God meant them to have. The leaders saw this evidence, heard and observed it, and yet they shut their minds to what Jesus and God the Father declared.

Grab the opportunity that God gives you to know His salvation in Jesus Christ. Accept Him as Your Savior and Redeemer, and walk in His light now and forever.

Savior and Redeemer, I believe with all my heart and I trust You completely.

Help Will Come

"I will send you the Advocate – the Spirit of Truth. He will come to you from the Father and will testify all about Me" (John 15:26).

When a motorist has problems with their car and is far from home, they become very anxious. They stand at the side of the road, wondering what went wrong and what it will cost to repair the car. As the time goes by, they wonder if help is ever going to come. There are so many people, in a wide range of circumstances, who wonder if help will ever arrive for them.

Jesus knew that the disciples would be left completely on their own once He ascended to heaven. They would be confused, worried and anxious. Help would, however, arrive in the form of the Holy Spirit, the Advocate who God would send.

He would come to them as light in their darkness, comfort in their sorrow, guidance in their confusion and faith in their doubt. They would not have to take on the world alone. The fact is, before they even knew it, they would be on their way, taking Jesus' message to the world. Some would be burnt at the stake and others savaged by lions in arenas.

> Courage consists not in blindly overlooking danger, but in seeing and conquering it.
> JEAN PAUL RICHTER

Whatever situation you face, believe this promise: A Helper will come from God. It might not be in the exact form you think, but God will come and give you strength, and lead you and support you. Jesus said He would be with His disciples to the end. And so it is with you and me!

I praise Your name, Lord Jesus, because You will be with me to the very end.

The Spirit Comes from the Father

"I will send you the Advocate – the Spirit of Truth. He will come to you from the Father" (John 15:26).

～✺～

A number of years ago many Christians became seriously confused about the Holy Spirit. The Christian church failed dismally to teach its members about Him. When people thought He had gone missing, it suddenly seemed as if He appeared out of nowhere. Some said they knew Him and that He made a great difference in many people's lives. Others were confused, afraid and hesitant.

It is important to understand that the Spirit was not another God who was suddenly raised from the dead and became known by those who spoke about Him often. The fact is that He was the same God who created the world, because the story of creation says, "And the Spirit of God was hovering over the surface of the waters" (Gen. 1:2).

> We share in Holy Nature by our participation in the Holy Spirit.
> St. Athanasius

Therefore the present revival of the Holy Spirit can be seen as a visit from God in which He renews people's faith and deepens the corporate life of the church. He revives people's faith and shakes the church awake again. In this way, the Spirit has brought many people into a new relationship with God.

At any point in time, the work of the Holy Spirit is not the act of some mysterious ghost that has been hiding behind the curtain and decided to come out. He is the Gift of God the Father, who comes to live in us to shape the personality of Christ in us. He is the inner transforming agent of God. Welcome Him and rejoice in His presence.

Lord Jesus, fill me with the Holy Spirit.

The Spirit of Truth

"He will come to you from the Father and will testify all about Me" (John 15:26).

The universe is overflowing with information about the world and its inhabitants, as well as events taking place. Information is available like never before, thanks to what we call modern technology. But there is much more to the truth than simply masses of facts. Truth is to develop the right insight and to understand the facts correctly so that we know what they mean.

It would have been impossible for the human mind to establish what, how and who God is. Thus, true to His nature, He revealed Himself to us. He revealed the facts about Himself and helped us to understand them, and consequently Him. He started by creating the world and the people in it. He spoke through prophets and revealed great insights about His nature. Then He became human in Jesus Christ; a Person who lived and walked among us. But the only way in which God could let our sluggish minds understand who He is, was by giving His Spirit to the world, so that He could work in our hearts and minds. He helps us to understand God and teaches us about Him.

> The God of Christians is a God of love and comfort, a God who fills the soul and heart of those whom He possesses.
> BLAISE PASCAL

If you would like to increase your knowledge of God, ask the Spirit to enlighten your mind. He will do it, not by cramming your brain with theological truths, but by the embodiment of Jesus Christ in you. You get to the truth by living in Christ and walking with Him every day. There is no other way to get to know the truth about God.

Spirit of Truth, lead me in the full truth of God.

The Spirit of Jesus Christ

"When the Advocate comes, whom I will send to you from the Father – the Spirit of Truth who goes out from the Father – He will testify about Me" (John 15:26 NIV).

We all know people who will ask in an ordinary everyday conversation how we are, and before we can answer, they will give us a long list of their aches and pains. Most people like talking about themselves and they have no idea how boring they are in the process. Just sometimes, and far too seldom, someone will tell you about another person, but then it is usually gossip.

Jesus spoke a lot about His heavenly Father and His main theme was the kingdom of God! When He was on the verge of leaving them, He promised His disciples to send them the Holy Spirit. The Spirit would lead them into the full truth of the Father – and He would also tell them about Jesus Christ. The Holy Spirit's role and calling was to make known the other members of the Holy Trinity. His task was in fact to direct people away from Himself, to the Father and the Son.

> Happy the man whose words come from the Holy Spirit and not from himself.
> ANTHONY OF PADUA

When someone speaks a lot about the Holy Spirit, just make sure that the conversation always focuses on Jesus. If it's all about Jesus, then the Spirit is leading the conversation. The Holy Spirit diverts conversations away from Himself and puts Jesus in the limelight. And He leads you to a greater understanding of Jesus while He shapes Jesus in your life more and more. His purpose is to make you a reflection or replica of Jesus. In addition, He inspires the written report of what Jesus said – the Bible.

Holy Spirit of God, help me to focus on You more regularly.

Testifying for Jesus

"You must also testify about Me because you have been with Me from the beginning of My ministry" (John 15:27).

Many people have only one topic they talk about. For some parents it is their children – or only one of their children. Others will talk about sport and their favorite team. Some people will chatter away non-stop about money; others about books they have read, food they have eaten or places they have visited. And then there are those who will drive you to distraction with their aches and pains if you are unfortunate enough to be cornered by them.

Jesus knew that, ignorant as His disciples were about Him before His death and resurrection, everything would change. He would become the topic and focus of all their conversations when the Holy Spirit would take possession of them at Pentecost. They would overflow with Christ and His deeds. They would tell people about Him on the market squares and in their homes, along the road and at wells where people gathered. They would preach about Him in the synagogues and courts, in prisons and in temples, before kings and in the presence of judges.

> Our power in drawing others after the Lord mainly rests in our joy and communion with Him ourselves.
> JOHN G. BELLETT

The Holy Spirit would empower them to do all this and He would give them the boldness to spread the gospel among all people. And it would be all about Jesus. Don't be a disciple only. Become an apostle: someone who is sent with a message. Give a Bible to someone who doesn't read it and encourage conversations about Jesus. Allow the Spirit to give you the words that you should share with others.

Master and Lord, open my mouth to testify about You.

Warnings and Challenges

"The time is coming when those who kill you will think they are doing a holy service for God ... I'm telling you these things now, so that when they happen, you will remember My warning" *(John 16:2, 4).*

Jesus warned His disciples beforehand about what the future held for them. He wanted them to realize what discipleship would demand from them. They would be banned from the synagogues, a cruel fate for any Jew because the synagogue occupied a special place in the lives of the Israelites. The disciples had to learn that it was better to be alone with God, for the sake of the gospel.

> The ultimate measure of a man is not where he stands in moments of comfort and convenience, but where he stands at times of challenge and controversy.
> MARTIN LUTHER KING, JR.

They would also be killed. The Jews thought they were doing God an honor by killing His disciples. Jesus certainly knew how to work with people! He was in fact telling His disciples, "I am offering you the most difficult task on earth. Are you willing to carry it out?" Their choice was either the world with its safety, or Christ with His suffering and sacrifice.

Everyone knows the words of Garibaldi to his soldiers after the siege of Rome in 1849: "Soldiers, all our efforts against superior forces have been unavailing. I have nothing to offer you but hunger and thirst, hardship and death; but I call on all who love their country to join with me." And they came in their thousands!

Jesus offers us not a road of comfort, but a road of glory. He is looking for people that will accept the challenge in His name.

Jesus, I hear Your challenge and accept it in Your glorious name.

The Work of the Holy Spirit

"When He comes, He will convict the world of its sin, and of God's righteousness, and of the coming judgment" (John 16:8).

⌒⍥⌒

The disciples were bewildered and distressed because they were going to lose Jesus. But Jesus told them that it would be a good thing, because when He left, the Holy Spirit, the Counselor, would come to them. While Jesus was in His body He couldn't be with them everywhere; He was limited to the human boundaries of place and time. But there were no limitations to the Spirit. He would always be with them. Jesus' Spirit would constantly bring them into contact with Him. Wherever they proclaimed Christ's name, the Spirit would be with them.

Here we have an almost perfect summary of the Holy Spirit's work. In the first place, He convinces us of our sin. When the Jews crucified Christ, they didn't think they were committing a sin; they believed they were serving God. But when they heard the story of the crucifixion later on, it broke their hearts: "When the people heard this, they were cut to the heart" (Acts 2:37 NIV). They were suddenly convinced that they had been part of the greatest injustice in history. We cannot understand our need of a Savior without an awareness of our sins. It is the work of the Holy Spirit that convinces people of sin.

> I was baptized with the Holy Spirit when I took Him by simple faith in the Word of God.
>
> R. A. TORREY

The Holy Spirit also convinces a person of righteousness. This means that we will discover Jesus' righteousness. It is incredible to think that, through all the ages, people would place their trust in a crucified Jewish criminal. The Holy Spirit convinces people that this criminal was the Son of God.

Spirit of God, do Your work in my heart and life, and convince me of my sin.

The Coming Judgment

"He will convict the world of its sin, and of God's righteousness, and of the coming judgment" (John 16:8).

The Holy Spirit also convinces people of the justness of God's judgment. There on the cross, sin was condemned and destroyed. The Spirit confronts us humans with the inevitability of the coming judgment. He tells us that we may not do what we please, but convinces us that a righteous judgment awaits us.

It is the Spirit who gives us the inner conviction and certainty that we will all stand before the judgment seat of God to account for our deeds.

But there is something else the Holy Spirit does that John doesn't mention here. When we are convicted of our sins and the justness of Jesus Christ; when we are convinced of the coming judgment, the Holy Spirit gives us the assurance that our salvation lies in the Cross of Jesus Christ.

> The Spirit breathes upon the Word, and brings the truth to sight.
> WILLIAM COWPER

Because of Christ, our sins are forgiven and we are saved from condemnation. This is also the work of the Holy Spirit, because it is the Spirit who convinces us and assures us that we can find our Savior and Redeemer in the crucified Figure. The Holy Spirit shows us our sins, but also assures us of our salvation. Let this be your glorious consolation in dark times.

Thank You, Holy Spirit of God, for the assurance and comfort You give me.

Revelation

"When the Spirit of Truth comes, He will guide you into all truth" (John 16:13).

Jesus says here that the Holy Spirit is the Spirit of Truth, and the major work of the Spirit is to bring God's truth to people. This is called revelation, and nowhere in the Word is the revelation of the Spirit highlighted more clearly than in this portion.

Revelation is inevitably a progressive process. Jesus knew many things, but He couldn't share everything with His disciples at that stage because they weren't ready. You can explain just as much to people as they are able to understand at a given moment in time.

There is no end to the revelations of God. One of the mistakes people make is to think that God's revelations end with the last book of the Bible; that since approximately AD 120, when the last book of the New Testament was written, there are no more revelations of God.

> We do not need to wait for the Holy Spirit to come: He came on the Day of Pentecost. He has never left the church.
>
> JOHN STOTT

The Spirit of God is *always* actively revealing God to humankind. Admittedly, the climax of God's revelation came in the form of Jesus Christ. But He is not a character in a book; He is a living Person and God's revelation continues through Him.

Revelations of God to humankind are the truth, the whole truth and nothing but the truth. All truth is God's truth, and the revelation of all truth is the work of the Holy Spirit.

I praise and thank You, O Holy Spirit, for all the truths of God that You reveal to me.

God Reveals All

"When the Spirit of Truth comes, He will guide you into all truth" (John 16:13).

Take note of another principle of revelation. That which is revealed comes from God. God is the owner and also the giver of all truth. Truth is not a human being's discovery; it is a gift of God. It is the truth of God that the Holy Spirit brings us.

Truth is not something we can create by means of a process in our minds; it is something already waiting to be discovered; something we accept, and not something we create ourselves. God is behind all truth.

Revelation is to take the things of Jesus and to make known their inherent truth. The greatness of Jesus lies in His inexhaustibility. No human being has understood everything Jesus came to say. No human being has uncovered the full meaning of Jesus' teachings. No human being knows what they mean to life and to faith; to humanity and to the individual; to the community and to the nation. Revelation is a continuous "opening up" of the meaning and importance of Jesus Christ.

> I surrender unto Him all there was of me; everything! Then for the first time I realized what it meant to have real power.
> KATHRYN KUHLMAN

Revelation comes to us not from a book or credo, but through a living Person. The closer we live to Jesus, the better we get to know Him. The more we conform to Him, the more He reveals to us. In order to enjoy His revelation, we must acknowledge His majesty. Submission to, and knowledge of Jesus, go hand in hand. It is only to the Man of God that God makes His revelation known.

I thank You, O Holy Spirit, for the revelation Jesus gives me.

Sorrow Becomes Joy

"In a little while you won't see Me anymore. But a little while after that, you will see Me again" (John 16:16).

❦

Here Jesus was looking beyond the present century to the new period that would come. He used an image that was deeply rooted in the Jewish mind. They believed that all time was divided into two parts: the present time and the time to come. The present was altogether bad and subject to damnation. The time that would come would be the Golden Age – the time of God. The time in between was called the time of the Messiah.

Jesus knew the Scriptures and He knew about these images. He said to His disciples, "I am leaving you now, but I will come back again when My kingdom comes and I start to rule. Before this, however, you will have to suffer hard times." Jesus went ahead to outline all that the Christian would have to endure.

There would be times when Christians would experience sorrow, but their sorrow would be changed to joy. And the day would come for a turnabout. The world's reckless joy would change to sorrow, and the Christians' apparent sorrow would change to joy. Christians should always remember this when their faith is costing them.

> Desire joy and thank God for it. Renounce it, if need be, for other's sake. That's joy beyond joy.
> ROBERT BROWNING

There are two exceptional things about Christian joy: First, it can never be taken away because it is rooted in God. For this reason, this joy will be complete, while there is always something missing in the pleasure the world knows. Second, the sorrow that went before Christian joy is forgotten like a mother forgets labor pains; like the martyr forgets their suffering in the glory of heaven.

Holy Lord Jesus, thank You for the lasting joy that You give me.

Lasting Joy

"You have sorrow now, but I will see you again; then you will rejoice, and no one can rob you of that joy" (John 16:22).

There will be fullness of knowledge the day Jesus is talking about. Jesus says to His disciples, "At that time you won't need to ask Me for anything" (John 16:23). There are always unanswered questions and unsolved problems in life. We must walk this path of life by faith, and not by seeing. We must accept the things we cannot understand. We are only able to grasp a fragment of the truth about God, but when Christ comes again, there will be complete knowledge. If we walk with Christ, the questions will disappear and the time of answers will dawn.

> Rejoicing is clearly a spiritual command. To ignore it is disobedience.
> CHARLES SWINDOLL

There will also be a new relationship with God. When God really knows us, we can ask Him anything; we know that the door to God is open and that He has a heart of love. Jesus says that in this relationship we will be able to ask God anything. If a child loves his father, he knows very well that his father sometimes says no, because a father's knowledge and a father's love knows best. We can become so intimate with God that we may go to Him with everything, as long as we end with, "Let Your will be done!"

This new relationship with God is made possible through Jesus. It is because of who Jesus is and what Jesus did that our joy is complete and indestructible. Everything we have comes to us through Jesus. It is in His name that we ask and receive; in His name that we approach God and are welcomed.

I thank and praise You, my Savior, that You opened the door to the Father's heart for me.

The Glory of the Cross

After saying all these things, Jesus looked up to heaven and said, "Father, the hour has come. Glorify Your Son so He can give glory back to You" (John 17:1).

It is one of the noteworthy facts of history that truly great people often found their glory in death. It was when and how they died that revealed their greatness. Even if people misunderstood them and condemned them as criminals, their death displayed their real nobility and their true place in the scheme of things. This was the case with Abraham Lincoln, Jeanne d' Arc and many others. Time and again, the majesty of martyrs is revealed in death.

This is also true of Jesus' death on the cross. The Roman officer remarked at the crucifixion, "This Man truly was the Son of God!" (Matt. 27:54). The cross revealed the glory of Christ because He was never more majestic than in His death. The cross was His glory because the magnet of the cross attracted people to Christ like His life never did – and it continues to do so.

> Jesus came to pay a debt He didn't owe, because we had a debt we couldn't pay.
> NORMAN VINCENT PEALE

The cross revealed the majesty of Christ because it was the completion of His work. He completed the task God gave Him to do. If Jesus hadn't gone through with the crucifixion, it would have meant that His task was left unfinished. This proved to people that there was nothing God wouldn't do to bring about salvation for them, and that there was no limit to God's love. On the cross Jesus reassured humanity of God's love.

Lord Jesus, thank You for saving my soul on the cross and assuring me of the Father's love.

The Cross that Saves

"Father, the hour has come. Glorify Your Son so He can give glory back to You" (John 17:1).

A question many people might want to ask is how the cross of Jesus could glorify God the Father. There is only one way to glorify God and that is through obedience. Children honor their parents when they obey them. The gospel makes it very clear that Jesus could have avoided the cross if He had wanted to. Humanly speaking, He could have turned His back on it and never gone back to Jerusalem. Jesus glorified God on the cross by His absolute obedience and perfect love for His Father.

> The cross means this: Jesus taking our place to satisfy the demands of God's justice and turning aside God's wrath.
>
> JAMES M. BOICE

But there is more: Christ prayed to God to glorify Him so that He could glorify God in return. *The cross was not the end!* The resurrection would follow. This proved that people could do their worst and that Jesus would triumph over it. It was as if God pointed to the cross and said, "This is what people think of My Son," and then to the empty tomb, saying, "This is what I think of My Son!" The worst that humankind could do would not succeed in getting rid of Him, neither in defeating or breaking Him.

The cross was the way back for Jesus: "Now, Father, bring Me into the glory we shared before the world began" (John 17:5). Jesus was like the Knight who left the King's palace to carry out the King's command. Now He was back to enjoy the glory of victory. Jesus came from God and returned to God. The cross was the gate to glory for Him.

I glorify You, Lord Jesus, because You were obedient to God and suffered for my sake.

The Meaning of Discipleship

"I have revealed You to the ones You gave Me from this world. They were always Yours. You gave them to Me, and they have kept Your word" (John 17:6).

D iscipleship is based on the realization that Jesus came from God. A disciple is principally a person who accepts that Jesus was God's ambassador, and that we hear the voice of God in Jesus' words and see the acts of God in Jesus' deeds. A disciple is someone who sees God in Jesus and knows that there is no one in the entire universe who is one with God in the way Jesus is.

Discipleship means obedience. A disciple is someone who keeps to God's Word and hears that Word in Jesus. There can be no discipleship without obedience. Disciples are people who have accepted the mastership of Jesus Christ and

> The final test of love is obedience.
> A. W. Tozer

have made Christ's words the law of their lives. As long as we insist on independence we cannot be disciples.

Discipleship is something that is determined beforehand. Jesus' followers are given to Him by God. These people are meant for discipleship in God's plan. God has His plan, His dream and His final destination for each person. We are not in the hands of fate, but in the hands of God. In this whole Scripture reading Jesus' faith in the future resounds. He never doubted that the disciples would continue with His work. He believed in God and He believed in people. He trusted God and He trusted people. We must not be kept back by human weakness, but go forward with Jesus.

I praise You, Father God, that You call me to discipleship and service in Your name.

Jesus and His Disciples

"My prayer is not for the world, but for those You have given Me" (John 17:9).

～✺～

This Scripture reading is laden with truths that are sometimes too big for us to comprehend. God gives Jesus the disciples. This means that the Spirit moves our hearts to answer Jesus' appeal. When our hearts go out to Jesus in love and worship, it is the Spirit of God working in us.

The work of the disciples brought glory to Jesus. As a result of the patient who was healed, the doctor is honored. Because of the athlete's success, his trainer is honored. It is the human being who was saved and redeemed by Jesus that brings Him glory.

> The decision we all face is this: whether to consciously lock God out of our lives or open the door of our heart and invite Jesus Christ to come in.
>
> LUIS PALAU

A disciple is someone who is given a task. Like God sent Jesus, Jesus sends His disciples into the world, to lead the world back to God. He prays for His people, for the ability to lead people back to God.

Jesus promised His disciples two things. He promised them joy through everything He said to them. But He also promised them a warning. He told them that they were not the same as the world; they had to uphold other values and standards. But there would be joy in the battle against the storm and the struggle against the tide. Facing up to the opposition of the world brings the disciple great joy.

I am overwhelmed because I know that You, Lord Jesus, pray for me.

Jesus Prays for His Disciples

"My prayer is not for the world, but for those You have given Me, because they belong to You" (John 17:9).

The sacred importance of this Bible verse is that it tells us about the things Jesus prayed for His disciples. Firstly, He didn't pray for the disciples to be taken out of the world. He never prayed for escape, but for victory. It was Jesus' conviction that we should put our faith into practice in the hustle and bustle of the world. Naturally there must also be prayer, meditation and quiet times when we lock the door to the world to be alone with God. But in the end, we live to demonstrate to the world the ultimate goal of life. Christianity was never meant to withdraw people from the community; it was to equip Christians better for the struggle of life.

> The devil tempts that he may ruin and destroy; God tests that He may crown.
> St. Ambrose

Jesus prayed for unity among the disciples, like He and the Father were united. The gospel couldn't really be preached in a congregation where all the members weren't one solid brotherhood. The world cannot be evangelized by warring churches. Jesus also prayed that His Father would protect His disciples from evil. The forces of evil are in conflict with the power of God, and Satan wants to lure people away from God.

It is an inspiring feeling to know that God keeps watch over our lives to protect and keep us from Satan's onslaughts. We so often fail because we try to resist evil in our own strength instead of seeking the help of Almighty God.

I kneel in gratitude, my Father, for You protect me against Satan's onslaughts.

A Glimpse into the Future

"I am praying not only for these disciples but also for all who will ever believe in Me through their message" (John 17:20).

In today's Scripture, Jesus' prayer reaches out to the farthest ends of the earth. First He prays for Himself, with the cross looming ahead of Him. Then He prays for His disciples. Now His prayer focuses on the future, and He prays for those who will accept the Christian faith in distant countries and in future centuries.

Here we see Jesus' absolute faith and His unwavering certainty. His faith is intact, even in the face of the cross. He prays for those who will believe in Him in coming centuries. This is Jesus' prayer for us too. He prays for unity in His church on earth: that it will unite people. It was in fact this unity that convinced the world of the truth of Christianity and Jesus' place in it.

> We must all hang together, or assuredly we shall all hang separately.
>
> BENJAMIN FRANKLIN

It is common practice for people to scatter in different directions, instead of staying together and becoming united. Unity among all Christians would be a supernatural achievement that could only be made possible by God. It is a tragic fact that the church has never shown the world this united front. Because of the division of Christians, the world struggles to accept the merit of the Christian faith. It is our individual duty to confirm that unity through love for our fellow Christians. This would be the answer to Jesus' prayer.

Lord Jesus, make me an instrument of Your peace and love.

Love One Another

"This is My commandment: Love each other in the same way I have loved you" (John 15:12).

If anyone should ask you which simple rule summarizes the Christian faith, your answer would probably be: love! And you would be absolutely right. It is so simple to remember, so easy to talk about – and yet so difficult to do. It is because we confuse God's kind of love with human emotions and because we are so selfish by nature; and this is the exact opposite of love.

As Christian disciples we don't love others because we necessarily like other Christians. Liking someone is the underlying principle of human friendship and love, and that is something completely different. We love each other because God commanded us to do so, and because He placed His love in our hearts. This means that we might detest some Christians, but we must still love them with the love that Christ awakens in us. God's kind of love is just like that of the Holy Spirit of God that stirs joy in us. To love someone with God's kind of love is not necessarily to enjoy that person, but to strive for what is best for them. This always leads to their spiritual growth.

> For the love of God is broader than the measures of man's mind; and the heart of the Eternal is most wonderfully kind.
>
> F. W. FABER

We have no option in this matter. Christ commanded us to love, whether we feel like it or not. Most of the time we don't feel like it and we find it difficult to love. Yet we must do it, because Jesus instructed us to do so. It is the task God has assigned us: to love like He loves us. He is our motivation and our model.

Lord of Love, help me to love others the way You love me.

November

The Future Is Assured

For Christ must reign until He humbles
all His enemies beneath His feet.
~ 1 Corinthians 15:25

In God, time and eternity are one and the same thing.
~ Henry Suso

Eternal and unchanging God,
we worship You as the Alpha and the Omega;
the Beginning and the End; the First and the Last.
Bless those for whom this was a good year
and let them thank and praise You!
Bless those for whom this was a sad year
and keep them from despair and frustration.
In Your grace, let us all approach the future with a firm step,
our eyes focused on Jesus, the Leader and Finisher of our faith.
Merciful Father and God of comfort, be with those whose joy
was turned into tragedy and grief this year;
those who lost loved ones on the roads,
through illness or through sudden and unexpected death.
Help us never to forget that somewhere, someone is unhappy;
that morning never reaches evening
without a heart breaking somewhere.
Accompany us the rest of this year:
console our hearts and ease our longing;
renew our spirit and our thoughts.
Forgive us when we, with self-loathing,
confess lost opportunities, unconfessed sin,
love we could have given but never did.
Strengthen us in our intentions to seek
Your will for the New Year,
and to do it conscientiously so that we glorify Your name.
In the name of Jesus, our Savior and Redeemer.

Amen.

How to Forgive

"No, not seven times," Jesus replied, "but seventy times seven!"
(Matt. 18:22).

～ つ ⌒ ⌒

It was a rabbinical doctrine that a person had to forgive their fellow man three times. They believed that God's forgiveness covered three transgressions and that He punished the fourth. Peter, the rash disciple with his impulsive nature, answered his own question by saying that we should forgive seven times. Peter expected Jesus to compliment him, but Jesus answered that the Christian should forgive seventy times seven. There is indeed no limit to the Christian's forgiveness.

Jesus tells the story of a servant who was forgiven an enormous debt, yet soon afterwards he had no mercy on a fellow servant who owed him a much smaller debt. This message runs through the entire New Testament like a golden thread: You must forgive others to be forgiven yourself. Those who cannot forgive others dare not expect God's forgiveness. Godly and human forgiveness must go hand in hand.

> Forgiveness of sins is the very heart of Christianity, and yet it is a mighty dangerous thing to preach.
> **MARTIN LUTHER**

In Jesus' story the fact that stands out is the size of the two people's debt. The point Jesus is making here is that nothing we do can be compared to what humankind did to God. If God forgave us our sins, we must also forgive others. We were forgiven an enormous debt that we would never have been able to pay, because our sins brought about the death of the Son of God. We can find mercy in God's eyes only if we forgive others like God forgave us.

Holy God, grant me the mercy to forgive like You forgive.

Jesus Welcomes the Children

Jesus said, "Let the children come to Me. Don't stop them! For the kingdom of heaven belongs to those who are like these children." And He placed His hands on their heads and blessed them before He left (Matt. 19:14-15).

Here we have one of the most beautiful pictures of the gospel. The characters in it stand out clearly and the story is only two verses long. First, there are the people who brought the children – undoubtedly their mothers. It is not surprising that they wanted Jesus to lay His hands on them, because they had already seen Him make bad things disappear with His hands: He opened blind eyes; He made pain and sickness disappear. Here we clearly see the glory of Jesus.

Secondly, there were the disciples who sounded stern and unfriendly. But it was because of their love for Jesus. They were only trying to protect Him. They saw how tired He was and the price He paid for performing all the healings, power flowing from Him every time. They did not want Jesus to get too tired. So many demands had already been made on Him.

> The soul is healed by being with child.
> FYODOR DOSTOEVSKY

Then there was Jesus Himself. The story tells us so much about Him. He was the kind of friendly adult that children love. This goes to show that no one who needed Jesus was unimportant to Him. The road to Jesus is clear for the most humble person, and even for little children.

Finally, there were the children. Christ says that they are nearer to God than anyone else, because of their humility. This is the tragedy in life: the older we get, the farther we move away from God.

Lord Jesus, give me the heart and the attitude of a child.

Love's Answer to a Cry for Help

Two blind men were sitting beside the road. When they heard that Jesus was coming that way, they began shouting, "Lord, Son of David, have mercy on us!" (Matt. 20:30).

Here we have the story of two people who found their way to a miracle. It portrays the type of spirit and attitude of mind and heart that receives God's most precious gifts. These two blind men waited and when their chance came, they grabbed hold of it with both hands. They had probably heard of Jesus' miracles and wondered if that power would also be available to them. If they let Jesus pass them by, they would never have another chance. But they grabbed the opportunity. There comes a time in our lives that we must decide and act.

These two men would simply not be discouraged. The crowds told them to stop shouting because they were making a nuisance of themselves. But nothing could stop them because to them it was either blindness for the rest of their lives or the ability to see. We are so easily discouraged to seek out the face of God. It is the person who cannot be kept away from Christ that eventually finds Him.

> The very limit of human blindness is to glory in being blind.
> St. Augustine

These blind men had imperfect faith, but they were determined to make use of the faith that they had. They acted in their faith and Jesus accepted it. No matter how imperfect, if there is any measure of faith at all, Jesus will accept it. No request is too big for God. The blind men were also thankful people. They received what they desired with all their hearts and were deeply thankful. Afterwards they followed Jesus. Being unthankful is a horrible sin. These people followed Jesus out of gratitude.

Miracle-working Jesus, give me perseverance, faith and gratitude because I have been saved.

The Wisdom of a Simple Heart

The leading priests and the teachers of religious law saw these wonderful miracles and heard even the children in the Temple shouting, "Praise God for the Son of David." But the leaders were indignant. They asked Jesus, "Do You hear what these children are saying?" "Yes," Jesus replied. "Haven't you ever read the Scriptures? For they say, 'You have taught children and infants to give You praise'" (Matt. 21:15-16).

We read in Psalm 8:2: "You have taught children and infants to tell of Your strength, silencing Your enemies and all who oppose You." On this particular day, a few things happened in the Temple that had never happened before. The merchants and their customers were driven out of the Temple by Jesus, two blind men regained their eyesight, and a paralyzed person was healed. Possibly, there wouldn't always have been children present, but this day was no ordinary day.

> You can learn many things from children. How much patience you have, for instance.
> FRANKLIN P. JONES

We accept the story just as it is written in the Scriptures and listen to the fresh, clear voices of jubilant children rejoicing and praising God. Then we are confronted with one great truth: There are certain truths that only the simple-hearted can understand and which are hidden from the wise. There are times when heaven is nearer to the heart of a child than to the most sensible adult. Children test the truth in their own special way.

George Macdonald said that he sets great store by the Christianity of the person who has children playing at his door and garden gate, because they aren't afraid to do so. If a child thinks a person is good, that person probably is.

Lord Jesus, Friend of children, grant that I pass the test of a child's eyes.

Let Your Joy Overflow

"I have told you these things so that you will be filled with My joy. Yes, your joy will overflow!" (John 15:11).

Is your joy overflowing today? When something overflows there isn't really room for anything else. It is a feeling of complete fulfillment. God wants our joy to be perfect. But too many of us plod through the day with sour faces, lacking enthusiasm. We hardly smile, let alone laugh. Everything seems to be a problem and a burden to us.

God didn't create us to merely endure life. He created us to enjoy it with gladness. We are not meant to go through life with long faces; negative, sour and irritable human beings. As believers and redeemed people, you and I should be the most cheerful people on earth. We should radiate joy wherever we go so that we brighten the day of others, filling it with joy.

The key to this is choosing love by choosing God, and by accepting and keeping His commandments. This is how joy starts overflowing. Is there an area in your life that you know you need to change so that you can live in obedience to His Word? Do it now. Don't become disconnected from God, even for a moment, because it is a wasted moment. Rather choose to obey Him, and choose love so that your joy can overflow.

> Joy is the experience of knowing that you are unconditionally loved and that nothing – sickness, failure, emotional distress, oppression, war, or even death – can take that love away.
> HENRI NOUWEN

Father God, I humbly plead that You would give me peace and wisdom to do what is right in Your eyes. Thank You that You make my joy perfect when I chose to obey Your Word.

Whatever You Ask For

"The Father will give you whatever you ask for, using My name"
(John 15:16).

This Bible verse is one of Christ's greatest pronouncements and we must make sure that we understand it correctly. A superficial reading of Jesus' words might make us misunderstand them, so that it sounds like those who are chosen by God, His reborn children, can ask just for anything, and they will receive it. However, the New Testament very clearly lays down definite and decisive principles about prayer.

Prayer must be offered in faith (see James 5:15). When prayer is merely a formality, a routine repetition of the same words and requests, it cannot be answered. When prayers are without hope, they cannot be answered. In order to pray powerfully, we must have unwavering faith in the omnipotence and love of God.

> The purpose of all prayer is to find God's will and to make that our prayer.
> CATHERINE MARSHALL

We must pray in the name of Christ. We cannot pray for things we know Jesus will disapprove of. The moment we ask for something that will enable us to achieve our own ambitions and desires, the prayer becomes powerless.

Prayer must declare: "Let Your will be done!" True prayer shouldn't always ask for what we want, but rather what Jesus wants. Prayer must never be selfish. Jesus once said, "If two of you agree here on earth concerning anything you ask, My Father in heaven will do it for you" (Matt. 18:19). This means that no one should think only of their own needs when praying. The greatest danger of prayer is that we pray as if no one but ourselves matter. The more we love God, the easier it is to pray correctly.

I praise and thank You, Lord Jesus, that You are my perfect example, also in prayer.

The World's Hatred

"If the world hates you, remember that it hated Me first" (John 15:18).

The world hated the early Christians for different reasons, and unfortunately it is true that the world still hates Christians today. By "the world" John meant the human community trying to function without God. There is obviously a difference between the person who regards God as the only reality in life, and the person who regards Him as irrelevant to life.

The world is wary of people who are "different." This can be caused by the most trivial of things. One of the most common items in the world today is the umbrella. Yet when Jonas Hanway introduced it to England by walking down the street holding one, he was bombarded with stones and mud. All people who are different, who wear unusual clothes or who have their own ideas about things, are automatically branded as crazy, eccentric, or a danger to society.

> For Paul the Spirit was the absolutely crucial matter for Christian life from beginning to end.
> HERMANN GUNKEL

The world disapproves of those whose lives appear to be a condemnation of their own. The fact is that it is dangerous to be "good." Aristides of Athens was known as "Aristides the Just" and yet he was banished.

In its broadest sense, one could say the world hates those who do not conform. The world likes a pattern; it likes to classify people by labeling them. Being different is dangerous, but nobody can be a Christian unless they take up this challenge. There will always be a difference between Christ's followers and the "world's" followers.

O Holy Spirit of God, give me the courage and conviction to be different.

Inner Conviction

"When the Counselor comes, whom I will send to you from the Father, He will testify about Me. And you must also testify, for you have been with Me from the beginning" (John 15:26-27 NIV).

Here Jesus mentions two aspects that were very important to Him. The first is the testimony of the Holy Spirit. What does Jesus mean by this? What is it that makes people feel, when they hear Jesus' stories and when His teachings unfold before them, that they are about the Son of God? What is it that enables us to say instinctively that there is godly wisdom in it? This is the work of the Holy Spirit inside us, helping us to respond to Jesus.

The second is the testimony about Jesus that people are to take into the world: "And you must also testify." Christian testimonies are borne of a long and intimate relationship with Christ. The disciples were His witnesses because they were with Him from the very beginning. A witness is a person who testifies: "This is the truth *and I know it.*" Without personal experience there can be no witnessing. We can only testify about Christ if we have a real relationship with Him.

> It is the signature of the Holy Ghost upon our work and witness that makes all the difference.
> DUNCAN CAMPBELL

Our Christian testimony comes from a place of inner conviction. We can tell when someone has hardly begun speaking if what they are saying is credible or not. A witness is not only someone who *knows* something is true; they are willing to say that they are *convinced* it is true. These people don't want to be the only ones who know Christ; they want others to get to know Him as well.

Lord Jesus, help me to be Your faithful witness wherever You put me in the world.

The Work of the Holy Spirit

"It is good for you that I am going away. Unless I go away, the Counselor will not come to you; but if I go away, I will send Him to you" (John 16:7).

T he disciples were in low spirits, because all they knew was that they were going to lose Jesus. But He reassures them that it will be better for them, because if He went away, the Holy Spirit would come. If Jesus stayed with them, they would not have been able to follow Him wherever He went. If He remained in human form, He would not be able to enter into the thoughts, hearts and minds of people. He would be limited to human restrictions of place and time. But the Holy Spirit has no such restrictions. Wherever we go, the Holy Spirit goes with us.

Jesus' words are a perfect summary of the Holy Spirit's work. The word that John uses here for the work of the Spirit is *elegchein*. Some translations interpret it as "reprimand" and others to "convince." The problem is that the word *elegchein* cannot be translated in a single word.

> The Holy Spirit came on the Day of Pentecost. He has never left the church.
>
> JOHN STOTT

It is a word that is used in the cross examination of a witness, or the trial of a criminal, or of an opponent in an argument. Such a cross examination may have two outcomes: It can reprimand a person for the wrong they have done, or it can convince them that the case has little merit. In our verse for today, we see both these meanings: We need to be both convinced and reprimanded. Now we can go forward and understand what Jesus wants to tell us about the work of the Spirit.

Holy Spirit of God, help me to hear what Jesus wants to say to me personally.

The Conviction of the Holy Spirit

"When He comes, He will convict the world of guilt in regard to sin and righteousness and judgment" (John 16:8).

The Holy Spirit will convict the world of guilt. When the Jews crucified Jesus, they didn't believe they were committing a sin. But when the story of the crucifixion was preached later, they were "cut to the heart" (Acts 2:37). They were deeply convinced that the crucifixion had been the greatest sin in living memory. We cannot be aware of our need for a Savior without the conviction of sin. Why would the story of the crucifixion of a man two thousand years ago break the hearts of people all over the entire world? It is the Holy Spirit's influence in our hearts.

> Every time we say, "I believe in the Holy Spirit," we mean that we believe that there is a living God able and willing to enter human personality and change it.
>
> J. B. PHILLIPS

The Holy Spirit will convict us of righteousness. What does this mean? We will understand it once we are convinced of Christ's righteousness. Jesus was crucified as a criminal. He stood trial and was found guilty. He was regarded by the Jews as an evil person who taught false doctrines, and the Romans saw Him as a dangerous troublemaker. He was given the most severe punishment and branded an enemy of God. What changed everything? What made people see the Son of God in the crucified man, like the Roman officer, who said, "This man was truly the Son of God!"? (Matt. 27:54). When one reflects on this, it is amazing to think that people would put their trust for their eternity in a Jewish criminal. It is the work of the Holy Spirit that convinces us of Jesus Christ's righteousness, supported by the fact that Jesus was raised from the dead and ascended to the Father.

Thank You, Spirit of God, that You also made me see and confess my sins and unbelief.

God's Righteous Judgment

"When He comes, He will convict the world of guilt in regard to sin and righteousness and judgment" (John 16:8).

〜〜

The Holy Spirit convinces people of God's righteous judgment. There on the cross hung evil and sin: tried, condemned and defeated. What gives us the certainty that there is something called "the wrath of God"? How do we know for sure that there will be a coming judgment? Why can't we just do what we want? What convinces us that judgment awaits us? Once again it is the Holy Spirit at work.

There is still one more thing about the Holy Spirit that John doesn't go into here. After we have been convinced of our sin, assured of Christ's righteousness and convinced of God's coming judgment, what gives us the certainty that our salvation lies in the cross? That we are forgiven in Christ and will be saved from condemnation? *This is also the Holy Spirit's work.*

> The Holy Spirit, object of faith, is also an object of prayer: we must not only pray that we receive the Holy Spirit. We must pray to Him.
> KARL BARTH

It is the Holy Spirit who convinces us and assures us that this crucified figure is also the object of our salvation: our Savior and Redeemer. The Holy Spirit convinces us of our sin, but also that our Savior and Redeemer is Jesus, the living Christ. Does the Holy Spirit have His rightful place in your life so that He can carry out His important work? May God enable you to honestly answer, "Yes"!

Come, O Spirit of God, and continuously do Your convicting work in my life.

The Glory of the Cross

"I brought glory to You here on earth by completing the work You gave Me to do" (John 17:4).

For Christ the cross was the glory of life and the glory of eternal life. He often spoke about the glory of the cross and His transfiguration. This is one of the great facts of history that is proved over and over again; that genuinely great people find glory in death. They might have been misunderstood in their lifetime, unappreciated, branded as criminals; but in death they find nobility and their true calling. Time and time again it has been proved that the glory of martyrs is demonstrated in death. It was the same with Jesus when the Roman officer declared at the foot of the cross, "This Man truly was the Son of God!" (Matt 27:54). Jesus was never as majestic in life as He was in death, and this is why the cross brought Him glory.

> By the cross we know the gravity of sin and the greatness of God's love towards us.
>
> JOHN CRYSOSTOM

Furthermore, the cross brought glory to Christ because it concluded His task: "I brought glory to You here on earth by completing the work You gave Me to do." If Christ had ended His mission before reaching the cross, it would have meant that His task remained unfinished. Jesus came to the world to tell people – and to show them – the great love of God. Stopping with this work before the cross would have implied that Jesus felt the love of God would go a certain distance, but no farther. By taking up the cross, Jesus told the world that nothing would stand in the way of God's great love for humanity – His love really knows no bounds.

I bow before You as I worship You, Lord Jesus, that You were faithful to the love of God till death.

God Glorified

"I have glorified You down here on the earth by completing the work that You gave Me to do" (John 17:4 AMP).

⌒ ◯G ⌒

How was God glorified through the cross of Jesus? There is only one way of glorifying God, and that is by obeying Him. Children honor their parents when they obey them. Citizens bring honor to their country when they obey its laws. Learners bring glory to their teachers when they are obedient. Jesus brought glory to God by His absolute obedience. Jesus could have evaded the cross by not returning to Jerusalem. If we look at Jesus' last days and His crucifixion, we are inclined to say, "Look how He loved God. Look how far His obedience went." It was perfect love and perfect obedience.

> Christ's blood is heaven's key.
> THOMAS BROOKS

But there is more: Jesus prayed that God would glorify Christ and also Himself. The cross was not the end! The resurrection would follow the crucifixion. The resurrection was Jesus' absolution. It was the proof that people could do their absolute worst, but that nothing could eliminate, defeat or break Him. The glory of the resurrection erased the shame of the cross.

The cross was the way back for Jesus: "Now, Father, bring Me into the glory We shared before the world began" (John 17:5). Jesus was like the knight who left the king's court to go on a dangerous mission. After He had accomplished it, He returned home triumphantly to celebrate the glory of the victory. Jesus came from God and returned to God. The link between His coming from the Father and His return, was the cross. For this reason the cross was His entrance to the glory of victory and triumph.

Lord, when I see the cross on which the King of heaven hung, all my efforts are delusions and so am I. And then I detest pride and self-interest.

Jesus' Work

"I have revealed You to those whom You gave Me out of the world. They were Yours; You gave them to Me and they have obeyed Your Word" (John 17:6 NIV).

Here Jesus gives a definition of the work He did. There are two main ideas, which we'll discuss over the next day or two.

There was an essential and characteristic belief about names in the Old Testament. A person's name served a very specific purpose. It was an indication of the character of the person. "Those who know Your name trust in You, for You, O LORD, do not abandon those who search for you" (Psalm 9:10). This doesn't mean that those who know God's name will trust Him, but that those who know what He's like, who know God's character and nature, will put their trust in Him. The psalmist places his trust in the character and nature of God. He knew that he could trust God because he knew who God was: "I will proclaim Your name to my brothers and sisters. I will praise You among Your assembled people" (Ps. 22:22).

> Whether life is good or bad, God's goodness, rooted in His character, is the same.
>
> HELEN GRACE LESCHEID

The Jews believed that Psalm 22 was a prophecy of the Messiah and of the work He would do: revealing God to humankind. The following is Isaiah's vision of the new age: "I will reveal My name to My people, and they will come to know its power" (Isa. 52:6). In this golden period, humankind would fully and truly know God. Therefore, when Jesus said, "I have revealed Your name," He was in fact saying, "I have enabled people to see the true character and nature of God. It was another way of saying, "Anyone who has seen Me has seen the Father"! (John 14:9).

I kneel in worship before You, Lord Jesus, because You showed me who God truly is.

The Holy Name of God

"I have revealed You to the ones You gave Me from this world. They were always Yours. You gave them to Me and they have kept Your Word" (John 17:6).

Today's verse tells us something more about the name of God. When the Jews used the name of God in later times, they referred to the holy four-letter symbol; it was called the *tetragrammaton:* IHWH. The name was regarded as so holy that it was never spoken out loud, except by the High Priest when he went into the Holy of Holies on the Day of Atonement. It could not be expressed by the lips of ordinary people. These four letters represent the name *Jahweh* (there are no vowels in the Hebrew alphabet). Later, the vowel sounds were indicated by small signs that were added above and below the consonants. The vowels in the name *Adonai* were placed underneath them so that readers didn't read *Jahweh* when they got to IHWH, but *Adonai*.

> All things were made by Him; and without Him was not anything made that was made.
> St. Augustine

In Jesus' time, God's name was so holy that the man on the street was not even supposed to know it, let alone express it. God was the distant, invisible King whose name was not to be spoken. Thus Jesus was saying in today's text: "I have made known to you the name of God. Now it may be used because of the work I came to do."

This is Jesus' great claim: that He made the true nature and character of God known to people; and that He brought God into intimacy with the humblest of people. Christians can speak to Him themselves, and allow His name on their lips.

Mediator and Friend, thank You that You brought God and His love close to me.

The Meaning of Discipleship

"They were Yours; You gave them to Me and they have obeyed Your Word" (John 17:6 NIV).

～◯⌒◯～

This passage in Scripture sheds light on the meaning of discipleship. Discipleship is based on the realization that Jesus came from God. Disciples are in their very being people who realize that Jesus is God's ambassador. We become aware of the voice of God Himself in Jesus' words, and observe God's hand in Jesus' actions. Disciples are people who see God in Jesus, and who know that in the whole universe, nobody is as united with God as Jesus is.

Discipleship is born of obedience. Disciples are people who hold onto Jesus' words as they hear them; people who acknowledge Jesus' mastership and who have made Jesus' words their law of life. As long as we desire independence – following our own will – we cannot be disciples. Discipleship requires submission and is grounded in obedience.

> The strength and happiness of a man consists in finding the way in which God is going, and going that way too.
>
> HENRY WARD BEECHER

Discipleship is predetermined. Jesus' people are given to Him by God. In God's plan, they are chosen for discipleship. God has His plan, His dream, His destiny for every person. The fearsome responsibility is that we can accept or decline God's plan for our lives. We are not in the hands of destiny, but in the hands of God.

This whole portion of Scripture resounds with a harmonious trust in Jesus' voice concerning the future. Jesus thanked God for the people God gave Him and He never doubted that they would carry on with the work He assigned them. Jesus had faith in God, as well as in people: the future possibilities are unlimited!

Holy Spirit, I praise You that You allow me to hear and obey the call to discipleship.

Jesus' Prayer

"My prayer is not for the world, but for those You have given Me, because they belong to You" (John 17:9).

✦⁓◯⌒✦

This section of the Bible is so packed with truths that we can grasp only fragments of it. First it tells us something about Christ's disciples: that God gave them to Jesus. This means that the Holy Spirit moves people's hearts, causing them to respond to Jesus' appeal. When our hearts go out to Jesus in love and worship, it is the Spirit of God working in us. Jesus is glorified through His disciples. It is like a student's gratitude towards their teacher when they have passed with flying colors, or a successful cricketer who praises his coach. It is the people Jesus has saved and set free who contribute to Jesus' glory.

A disciple is a person who has been given a task. Just as God sent Jesus, Jesus sends out His disciples. In this Bible verse, we also find the explanation of a puzzling matter. Jesus starts off by saying He doesn't pray for the world, and yet He came to the world because God loved the world so much. But as we have already seen, John uses the phrase "the world" to indicate the human community that wishes to live without God. What Jesus does for the world is to send His disciples into it, to lead the world back to God again and to give them a new awareness of God.

> Preach the gospel every day; if necessary, use words.
> St. Francis of Assisi

Jesus offers His disciples two things: joy, and a warning. Everything He says to them will bring them joy and make them "different" from the world. It is by enduring the scorn of the world that we will experience Christ's love at its best.

Risen and glorified Lord Jesus, thank You that I may be Your faithful witness.

"Keep Them Safe"

"I'm not asking You to take them out of the world, but to keep them safe from the evil one" (John 17:15).

The significance of this portion in Scripture is that it tells us what specifically Jesus prayed for His disciples. The first aspect is that Jesus didn't pray for the disciples to be taken out of the world. He didn't pray for escape, but for victory. Christians who buried themselves in a cloister didn't look like disciples to Jesus at all. Christians who experience the essence of life in prayer and meditation, who withdraw from life and the world, have a type of misconception about faith.

Jesus insists that Christians witness in the hustle and bustle of the real world. Naturally we all need quiet times of meditation and prayer. Among other things, this quiet time is necessary to find strength and motivation to witness in the world. Christians should never wish to escape from life; rather, they should try to win the world for Christ.

> The unity of Christendom is not a luxury, but a necessity.
>
> CHARLES H. BRENT

Secondly, Jesus prayed for the unity of the disciples; that they would be one, like He and the Father are one. Where there is a group, people are excluded; where there is competition, there is division and discord. The gospel cannot be spread successfully as long as there is competition among churches. Jesus prayed that His disciples would be completely united, like He and the Father. The answer to this prayer, more than any other of Jesus' prayers, is hindered by individual Christians and churches. It is an unfortunate but indisputable fact.

Lord Jesus, help Your children and Your churches on earth to be one, like You and the Father are one.

Remain in the Truth

"My prayer is not that You take them out of the world but that You protect them from the evil one" (John 17:15 NIV).

∽♡∼

Jesus prayed that God would keep His disciples from evil and hold them close. The Bible is not a speculative book: It doesn't discuss the origin of evil, but assures us that evil is powerfully at work in the world. It is in direct opposition to God's authority, an evil authority with the purpose of luring people from the right road. It is encouraging to know that God watches over our lives and protects us from the onslaughts of Satan. The reason we so often stumble is because we try to do things in our own strength, forgetting to seek God's help. We need to remember the presence of our God watching over us.

Jesus prayed that His disciples would remain in the truth: "Make them holy by Your truth; teach them Your word which is truth" (John 17:17).

> Leadership is found in becoming the servant of all.
> RICHARD FOSTER

The word that is translated here as "holy" is from the word *hagios*. The meaning of *hagios* is "different" or "set apart." So the word means to be set aside for a specific purpose. When God called Jeremiah, He said, "Before you were born I set you apart and appointed you as my prophet to the nations" (Jer. 1:5). When God wanted to create the priesthood in Israel, He said that Aaron's sons were to be "set apart as holy" so that they could serve as His priests (see Exod. 28:41).

Thus God not only chooses people to serve Him, but He also equips them with the necessary skills. In His love and grace God chooses and equips us for the tasks we are given.

Holy God, help me to hear Your voice so that I may be set apart and equipped by You.

Into the Future

"I pray that they will all be one, just as You and I are one – as You are in Me, Father, and I am in You. And may they be in Us so that the world will believe You sent Me" (John 17:21).

J esus' prayer in today's Scripture gradually spreads to the ends of the earth. First He prays for Himself as He is faced with the cross. He prays for His disciples and for God's protective power over them. Then His prayer includes the distant future, and Jesus prays for those in distant lands and future generations who accept the Christian faith.

Two particular attributes of Christ are revealed here. First, we see His perfect faith and radiant certainty. At this stage, His followers were few, but even with the bleak prospect of the cross ahead of Him, His faith was undimmed and He prayed for those who would believe in Him in the future. This remains Christ's prayer for us today.

> I might worship in a different building from you, I may worship in a different style, but all we hold dear is God's gift in Christ Jesus, who is our Unity. In Him we have all and lack nothing.
> MICHAEL J. DAVIS

Secondly, we see Jesus' absolute trust in His disciples. He knew they didn't fully understand Him and that they would soon leave Him in His greatest agony. And yet it was these people He trusted to spread God's love. He never lost faith in God or His people. And what was His prayer for the future church? It was that the members should be one, like He and the Father are one. This oneness was not for unity in organization and administration. It was for harmony in a relationship of love and obedience.

Holy and loving Master, let the work of the Spirit continue and may unity be established among Your disciples.

The Gift and the Promise of Glory

"Father, I want those You have given Me to be with Me where I am, and to see My glory, the glory You have given Me because You loved Me even before the creation of the word" (John 17:24).

In today's Scripture passage, Jesus says He gave His disciples the same glory that God gave Him. Christ speaks about His glory in different ways. The cross was His glory. Therefore, more than anything, as Christians our glory lies in carrying our cross.

It is an honor to suffer for Christ. We must never think of the cross as punishment, but as a privilege. The harder the task the knight has to perform, the greater the glory. When we find it hard to be a Christian, we must see it as God's gift and promise of glory.

> The glory of God, and, as our only means to glorifying Him, the salvation of souls, is the real business of life.
> C. S. Lewis

Secondly, Jesus' absolute obedience to the will of God was His glory. We find our glory, our honor, our life, not by doing what we want, but by doing God's will. When we try to do what we want, it ends in sorrow and disaster for ourselves and others. The greater our obedience, the greater the glory.

Jesus' greatness lies in the fact that people saw an intimate relationship with God in His words, His life and His deeds. They knew that no one could live like that if they didn't have a special bond with God. Our honor is when people see God reflected in us. They see it in our service to others; in our love for others.

Holy Father God, may my fellow humans see Your love in my life.

Sharing the Cross

"Father, I want these whom You have given Me to be with Me where I am. Then they can see all the glory You gave Me because You loved Me even before the world began!" (John 17:24).

Jesus says He would like His disciples to see His glory in the heavenly realm. It is the Christian's conviction to share *all* Christ's experiences. If we are to share Christ's cross, we should also share in His glory: "If we die with Him, we will also live with Him. If we endure hardship, we will reign with Him" (2 Tim. 2:11-12) and "Now we see things imperfectly, like puzzling reflections in a mirror, but then we will see everything with perfect clarity" (1 Cor. 13:12).

The joy we know now is merely a poor foretaste of what is still to come. It is Christ's promise to His disciples that if we share in His suffering on earth, we will also share in the glory of His triumph when our life here is over. What greater promise could there be? When the commentator Bengel commented on this portion of Scripture, he proclaimed, "How great is the Christian's glory!" Yes, indeed.

> The great end of God's works, which is so variously expressed in Scripture, is indeed by one; and this one end is most properly and comprehensively called the glory of God.
> JONATHAN EDWARDS

After Jesus prayed this prayer, the betrayal of Judas took place and this was followed by His death on the cross. He would not speak to His disciples again. But it is wonderful and precious to know that before these horrific hours began, Jesus' last words were not words of despair, but of radiant hope.

Thank You, Lord and Master, for Your encouraging words to all Your disciples.

The Symbolism of the Cross

May I never boast about anything except the cross of our Lord Jesus Christ. Because of that cross, my interest in this world has been crucified, and the world's interest in me has also died (Gal. 6:14).

～ ♋ ～

Before we get to what Jesus' said on His path of Suffering, we must first understand the symbolism of the cross, otherwise we won't understand Jesus' words. The cross of reconciliation is, after all, the essence of our religious life. The cross dominates many churches, but it seldom has anything to do with Jesus' suffering. It adorns practically every Bible and takes a prominent place in many churches, especially at the altar.

Over the years, the cross became a root of superstition. Farmers painted it on their stables, not as a sign of godliness, but to protect the animals against sickness. People placed crosses on the borders of their farms so that no one would trespass or move the boundries. People believed in the power of the sign of the cross, instead of praying to God in heaven. All of this could have been prevented if people knew the Bible better.

> The death of Christ was the most dreadful blow ever given to the empire of darkness.
> WILLIAM S. PLUMMER

Moses erected the bronze serpent in the desert on God's orders, to heal those who looked up to it in faith. Jesus Himself declared in His conversation with Nicodemus that the bronze serpent was an image of Himself on the cross. Yet the bronze serpent later became an object of idolatry, to the detriment of the Israelites' faith. When Hezekiah became king, he got rid of all forms of idolatry – including the bronze serpent: "He smashed the sacred stones and cut down the Ashterah pole. He broke into pieces the bronze snake Moses had made" (2 Kings 18:4).

Lord Jesus, may Your cross always be the symbol of Your love.

The Sign of the Cross

Because of that cross, my interest in this world has been crucified, and the world's interest in me has also died (Gal. 6:14).

King Hezekiah gave a warning to stop all religious worship of the cross or to attribute magical powers to it. This did not apply to the cross only, but also to so-called holy relics that were revered. This is a fact that is confirmed by history. The sign of the cross will always awaken a feeling of reverence in the heart of every Christian. Its only function should be to remind us of what Christ achieved on the cross. Therefore it is understandable that the Reformists put aside the sign of the cross together with religious relics, to prevent Christians from focusing on something that was at most a symbol or a sign.

> The cross is God's truth about us, and therefore it is the only power which can make us truthful. When we know the cross we are no longer afraid of the truth.
> DIETRICH BONHOEFFER

It is noteworthy that Christ didn't leave us anything of Himself that is visible or tangible. His loin cloth and shroud do not exist anymore; the place where He was buried has never been identified with any certainty; nothing He ever wrote down remained. Would these objects then be meaningless? One cannot think this would be the case. There must be some godly order in the total absence of these things. In this lies an indication that our worship should not look for support in visible things. Should we cling to the visible, we follow the way of Thomas, who wanted to see and feel before believing. For this reason, the words Jesus spoke before and after His crucifixion are of the utmost importance, which we will examine over the next few days.

I thank and praise You, Lord Jesus, that the cross is bare and that the throne in heaven is occupied.

Jesus in Gethsemane

Then Jesus went with His disciples to a place called Gethsemane, and He said to them, "Sit here while I go over there and pray" (Matt. 26:36 NIV).

Gethsemane! How charged with holy perceptions this name is to the believer! Today we come to a stop at the Via Dolorosa – Christ's road of sorrow.

Gethsemane means "olive press." We tread on holy ground when we cross the bridge over the brook, Cedron, and move on into the shadows of the olive trees. Let us take off our shoes and bow our heads, for Jesus was here Himself to wrestle in prayer with God. Gethsemane symbolizes the crushing weight Jesus carried on the cross. Christ prayed His High Priest prayer for others, then He prayed for God to equip Him for His massive offering: to make the impossible possible; to bear the unbearable.

"Is this the only way to save the world?" asked our Savior. "Is it not possible to find another way?" Earlier, Satan showed Jesus the other, easier way. During Christ's temptation in the desert, Satan said, "I will give it all to You, if You will only kneel down and worship me" (Matt. 4:9). Jesus didn't want to take the easier way without God's approval. Here in Gethsemane it was not Jesus' body that was crucified, but His will. Our Lord placed all His wishes and desires on the Father's altar. Although the cup of suffering made Him shudder, He still accepted it from the Father's hand. He let His will become His Father's. He bowed in obedience and carried the burden of the world to Golgotha.

> If I cannot commit the matter and go on in peace and in silence, remembering Gethsemane and the cross, then I know nothing of Calvary.
> AMY CARMICHAEL

Grant, Lord Jesus, that when I arrive at my Gethsemane, Your example will be my inspiration.

The Victory of Gethsemane

Then Jesus went with them to the olive grove called Gethsemane,
and He said, "Sit here while I go over there to pray" (Matt. 26:36).

In Gethsemane Christ not only submitted to the will of His Father, but in doing so He showed that He was willing to suffer and die at Golgotha. Although He had to walk the Way of Suffering, the Son of God emerged from Gethsemane victoriously. "Because one person disobeyed God, many became sinners. But because one other person obeyed God, many will be made righteous" (Rom. 5:19). We must hear and understand: The disobedient will be accepted as righteous; children of wrath will become children of God.

> To endure the cross
> is not a tragedy; it is the
> suffering which is the fruit
> of an exclusive allegiance
> to Jesus Christ.
> DIETRICH BONHOEFFER

The victory of Gethsemane doesn't lie in the fact that we eventually settle for the unavoidable because we can't do anything about it. This is not surrender; it is fatalistic defeat. Such people are not in harmony with God's will. Victory is when we accept the glory of God's will above our own. It is never a disaster, but an indescribable blessing.

When everything doesn't revolve around our own will anymore, but around God's, we are winners. Even if it happens in a sea of blood and tears, all is still well. If we follow God's travel plan, we will reach the safe harbor. Gethsemane obedience ensures Gethsemane victory. Christ was able to bear the unbearable because of His obedience. The forces of Satan will be made powerless; his head will be crushed and lost humankind will be saved.

Lord Jesus, I kneel down and worship You, for Your obedience in
Gethsemane.

Weep for Yourselves

A large crowd trailed behind, including many grief-stricken women. But Jesus turned and said to them, "Daughters of Jerusalem, don't weep for Me, but weep for yourselves and for your children" (Luke 23:27-28).

〜♋〜

It was a sad and heart-stirring procession that made its way to Golgotha that Friday morning. Everything testified to hardness in people's hearts: Jesus' bleeding body, His thorn-covered head and the rugged wooden cross. The haughty Roman soldiers felt no pity for Him. The voices of the people were hoarse from shouting, "Crucify Him! Crucify Him!" Simon of Cyrene was forced to help Jesus carry His cross, not because of the people's compassion, but because they were worried Jesus wouldn't make it to Golgotha and they would be robbed of their brutal spectacle.

> What soap is for the body, tears are for the soul.
> JEWISH PROVERB

But in this world of pitiless harshness we suddenly see an exception: A group of women sorrowfully following Jesus, grieving His pain and humiliation. Their tears must have meant a lot to Jesus. It gave Him the assurance that not everyone had become hard and unfeeling. These tears were not without value. Human feelings are often the gate through which God's grace flows. They can be the bridge that blessedness crosses to enter a heart. It must have moved Jesus and filled Him with thankfulness: There were still tears in this merciless world.

And there along the road, Jesus stopped, turned to them and said, "Don't weep for Me, but weep for yourselves and for your children" (Luke 23:28). Why did Jesus tell them not to weep for Him? And why did He tell them to weep for themselves and their children? We will find out tomorrow.

Lord Jesus, grant that I may never become uncaring about Your sorrow for the sake of my own.

Man of Sorrows

Jesus turned and said to them, "Daughters of Jerusalem, don't weep for Me, but weep for yourselves and for your children" (Luke 23:28).

✦⟡✦

We concluded yesterday's devotion with two questions: Why did Jesus tell the women not to weep for Him? And why did He tell them to weep for themselves and their children? Jesus' path, no matter how painful, was the way of salvation for the whole world. His suffering wouldn't be in vain, but would bear wonderful fruit in the lives of millions of people, including yours and mine. One doesn't weep for the labor pains of a woman giving birth; this process is the beginning of new life. Thus Jesus' pain brought life for many – why then should they cry?

> The soul would know no rainbow had the eyes no tears.
> St. John of the Cross

At the end of Jesus' suffering a glorious reward awaited Him. It is the end result of our grief that is important and not the suffering of the moment. That is why Jesus told them not to weep for Him. Furthermore, the road of suffering was also the road of glorification. His road of humiliation was a long, dark road, but there's no doubt that it led to infinite glory. God would raise Him up to the heights of heaven and give Him a name above all names, so that in the name of Jesus every knee would bow and every tongue would confess that He is Christ, to the glory of God (see Phil. 2:5-11).

No, Jesus was definitely not the unhappiest person in that procession. While it is true that He was on His way to Calvary, that He was carrying a heavy cross, that He was the Man of Sorrows, He was certainly not pitiable. Everyone around Him was far worse off than He.

I bow before You, Lord Jesus, who walked the road of suffering with distinction.

Jerusalem

Jesus said, "Daughters of Jerusalem, don't weep for Me, but weep for yourselves and for your children" (Luke 23:28).

⌒◌⌒

Why did Jesus tell the women to cry for themselves and their children? Hadn't they just called out to Pilate, "We will take responsibility for His death – we and our children"? (Matt. 27:25). They had reason to cry because they were women and daughters of Jerusalem. Had Jerusalem not been the city of grace, the earthly Zion? Now the city of grace was going to become a city of blood! That was enough to make anyone cry! When people are given grace, they are also given responsibilities. Those who are not saved by godly grace bring a terrible judgment on themselves. And so it was with Jerusalem: They rejected God's grace.

> I did not weep, so
> like a stone had
> I become within.
>
> DANTE

They should also weep because they rejected Christ and because of that, they lost the chance of being saved themselves. Although they were drowning, they threw the only lifebuoy away. For these people salvation was no longer possible.

They should also weep because they sinned against the highest form of love and for this people would suffer an unthinkable punishment. Jesus walked down the streets and invited them, "Come to Me, all of you who are weary and carry heavy burdens, and I will give you rest" (Matt. 11:28).

There was a time when Jesus wept for Jerusalem and wanted to gather everyone together like a hen gathers her chicks, but they didn't want Him to. This meant death. When we think about these things we begin to understand why Jesus told these women to rather cry for themselves and their children than for Him.

Lord Jesus, I wept for my sins, and in Your grace, You forgave me and accepted me.

Crying Daughters

"Daughters of Jerusalem, don't weep for Me, but weep for yourselves and for your children" (Luke 23:28).

The judgment that was passed on Jerusalem was shattering, and some of these weeping women experienced it themselves. Thirty-seven years later, in the year AD 70, Jerusalem was besieged and tens of thousands died from hunger and the plague. People hid in the city's sewers to escape the enemy. Youths were crucified until there was no more wood to make crosses. Mothers killed their own children because they couldn't bear their suffering any longer. They called out: "Mountains, fall on us! Hills, bury us!" Anything was better than falling into the hands of the Romans. Do you see, dear reader, one can cry for Jesus and still not escape a horrific judgment. Our relationship with the Lord Jesus is a very serious matter.

> Heaven knows we need never be ashamed of our tears, for they are rain upon the blinding dust of the earth, overlying our hard hearts.
> CHARLES DICKENS

These crying daughters of Jerusalem have something to say to us. It would be good to listen well: We can feel compassion for the Man of Sorrows and yet not be saved! Tears of sorrow are not enough – God asks for tears of remorse. We mustn't cry *for* Jesus, but *to* Him. Our tears must not be for His suffering, but for our part in it. He asks us for our hearts and nothing less. We dare not think sentimental tears are sufficient; we need to be saved by His blood! Therefore, take refuge in the Lamb while there is still a time of grace. Cry tears of remorse at His feet for the grief you caused Him, for the sin that still rules in your life. Blessed are those who grieve like this, because Christ will comfort and save them.

Thank You, Lord Jesus, that there is salvation with You for all who repent.

December

The Salvation of Humankind

"I have come to save the world and not to judge it."
~ John 12:47

In His life Christ is an example showing us how to live; in His death
He is a sacrifice satisfying our sins; in His resurrection a Conqueror;
in His ascension a King; in His intercession a High Priest.
~ Martin Luther

Jesus, Savior and Redeemer,
who came into the world in Bethlehem:
We yearn for the serene beauty of Your arrival in our world;
for the familiar and eternal Scripture passages and the
songs that are emotional reminders of that wonderful night
when You lay in a manger as Baby Jesus.
We are on our knees before this tremendous mystery,
while in our spirit we follow the shepherds
and the wise men to pay homage to You,
and bring You the offer of our lives and love.
We confess with shame that our love for You is not what it
should be. Purify our love for You and for one another.
Help us to commemorate Your day of birth
in a way that is acceptable to You;
let Your Holy presence be felt among us anew,
each day of each year.
Today we want to rejoice with Mary:
"Oh, how my soul praises the Lord. How my spirit
rejoices in God my Savior!" (Luke 1:46-47).
Thank You that we may share this festive season
with friends and family; also with fellow believers
and with You, Lord, in Your house.
This we pray in the name of Immanuel,
who came to seek His own
and to make eternal life possible for us.

Amen.

Golgotha

They went out to a place called Golgotha (which means "Place of the Skull") (Matt. 27:33).

Golgotha, Scopus, Zion, Mount of Olives, Moriah: These are all hills that surround Jerusalem. To the Christian, Golgotha is the most precious of all the mountains on earth. Three crosses were planted on Golgotha: In the middle was Jesus Christ, our Savior, and on either side a murderer. On the face of it, all the crosses looked the same, but there was a world of difference between them, like the sunniest day differs from the darkest night. In the middle was the Cross of Reconciliation and Salvation, and on either side, the crosses of Warning and Encouragement.

First we take a look at the cross in the middle: The Cross of Reconciliation and Salvation! That cross was actually meant for Barabbas, the greatest criminal of his time. But it became the focal point on Golgotha – the focal point of the universe. "He was despised and rejected – a Man of Sorrows, acquainted with deepest grief ... He was despised, and we did not care" (Isa. 53:3). He was mocked, whipped, tortured and spat on. And yet it is before Him that the angels bow; for Him that they continuously sing, "Holy! Holy! Holy!"

> God proved His love on the Cross. When Christ hung, and bled, and died, it was God saying to the world, "I love you!"
>
> ANONYMOUS

The guilt of all people was nailed to the cross with Jesus – and yet He was unblemished and pure. His innocence was declared by Pilate, by Judas, by one of those crucified with Him and even the Roman officer. The cross in the middle was in fact meant for us. That is why we kneel before it, the gateway to the eternal city of refuge, the symbol of our salvation!

I praise and thank You, Lord Jesus, that You were willing to die on Golgotha so that I could live.

Prove It

One of the criminals hanging beside Him scoffed, "So you're the Messiah, are You? Prove it by saving Yourself – and us too, while You're at it!" (Luke 23:39).

Jesus died on Barabbas' cross and Barabbas was free! Sinner, whoever and wherever you are, whatever burden of guilt you bear, and however deep you may have fallen into sin – here at Golgotha all your debts are paid in full! Jesus' mediating blood reconciles you with God! Come to the cross in the middle. Complete salvation flows from it. There the weary traveler finds rest; there the guilty find forgiveness; there the enemy is reconciled with God. That is the Cross of Reconciliation and Salvation!

By the cross we know the gravity of sin and the greatness of God's love towards us.
JOHN CHRYSOSTOM

Let's look up for a moment at the cross on the left side of Jesus: This is the Cross of Warning. There hung a robber and a murderer; a shameful and godless life had come to its end. The Savior of guilt, the Redeemer of sinners hung next to Him. If only this poor man had called out for Jesus' grace. He hung next to the Almighty Savior and yet would be lost forever!

A person can live close to an Almighty and willing Savior, yet be lost forever. A rich source of grace may flow past you, and you can still die without receiving it. You can live next door to the gates of paradise, yet never enter. The Lord so often says to us what He said to Jerusalem, "O Jerusalem, Jerusalem! How often I have wanted to gather your children together as a hen protects her chicks beneath her wings, but you wouldn't let Me" (Luke 13:34). Let us take heed of this serious warning from this cross.

Father God, keep me, through the work of the Holy Spirit, from ignoring Your voice calling me to conversion.

Remember Me

The other criminal protested, "Don't you fear God even when you have been sentenced to die? We deserve to die for our crimes, but this man hasn't done anything wrong." Then he said, "Jesus, remember me when You come into Your Kingdom" (Luke 23:40-42).

Now we pay attention to the cross on Jesus' right-hand side: This is the Cross of Encouragement. This man was also a criminal, no better than the one on the left. He would also soon breathe his last. But, *he gained eternity!* This murderer turned to Jesus and admitted his guilt, as well as Jesus' authority. And so his night of sin was changed into the divine dawn of salvation: Death passed on into eternal life! Presently Jesus' eyes closed in death. He died before being given the merciful death blow. But Jesus waited for the saved man on the threshold of paradise and led him into heaven. There was joy among the angels over this one sinner who repented and was saved. He went from the shame of the cross to the paradise of Glory, because Jesus saved him.

> Fight the good fight for the true faith. Hold tightly to the eternal life to which God has called you, which you have confessed so well before many witnesses.
>
> 1 Timothy 6:12

Three crosses on Golgotha, each with its own unique message: Reconciliation and Salvation in the middle, and the Cross of Warning and the Cross of Encouragement on either side. May the Lord meet you at Golgotha today so that you are able to answer positively to the question: Are you hanging on Jesus' left or on His right?

Father, worthy of praise, thank You that I hung on Your right-hand side and received undeserved grace, so that I will spend eternity with You.

Place of the Skull

Then they went out to a place called Golgotha (Matt. 27:33).

Golgotha is where the greatest event of all time took place. It is the place where the gap between God and humanity was bridged; where human beings were lifted from the quagmire of sin and their feet placed on the steadfast Rock, Jesus Christ.

Christ spoke seven times on the cross: 1) To His Father on behalf of others: "Father, forgive them, for they don't know what they are doing" (Luke 23:34). 2) To one of the murderers: "I assure you, today you will be with Me in paradise" (Luke 23:43). 3) To His mother and beloved disciple, John: "Dear woman, here is your son" and "Here is your mother" (John 19:26-27). 4) To God, in His desolation: "My God, My God, why have You forsaken Me?" (Matt. 27:46). 5) To the bystanders: "I am thirsty" (John 19:28). 6) To His Father: "It is finished" (John 19:30), and 7) To His Father: "Father, I entrust My spirit into Your hands!" (Luke 23:46).

> If Jesus Christ be God and died for me, then no sacrifice can be too great for me to make for Him.
> C. T. STUDD

The seventh time He speaks, Jesus goes Home to rest in God. On that rugged cross, Jesus taught us how to die as children of God. The Emperor Julianus said that Christian martyrs die a dignified death. They learnt from their Savior! We must all die – and people die like they have lived.

The atheist Voltaire admitted on his deathbed to being afraid. Unbelievers fear death. Francis Bacon said, "Men fear death as children fear to go in the dark." If God is really our Father, we can die peacefully. We are safe in God's hands. Don't wait until you are dying; say today, "Father, I entrust my spirit into Your hands!"

My spirit, my soul, my body, I dedicate to You, O Lord.

"Father, Forgive Them"

Jesus said, "Father forgive them, for they don't know what they are doing" (Luke 23:34).

The seven times Jesus spoke on the cross are like seven windows that give us insight into the mind and heart of our dying Savior. In the first three, our Savior elaborates on the love in His heart for His enemies, His fellows on the cross and His mother. During the last three, He speaks of His consuming thirst; His triumphant, "It is finished!" and His acquiescent, "Father, I entrust My spirit into Your hands!"

Today, under the guidance of the Holy Spirit, we reflect on the words, "Father, forgive them, for they don't know what they are doing" (Luke 23:34). The crucifixion was a brutal act that was not only accompanied by humiliation and scorn, but also by terrible suffering. In those moments of His deepest agony, Christ speaks not a curse but a prayer; not a prayer of vengeance, but of sympathy and forgiveness. It is unbelievable but true!

> The practice of forgiveness is our most important contribution to the healing of the world.
> MARIANNE WILLIAMSON

However, Jesus has a haven amid His suffering: His Father. His Father is also our Father. In our worst grief we can pray to Him. Jesus prays a prayer of compassion: "They don't know what they are doing!" Jesus prays for others, not for Himself. He makes excuses for them rather than condemning them. He preached it, now He was doing it. It was a test of discipleship. He loves us until the very end. His prayer includes everybody: "Father, forgive them." And to this day, He intercedes for us. We learn to receive and grant forgiveness at the cross.

Lord Jesus, by Your wounds I was healed. Grant that I may follow Your example.

"You Will Be with Me in Paradise"

Jesus replied, "I assure you, today you will be with Me in paradise" (Luke 23:43).

~ ᴑᴒ ~

This is the second window through which we look into the depths of our dying Savior's heart. These words demonstrate the infinite power of remorse. Even in the face of death, Christ still grants forgiveness and saves us – and even when our lives depend on it, we can reject Him.

The sinner on this cross has deep remorse for a life of sin. He now realizes that he is unsaved and that the only One who can save him is hanging next to him. There were so many opportunities in his life that he didn't make use of, but not again.

> Humanity is never so beautiful as when praying for forgiveness, or else forgiving another.
>
> JEAN PAUL F. RICHTER

Sin drives us away from God while confession of sin brings us closer to God's heart – a heart that doesn't want the sinner's death, but wants them to repent and live.

This sinner who hung next to Jesus reveals a childlike faith. He trusts like a child and holds out his weak hand so that the Father's Almighty hand can take hold of it and pull him out of the mud and slime of sin, and place him on the steady Rock. His is a childlike surrender: trusting like a child, believing like a child and praying like a child. Jesus Himself said, "Unless you turn from your sins and become like little children, you will never get into the Kingdom of Heaven" (Matt. 18:3).

Because this sinner is remorseful, Jesus accepts him. He becomes part of a wonderful partnership where he will experience the most indescribable love imaginable: the forgiving love of the middle cross: Jesus our Redeemer and Savior. Paradise!

Praise and thanks to You, Lord Jesus, that You died so that I may live forever.

"Here Is Your Mother"

When Jesus saw His mother standing there beside the disciple He loved, He said to her, "Dear woman, here is your son." And He said to this disciple, "Here is your mother" (John 19:26-27).

⌒◯⌒

In the scene today, we see two of the most sacred sensations of the human heart: A mother's faithfulness and a child's love.

Mary's faithfulness started before Christ's birth when the angel Gabriel brought her the message of the strange birth. When scandalmongers wanted to humiliate her, she stayed faithful to the revelation God had given her. She kept all the words in her heart. She was always there at the highlights in Jesus' life, for instance when they welcomed Him in Jerusalem with: "Praise God for the Son of David!" (Matt. 21.9). But she was also there at the lows, when the same crowds shouted, "Crucify Him!" (Luke 23:21).

> A mother's heart is the child's classroom.
> HENRY WARD BEECHER

She was there when everyone fled and He hung on the cross alone. Mary saw His love for all people. She witnessed the hatred: how the people insulted, tortured and crucified Him. When everybody let Him down, she remained faithful. Her mother's heart went out to Him and bled for Him.

Who can put a mother's faithfulness into words? His disciples betrayed, denied and deserted Jesus. His people rejected Him and His enemies wanted His blood. In spite of all this, His mother was there, at the foot of the cross. The crowds jeered, and scorned Him; the priests' malice knew no limits; the soldiers were arrogant and heartless. Jesus was dying for others ... but His mother stayed with Him. What faith, what love, what courage! On that day Jesus gave new depth to the meaning of motherhood; an undying meaning.

Thank You, Lord, for women like Mary who set an example for mothers.

"Here Is Your Son"

"Dear woman, here is your son." And He said to the disciple, "Here is your mother" (John 19:26-27).

Our Scripture today illustrates love borne of the sincere heart of a child. Jesus was truly God but also truly human, yet without sin. He knew how much Mary had to suffer. Only love allows one to understand the suffering of another. The love of Christ always burnt brightly, for the entire sinful world, but also in tenderness for His own family – and especially His mother. His love remained true until the end. He didn't shirk His responsibilities but looked after His mother.

> Most of the stones for the buildings of the City of God, and all the best of them, are made by mothers.
> HENRY DRUMMOND

Christ's last command concerned His mother. He forgot Himself, His own needs, His own sorrow. Human love was an important priority in Jesus' life. In His dying hour and in His sorrow, He took care of His mother. If anyone dare say that they are taking care of their parents, let them look up at the cross on Golgotha and remember Jesus' example. Jesus was never more thankful, tender and sensitive than at that moment. He loved His own until the very end. Jesus had already saved the man on the cross next to Him, He had already prayed for His enemies, but He did not forget His mother!

Human bonds bring responsibilities – responsibilities that remain even after our death. Christ's suffering and death make us very aware of this. And so the cross on Golgotha connects the two richest words on earth: mother and Jesus!

Lord Jesus, help me through the Holy Spirit to respect my parents until the end.

Feeling Forsaken

"My God, My God, why have You forsaken Me?" (Matt. 27:46).

We are standing on Golgotha and watching in dismay how Jesus is dying a painful death, so that we may be united with God. Christ has prayed for His enemies; He has given a murderer the assurance of salvation; He has made provision for His mother and brother. Now a heavy silence rests on Golgotha, because darkness had descended. Then the air is split by an agonized cry: "My God, My God, why have You forsaken Me?"

Christ was not delirious – He was forsaken by God! He did not *think* He was forsaken by God: He *was* forsaken by God! This was all for our sakes. Forsaken! Is there a sadder word in any language in the world? Forsaken by your friends, your parents, your people and family? Jesus knew all this. But now He had experienced the greatest rejection: being forsaken by God! The soul of Christ's suffering was not the suffering of His body, it was the suffering of His soul.

> Crucified inwardly and outwardly with Christ, you will live in this life with fullness and satisfaction of soul, and possess your soul in patience.
>
> St. John of the Cross

Because He suffered, He is able to identify with us when darkness settles in our lives – and we all know such times. No torment we know could ever equal Christ's torment. When we suffer, we once again realize God's unshakable faith in His bottomless sorrow. Even if it was dark around Him and He felt God-forsaken, it was always, "My God!" He knew that He would never drift out of the sphere of God's love. Thus we should also believe without a doubt that because He died, we cannot drift away from God's love.

Crucified and forsaken Lord Jesus, thank You for suffering for my sake.

God Turns Away

"My God, My God, why have You forsaken Me?" (Matt. 27:46).

Christ died on Golgotha because our sins had been loaded onto Him: all the sins of all generations of all time. Therefore it was necessary for God to turn His back on Him. God's righteousness made it necessary; the sins of humanity made it necessary; our salvation and redemption made it necessary. Sin separates people from God. God is light and when Jesus was burdened with our sins, He had to enter into darkness, away from God, to carry our sins away. When Jesus called to God in His deepest anguish, the gates of paradise were unlocked and swung open again for humankind. Despite His sorrow, Jesus never wavered in His unshakable faithfulness towards His Father. He was unperturbed in His faith. It is easy to trust God in the sunshine, but the test comes when it gets dark.

> The death of Christ was the most dreadful blow ever given to the empire of darkness.
> WILLIAM S. PLUMER

Christ didn't cry out these words in desperation or as a curse. He knew what was at stake: the eternal salvation of all generations of all time. By His faithfulness Christ turned the shame of the cross into something holy. What profound meaning does this have for us? He did it all for us! We never have to suffer sorrow anymore – where the fire has already been, it doesn't come again. What will happen if we reject such a great salvation? A day will come when God will forsake us forever! Then even the entire world would be an insignificant sacrifice. The love of our God is magnificent, but it demands everything from us – body, soul and spirit.

God forbid that I would pride myself on anything, Lord. Let me be grateful for the blood You shed for me, and willingly lay all my pride at Your feet.

Jesus Thirsts

"I am thirsty" (John 19:28).

These words are said every day by millions of people all over the world. However, few people really know genuine physical thirst at its worst. Those who have experienced it, tell bloodcurdling tales of the suffering it causes. Think of a person lost in the desert without water, the scorching sun burning mercilessly down on them. In wartime, when ships had been torpedoed, the survivors were left adrift in lifeboats, surrounded by an ocean but without any water to drink.

This thirst is only part of human thirst; it is physical thirst. But then there is the other kind of thirst – spiritual thirst: thirsting for God, for salvation and for everlasting life! We are standing at Golgotha again today where we have brought our sin and have come for forgiveness. We have brought our corruption to receive perfection; our rebellion to learn humbleness. We

> As the deer longs for streams of water, so I long for You, O God. I thirst for God, the living God.
> PSALM 42:1-2

have come to the cross with our despair to receive faith; with darkness to receive eternal light; with our sorrow to receive joy. We have come to Golgotha with our physical and spiritual thirst to receive the Water of Life.

Christ was hanging on the cross and He couldn't live much longer. The darkness had passed and the sun was shining again. The pain of His wounds and the blistering eastern sun were accompanied by a consuming thirst. This was one of the most painful aspects of death on the cross. It is said that with a crucifixion, one's thirst is worse than the pain. Jesus had now been on the cross for three hours. After all the preceding suffering and scorn, He now had to endure also this unbearable thirst.

Lord, thank You for the sacrifice You made on the cross.

Spiritual Thirst

"I am thirsty" (John 19:28).

For whose sake did Jesus suffer this inhuman thirst? For whose sake did God turn His back on His Son? For yours and mine. It was to safeguard us from the eternal thirst of hell. "Let anyone who desires drink freely from the Water of Life" (Rev. 22:17).

This refers mainly to spiritual thirst. Jesus spoke to the woman at the well of Jacob and asked her, "Please give me a drink" (John 4:7), but she didn't understand ... the water was there, in the well. Jesus thirsted for her salvation and wanted her to desire the Water of Life. On Golgotha He was willing to lay down His life for this. Then, during the course of their conversation, Jesus moved towards her spiritual thirst: "Those who drink the water I give will never be thirsty again" (John 4:14).

> A revival is nothing else than a new beginning of obedience to God.
> CHARLES G. FINNEY

What a glorious invitation to godly grace! And at what price that water was made available to us! Jesus' thirst is for lost people (see Matt 23:37; Luke 19:10). He was thirsty for each one of us to find eternal life. What can you and I do about Jesus' thirst? We can go to Him and be given the Water of Life – without charge (see Isaiah 55:1).

People today thirst for riches, honor and status, achievement, pleasure, and fame. But at Jesus' fountain there is a sign that reads: "Those who drink the water I give will never be thirsty again" (John 4:14). If you persist in chasing the sinful worldly thirst, you will be thirsty forever. But if you yearn for God like a deer yearns for water, He will quench your thirst forever.

Lord, I hear about the rich blessings You pour out, that fall like a soft, gentle shower. Let Your generous rain fall also on me.

"It Is Finished"

"It is finished!" (John 19:30).

⌒ ♋ ⌒

Come with me to Golgotha again today, to the gray hill just outside the city gates of Jerusalem. This is where God revealed His heart of love to the world: "For God so loved the world that He gave His one and only Son, so that everyone who believes in Him will not perish but have eternal life" (John 3:16). Here we hear the sixth words Jesus spoke on the cross: "It is finished!" What is translated into three words in English is only one word in Greek: *Tetelestai*. It is a triumphant cry; an exclamation of victory. It does not indicate defeat, but glorious victory!

These are the only words spoken on the cross that are not directed at a specific person. They are meant for all nations – a triumphant cry of victory!

> Let the fact of what our Lord suffered for you grip you, and you will never again be the same.
> OLIVER B. GREENE

The Old Testament prophecies had been fulfilled. A virgin gave birth to Jesus in Bethlehem; He was from the lineage of David; He was called Immanuel and His parents did flee to Egypt; He was numbered among the poor and the simple; He found His place among criminals; His hands and feet were pierced; His side was pierced with a spear; they gambled for His clothes by throwing dice; He made the disabled walk, the blind see, the deaf hear and He raised the dead. Everything happened as it had been prophesied. The people of that time must have asked themselves, "Why didn't we believe? Why didn't we see it?" And we? What about Jesus' predictions about His second coming? Will the prophecies come true again? "He came to His own people, and even they rejected Him." (John 1:11).

I bring You praise, thanks and honor, Lord Jesus, because You were faithful and obedient until death.

Spiritual Victory

When He had received the drink, Jesus said, "It is finished" (John 19:30 NIV).

❖❖❖

Judas betrayed Jesus ... Jesus sacrificed Himself to become the perfect Lamb, laid on the altar – the perfect offering to measure up to all of God's requirements. The enemies were defeated! Darkness turned into shining light. The power of Satan and darkness was broken and the triumphant Christ could now say, "I am the resurrection and the life. Anyone who believes in Me will live, even after dying" (John 11:25).

Sin won't rule over us anymore, because hell is concealed beneath us and heaven above is open to us. The devil's power has been destroyed forever for those who place their hope, love and faith in the Risen Savior.

> Spiritual victory comes only to those who are prepared for battle.
> ANONYMOUS

The work of salvation had been completed: "You are worthy to take the scroll and break its seals and open it. For You were killed, and Your blood has ransomed people for God from every tribe and language and people and nation" (Rev. 5:9).

Humanity's debt has been paid – the acknowledgement of debt has been nailed to the cross. God's demands have been fully met. We don't need to ask anymore, "What must I do to be saved?" Jesus did everything that was necessary. We must accept Him in faith – by His suffering on the cross He completed everything that leads to our salvation and blessedness. How can we be set free if we trample such a mighty salvation underfoot?

Crucified Lord Jesus, I am grateful that You could end the way of suffering with a cry of victory.

Jesus Dies

Then Jesus shouted, "Father, I entrust My Spirit into Your hands!" And with those words He breathed His last (Luke 23:46).

～◯◯～

Today we come to the end of Christ and Golgotha. The first three times Jesus spoke about His love for humankind. Then came the godforsaken cry; the heartrending, "I am thirsty!"; the triumphant, "It is finished!"; and in conclusion, "Father, I entrust My Spirit into Your hands!" The work of salvation was perfectly and finally concluded – we can now be taken to God and never be forsaken by Him.

Jesus' deathbed was a new cross, but there we learn how to die worthily. First, He bowed His head in humble obedience to God's will and with calm acceptance of what God inflicted upon Him. How readily we question God's will. Here Christ set the example of how to accept God's will; even if it was a merciless and brutal death on the cross.

> When my eyes shall close in death, when I rise to worlds unknown, and behold Thee on Thy throne, Rock of Ages, cleft for me, Let me hide myself in Thee.
>
> REV. A. M. TOPLADY

Secondly, Christ surrendered His Spirit to God. With this He, without uttering a word, said that His death was not His fate, but His privilege. This differs dramatically from those who don't know God as Father. In their dying hours they are filled with anxiety and are deeply disturbed in spirit.

Let us reflect on Jesus' words on the cross and rate them at their true value. They are at times more serious and deeper than the words He spoke in His lifetime. In order to understand and appreciate salvation and redemption, we must understand and appreciate what Jesus said in His dying moments.

How precious, Lord Jesus, are Your words. Thank You that Your words were also for my sake.

Christian Unity

"I have given them the glory You gave Me, so that they may be one as We are One. I am in them and You are in Me. May they experience such perfect unity that the world will know that You sent Me and that You love them as much as You love Me" (John 17:22-23).

Christian unity surpasses all things and binds people in love. Unfortunately, Christian unity is marred, shamed and thwarted in present times, because people love their own Christian organizations more than they love one another. If we really loved each other, no Christian would be refused access or membership to any church. Only the love that is planted by God in the human heart can break down the dividing walls that people put up between churches.

> Unity without the gospel is a worthless unity; it is the very unity of hell.
>
> J. C. RYLE

As Jesus viewed it and prayed for it accordingly, it is Christian harmony that is necessary to convince the world of the truth of Christianity and of Jesus' place in it. It is more common for people to be divided than united. Human nature tends to forge apart rather than stand together. True unity among all Christian churches requires a superhuman effort.

It is a tragic fact that it is specifically this united front that humanity has never seen demonstrated by the church. The discord among Christians and Christian churches prevents the world from seeing the worthiness of the Christian faith. It is our individual duty to demonstrate this unity in love as our answer to Christ's prayer. Perhaps the ordinary Christian should do what Christian leaders can't or won't do.

Holy Spirit, work in my heart so that love will make us one with Christ.

Peace Be with You

Suddenly, Jesus was standing there among them! "Peace be with you," He said (John 20:19).

⌐⟀⌐

On the first day of the week, the Risen Jesus appeared to His disciples. They were heartbroken, in low spirits and afraid of the Roman authorities. The disciples must have been overjoyed at Jesus' appearance. Amid their indescribable heartache, the living Jesus appeared to comfort them in their sorrow.

His appearance also coincided with a time when the disciples lived in great fear. They didn't want the godless world to witness their raw grief and sorrow for the loss of their beloved Master.

Jesus appeared when His disciples were at a point where a deep sense of despair threatened to overwhelm them. There were countless questions in their hearts that cried out for answers: Why? Why did He have to suffer so? Why did He have to die so brutally? And in the meantime doubt was eating away at their hearts. But now, with Jesus there, everything was good again: "Peace be with you!" There are times in each of our lives when we are threatened by despair and doubt, but in the presence of Jesus there is rest and peace.

> Our peace and confidence are to be found not in our empirical holiness, not in our progress toward perfection, but in the alien righteousness of Jesus Christ that covers our sinfulness and alone makes us acceptable before a holy God.
> DONALD BLOESCH

The disciples were together when Jesus appeared to them. It is comforting when like-minded people are together to share their sorrow or doubt. It is called the fellowship of believers. Christ comforts them with the words, "Peace be with you!"

Father God, I praise You for the peace You brought about for me through Jesus.

Indescribable Comfort

"Be sure of this: I am with you always, even to the end of the age"
(Matt. 28:20).

Today's Scripture gives us the assurance of the holy and continuous presence of the living Christ. Our Savior makes sure there is no doubt about it. Christ appears to the disciples beside the Sea of Galilee. These apostles were the founders of the universal church.

Would this small group be able to carry out such a challenging task? To found and expand the church? Not if it depended on their own abilities, but it was possible with the omnipotence of the Master, who said, "I have been given all authority in heaven and on earth" (Matt. 28:18). Christ rules His church through His Word and leads it through His Spirit. Our task is merely to contribute towards it.

> I have a great need for Christ; I have a great Christ for my need.
> CHARLES H. SPURGEON

When is Jesus with us, in the church and in the hearts of His believing children? Our Scripture says "always"! His promise is that He will always be present in our lives with His Spirit and with His grace: an enduring and uninterrupted Presence.

We know that all days are different: There are sunny days, but also ominous and dark days; there are days when our hearts sing with joy, but also days when our hearts sob with misery and grief. There are days of firm and unshakable faith, but also days of doubt and stumbling, when we need to plead, "Help me overcome my unbelief!" (Mark 9:24). In His supreme wisdom God broke our lives up into pieces that we call days. The days all differ, but Christ promised, "I am with you always!"

Holy Lord Jesus, thank You for the assurance that You are always with me.

"Even to the End of the Age"

"And be sure of this: I am with you always, even to the end of the age" (Matt. 28:20).

⁂

How long can the children of God rely on Christ's holy presence? Always! He will be at the center of our lives and His church, even to the end of the world. The promise is that He will always be present with us, with His Word and His Spirit, with His love and grace: A lasting and continuous presence until He comes again on the clouds in all His glory.

He uses ordinary people to sustain His church on earth. When Moses died, God had already trained Joshua. When Elijah ascended to heaven, the prophet's cloak had already fallen on Elisha. God always lays His hand on someone to carry on with His work. Even if the builders vary, the heavenly Architect stays the same: Jesus Christ! He will always be present to preserve His work, even if the mountains stagger in the heart of the sea.

This is why nothing can separate us from God's love! He will always be with us, every day! Undeserved and glorious grace! To be with Christ, always! This is salvation and it stands firm and certain. But then we must always be with Christ. He will temper our sorrow and fear and make these feelings more bearable.

> Immanuel, God with us in our nature, in our sorrow, in our lifework, in our punishment, in our grave, and now with us, or rather we with Him, in resurrection, ascension, triumph, and Second Advent splendor.
>
> CHARLES H. SPURGEON

And at the end of the age we will meet each other again at His feet, the King of kings and the Lord of lords; He who said, "And be sure of this, I am with you always."

Lord Jesus, Your holy presence makes all the difference in my life.

Resurrection Comfort

The angel said, "He is risen from the dead! Look, this is where they laid His body. Now go and tell His disciples, including Peter, that Jesus is going ahead of you to Galilee" (Mark 16:6-7).

According to the Bible, our risen Savior appeared to different groups and individuals before ascending to the Father. It was not a random coming and going, but specific encounters to teach us certain things. This took place during the period between Easter and Pentecost; between the Resurrection and Ascension.

In today's Scripture verse, Jesus gives us some "resurrection comfort." When the men who walked to Emmaus were back in Jerusalem with the joyful news of their encounter with the risen Jesus, the other disciples replied, "The Lord has really risen!" (Luke 24:34). Paul says, "He was seen by Peter and then by the Twelve" (1 Cor. 15:5-6).

> However many and however great and burdensome your sins may be, with God there is greater mercy.
>
> TIKHON OF ZADONSK

All these pronouncements tell us that, firstly, the Risen Lord wants to give the remorseful sinner back his self-respect. The first apostle He appeared to was the one who denied Him. Here the greatness of Christ's love is demonstrated: He thought about the bitter grief of the person who wronged Him, instead of the wrongs and grief He Himself suffered. Put yourself in this situation. Imagine with how much trepidation Peter received this message! Could it be true? Did he hear correctly? Did Jesus really mention his name? He had been the cause of so much of Jesus' sorrow. He had denied Him three times! But this is how Jesus treats the sinner. Who will ever be able to fathom the depth of God's forgiving grace?

How great and amazing is the grace that You show me, Lord.

Risen from the Dead

The angel said, "Don't be alarmed. You are looking for Jesus of Nazareth, who was crucified. He isn't here! He is risen from the dead! Look, this is where they laid His body. Now go and tell His disciples, including Peter, that Jesus is going ahead of you to Galilee. You will see Him there" (Mark 16:6-7).

A gainst the dark background of Peter's denial, the light breaks through in the disciples' words to the men from Emmaus: "The Lord has really risen! He appeared to Peter" (Luke 24:34). A jewel glitters so much brighter on a dark background. Likewise, the grace of God and His saving omnipotence are best seen in a deeply fallen sinner. This short extract from history should encourage even the greatest sinner to go to the Father and confess their sins.

> Nothing less than unconditional surrender could ever be a fitting response to Calvary.
>
> JOHN FLAVEL

The gospel gives us no sensational or gripping detail of the conversation between Christ and Peter. Peter didn't tell anyone what happened between him and Jesus. In life there are intimate and personal things that cannot bear up under the harsh glare of public exposure. There are spiritual experiences that must remain private because they are part of one's personal fellowship with God. We dare not reveal every spiritual blessing to inquisitive publicity seekers, or shout it from the rooftops.

The undeserved goodness of God and His grace and majesty sometimes leave us at a loss for words. We can draw quite a few conclusions from this historical snippet that should serve to strengthen and comfort us spiritually. We deal with that in our next devotion.

Risen Lord Jesus, I praise and exalt Your Holy name because You call sinners to repentance.

True Remorse

"He isn't here! He is risen from the dead! Now go and tell His disciples, including Peter, that Jesus is going ahead of you to Galilee. You will see Him there, just as He told you before He died" (Mark 16:6-7).

Peter was the first of the apostles to see Jesus after His resurrection. You might think Peter didn't deserve this! The gentle John, the apostle of love, was passed by to meet the unfaithful Peter. This is what human nature tells us: we move the worthiest into the limelight while the unworthy must remain behind the scenes. But in the kingdom of God many of those who are last will be first. Christ doesn't judge by the yardstick of worthiness, where human merit plays a decisive role, He uses the genuine need of a person's heart.

When sin is your burden, Christ will be your delight.
THOMAS WATSON

Who had greater need than Peter? He was not only aware of his unrighteousness, but had also shed bitter tears over it.

Three long nights of consuming grief followed Golgotha as well as the shock of Judas' gruesome death. The offering that God seeks is a broken heart and a downcast spirit; He will not break those who are struggling. Peter discovered what true remorse meant: being tearful, unsure of his next step, knowing he was a fallen sinner, with hands outstretched to heaven in an impassioned plea for grace. And Christ in His unfathomable love and mercy is there, a place of true repentance. He meets in quiet reclusion with the remorseful sinner.

Lord Jesus, thank You for holy moments alone with You.

"You Will See Him"

The angel said, "Jesus is going ahead of you to Galilee. You will see Him there, just as He told you before He died" (Mark 16:7).

Jesus had something He wanted to say to Peter that was not meant for others to hear. He wanted to meet Peter without any inquisitive witnesses present – alone. There was an inner breach between them that needed to be healed. Peter's fall was an intimate matter between him and his Lord.

Alone with Christ! What magnificent grace it is that Jesus, the King of kings, wants to be alone with sinners. This is restorative to the burdened sinner's heart. Then one dares to share, or rather whisper, one's burdens, without holding anything back. The anguish and sorrow of a stormy heart can be poured out, laid bare. We can kneel down humbly and, without fear of people, shamelessly weep tears of remorse.

> Sin is sovereign till sovereign grace dethrones it.
> CHARLES H. SPURGEON

When we are alone with Jesus we can open our book of life to His understanding, exposing its dirtiest pages. Then we can fearlessly confess, "I have sinned against You."

There in the glow of His godly majesty, a new faith begins: a new life, a new future and a new song in the heart. There under His wings we can know safety, rest and peace for the first time. This is how it was with Peter, and it can be the same for each of us. Make time to be alone with Jesus.

Lord Jesus, thank You for Your throne of grace that is always available for me to be alone with You.

Jesus Is the Answer

"Go and give this message to His disciples, including Peter, that Jesus is going ahead of you to Galilee" (Mark 16:7).

Meeting alone with Jesus always has three important and essential moments: 1) "Oh, what a miserable person I am!" 2) "Who will free me from this life that is dominated by sin and death?" 3) "Thank God! The answer is in Jesus Christ our Lord" (Rom. 7:24-25). People today are terribly afraid of loneliness. But everything changes when we hear Jesus' footsteps. Peter wasn't looking for Jesus – Jesus came to Peter. Do you hear? Christ is waiting for you so that He can bless you through His grace.

> Forgiveness is always free. But that doesn't mean that confession is always easy. It is painful to admit our sins and entrust ourselves to God's care.
>
> ERWIN LUTZER

Jesus has made ample provision for every individual in His godly plan. It is good to take note of this in an age where humans are losing their individuality. We hear of partnerships, companies, syndicates, world trusts, ecumenical movements and mass meetings. The individual is disappearing: the masses dominate.

But in the kingdom of Jesus Christ another rule is in force. There the individual – the person – is of prime importance. It's not so much about the ninety-nine, but rather the one lost sheep. Jesus still has an open heart for the individual. This is the resurrection comfort for the sick person, the addict, the prostitute, the AIDS sufferer – for everybody who has had enough of this fallen world. In the glory of His grace, Christ knows how to find the individual and redeem them. Alone with Christ: this is our comfort in life and in death.

You gave me undeserved grace when You came looking for me, Lord Jesus.

Christ's Words

So the Word became human and made His home among us. He was full of unfailing love and faithfulness. And we have seen His glory, the glory of the Father's one and only Son (John 1:14).

Immanuel! God with us! Christ was born and we celebrate Christmas. God shares His entire creation with us: the sun and the moon; the rain and wind; the changing seasons; the plants and animals. He also gives us joy, love, the ability to pray and the victory over trials and temptations. He also gives us a noble ideal to strive for: profound fellowship with Him, our Father, who will lead us into Christ-likeness. When we strive after this ideal, we glorify God and experience true spiritual fulfillment.

When we believe in the heavenly Father as the One who controls our lives, Jesus Christ's attitude takes possession of us. He did, after all, come to this world in absolute obedience to the Father's will ... and He was obedient until death. When we strive to reveal the same attitude as Christ, we will no longer be the ones who live, it will be Jesus Christ who lives in us.

> Bethlehem and Golgotha, the Manger and the Cross, the birth and the death, must always be seen together.
> J. SIDLOW BAXTER

The Baby who was born in Bethlehem can be your Savior too, if He is born anew in your heart. You can become aware of His presence; you can know His peace, experience His power, enjoy His forgiveness and continually experience His love and joy. In this way, He becomes part of your life and your faith becomes practical and dynamic. Have a blessed Christmas Day.

Savior and Redeemer, this Christmas I give my life to You anew. Come and live in my heart and change my life as You will, and as it pleases You.

"Love the Lord Your God"

Jesus replied, "'You must love the Lord your God with all your heart, all your soul, and all your mind.' This is the first and greatest commandment. A second is equally important: 'Love your neighbor as yourself.' The entire law and all the demands of the prophets are based on these two commandments" (Matt. 22:37-40).

✦ ✧ ✦

We can say with reason that with this Scripture, Jesus gives us the perfect definition of Christianity. Christianity consists of love for God. Jesus refers to Deuteronomy 6:5. This verse was part of the *shema* that was the basis and precondition of Judaism. Jewish services still start with it and this is the first Scripture text that every Jewish child must learn. It means that we must give God all our love: love that controls our emotions, that directs our thoughts. All Christianity starts with the type of love that is the total surrender of our lives to God.

> Take away love and our earth is a tomb.
> ROBERT BROWNING

The second commandment that Jesus refers to is Leviticus 19:18. Our love for God must spill over into love for our neighbor. The only way in which we can prove that we love God is to show that love for others. We must, however, pay attention to the sequence in which the commandments are given. First it is love for God, and secondly, love for our neighbor. It is only when we love God that we are able to love others. The true basis of democracy is a love for God. The basis of love for our neighbor is grounded on this love for God.

God of love, grant that I will love You more than anything, and my neighbor like myself.

The Disciples' Assignment

Then He breathed on them and said, "Receive the Holy Spirit. If you forgive anyone's sins, they are forgiven. If you do not forgive them, they are not forgiven" (John 20:22-23).

Jesus breathed on His disciples and gave them the Holy Spirit. John undoubtedly had the story of creation in mind when he wrote, "Then the LORD God formed the man from the dust of the ground. He breathed the breath of life into the man's nostrils, and the man became a living person" (Gen. 2:7).

Ezekiel saw this same picture in the valley of dry bones when God said, "Speak a prophetic message and say: 'This is what the Sovereign LORD says: Come, O breath, from the four winds! Breathe into these dead bodies so they may live again'" (Ezek. 37:9). When the Holy Spirit came it was like a new creation; like waking from death to life. When the Holy Spirit comes over a church, it is awakened and re-created for its task.

> God has cast our sins into the depths of the sea, and He's even put a "No Fishing" sign over the spot.
> DWIGHT L. MOODY

Jesus told His disciples, "If you forgive anyone's sins, they are forgiven. If you do not forgive them, they are not forgiven." It is important that we understand the correct meaning of these words. One thing is clear: no person can forgive another person's sins. But it is the special privilege of the church to proclaim the message of God's forgiveness to all people. God forgives, but the church is responsible for proclaiming the truth of His forgiveness. It is the church's duty to affirm the forgiveness of sins to the repentant, and the denial of God's forgiveness to those who choose to deny Him.

God of love and grace, I bow before You in worship because I know my sins are forgiven.

The Doubter Is Convinced

Then He said to Thomas, "Put your finger here, and look at My hands. Put your hand into the wound in My side. Don't be faithless any longer. Believe!" (John 20:27).

~ ⦿ ~

Thomas experienced the cross just as he expected. When Jesus suggested they go to Bethany when they heard the news that Lazarus was ill, his reaction was, "Let's go, too – and die with Jesus" (John 11:16). Thomas never lacked courage, but he was a pessimist by nature. There can be absolutely no doubt that Thomas loved Jesus – enough to go to Jerusalem to die with Him, while the other disciples were hesitant and frightened.

What Thomas expected, happened. He was so distraught that he couldn't bear to be with anyone. All he wanted was to be left alone in his grief. He wanted to deal with his suffering and sorrow alone. So it happened that when Jesus came back to His disciples, Thomas wasn't with them. The news that Jesus had returned to life was just too good to be true. He refused to believe it. In keeping with his pessimism, he said that he would not believe it until he had touched the marks of the nails.

> Jesus was God spelling Himself out in language humanity could understand.
> S. D. GORDON

Another week passed before Jesus saw His disciples again and this time Thomas was there. Jesus knew Thomas' heart. He repeated Thomas' own words and invited Him to do what he suggested and touch the wounds. Thomas' heart reached out in love and worship and all he could say was, "My Lord and my God!" (John 20:28). Then Jesus said to him, "You believe because you have seen Me. Blessed are those who believe without seeing Me" (John 20:29).

I praise You, Lord Jesus, that through the Holy Spirit, I may believe without having seen You.

Doubting Thomas

"You believe because you have seen Me. Blessed are those who believe without seeing Me" (John 20:29).

Thomas made a big mistake: He withdrew from the Christian brotherhood. He chose to be alone. Because he was not with his other brothers, he missed Jesus' first appearance to them. We do ourselves great harm when we isolate ourselves from the Christian community. We experience things during fellowship with other believers that don't happen when we're alone. It is precisely when we are overcome with sorrow and pain that we need the fellowship of believers. It is also the most likely place to meet Jesus.

But Thomas did have two very good characteristics: He refused point-blank to say he believed when he didn't; that he understood when he didn't. Thomas' honesty was admirable. He would never try to still his doubts by pretending they didn't exist. He would not support a dogma if he didn't know what it was

> It is not as a child that I believe and confess Jesus Christ. My hosanna is born of a furnace of doubt.
>
> FYODOR DOSTOEVSKY

about. Tennyson said, and quite rightly so, "There lives more faith in honest doubt, believe me, than in half the creeds." There is more faith in the person who insists on making sure than in those who support things they don't really believe. It is doubt like Thomas' that leads to faith in the end.

Once Thomas was certain, he was willing to walk all the way with Jesus. He said, "My Lord and my God!" Thomas doubted before he was certain, but once he was convinced, he was prepared to give his all. Working through your doubts up until the end gives you the certainty that Jesus is Lord and God.

Holy Spirit of God, You lead me through doubt to glorious victory. I thank You for this, Lord.

A Glorious Final Promise

"Be sure of this: I am with you always, even to the end of the age"
(Matt. 28:20).

～✺～

We reach the end of the Gospel story with this Scripture verse, listening to Jesus' last words to His disciples. Jesus did three important things at this last meeting:

He assured them of His omnipotence. What could be above the power of He who died, was raised from the dead and defeated Satan? They were now servants of a Master whose authority could not be questioned in heaven or on earth.

He assigned them a lifelong task: sending them out to make disciples of all people. Baptism may be the topic of discussion, and various viewpoints are held about it. But one fact is glaringly obvious: Jesus' instructions were that they were to go out and win all people for His kingdom by making them disciples.

> It is the duty of every Christian to be Christ to his neighbor.
> MARTIN LUTHER

He promised them His eternal presence. It must have been an amazing privilege for the eleven humble disciples of Galilee to be sent out to conquer the world for Christ. It must have been difficult for them to believe when they heard it. But as soon as the assignment had been given to them, the glorious promise followed. They were sent out – just like us – to perform the greatest task on earth, but with Him, the greatest Presence in the world, always with them. Even if we are weak and insignificant, the Lord, who gives us this command, is almighty and eternal. And this is the guarantee of our victory.

I rest in Your glorious presence, Lord and Master, and strive to carry out Your instructions.

Eternal Assurance

"When everything is ready, I will come and get you, so that you will always be with Me where I am" (John 14:3).

L et's end where we started. The Lord Jesus has taught us so many rich lessons, like the Parable of the Prodigal Son, who undertook a long journey to a distant land where he hoped to find freedom and pleasure. The older brother was the sober-minded, exemplary, trustworthy son who stayed at home. However, he lived the life of a slave in ungratefulness. In a way, both sons were slaves. Both were hopelessly lost. The loving father wanted to give them freedom and a safe refuge. That is why he met them both halfway, just as Jesus came to meet each one of us this past month.

Did you recognize yourself? Perhaps in the younger son who makes demands, leaves his parents' house, and goes to live in a distant land in misery?

> Is it not wonderful news to believe that salvation lies outside of ourselves?
> MARTIN LUTHER

Or did you see yourself in the older son: self-righteous, ungrateful, proud, judgmental, jealous, without joy and love. Or is there something of both boys in your life? Luckily God doesn't leave us to fend for ourselves. In His love He meets us halfway. He pleads with us to come into the Father's house and to share in the abundance, to enjoy the privilege of the security and safety of the Father's house.

Let us say before God: I believe in God the Father; I believe in Jesus Christ, His only begotten Son; I believe in the Holy Spirit; I believe in the holy Christian church; I believe in the communion of believers; I believe in the forgiveness of sin; I believe in the resurrection of the body and everlasting life!

Hallelujah! Praise the Lord! I have come home and by love and grace I am safe in the Father's house! Amen!